Another Way Forward

Grassroots Solutions from New Mexico

Dede Feldman

Another Way Forward
Grassroots Solutions from New Mexico

PUBLISHED BY:
Dede Feldman Co./Books
Albuquerque, NM
www.dedefeldman.com

with support from
The Con Alma Health Foundation,
The McCune Charitable Foundation,
The Thornburg Foundation
and The Center of Southwest Culture

Trade Paperback ISBN: 978-0-9995864-0-2
eBook ISBN: 978-09995864-1-9
Library of Congress Control Number: 2017916043

248 pages, 63 photos, resources, end notes and index

Current Events • Community Development • Southwest

DESIGN: Charlie Kenesson

COVER PHOTO: Jim Caffrey

FRONT COVER INSET PHOTOS (top to bottom):
Rocky Mountain Youth Corps members at work (photo courtesy of RMYC);
Red Chile Harvest at Jemez Pueblo (Dede Feldman);
Don Bustos on the farm (Mark Feldman)

INTERIOR PHOTOS: Dede and Mark Feldman unless indicated otherwise

*"There's something about
people beginning to seek
solutions by doing things
for themselves, by deciding
that they are going to
create new concepts of
governance, new concepts
of education...that they
have the capacity within
themselves to create the
world anew."*

—Grace Lee Boggs,
A Century in the World
On Being with Krista Tippett
January 19, 2012

About the Author

Known as one of New Mexico's most progressive legislators, Dede Feldman represented the North Valley of Albuquerque in the State Senate for 16 years. A former journalist and teacher, she is the author of *Inside the New Mexico Senate: Boots, Suits and Citizens*, the winner of two book awards from the National Federation of Press Women and the Arizona New Mexico Book Awards Program. With a BA and MA from the University of Pennsylvania, Dede is currently a political commentator and non-profit consultant in Albuquerque, where she continues to live in the solar adobe home she and her husband, Mark, built in 1976.

Contents

Real Change Comes
From the Bottom Up

This book grows out of a realization that finally sunk into my weary noggin after hours of committee testimony, disappointing votes, and the frustrations of ordinary citizens I encountered during my sixteen years in the New Mexico Senate. No matter how hard I—and many others—tried, real progress seemed unattainable. The big solutions to social problems regularly failed, victims of partisan division and bureaucratic rigidity. And that was even before the bottom fell out of everything in 2016 with the election of a president and a Congress that ran on dismantling social reforms, cutting taxes, and reducing the role of government in every area!

Gradually, I realized that real change comes from the bottom up—from neighborhoods, rural communities, and individuals finding their own solutions to health-care inequities, affordable-housing shortages, or an achievement gap between low-income learners and those with more money. My mantra, which I repeated at neighborhood gatherings, on the campaign trail, and on the senate floor, became just that: "Real change comes from the bottom up, not the top down."

It is even truer now, in 2017, than it was then. During the first six months of President Trump's term, cities, states, and local governments are resisting federal efforts to round up illegal immigrants, restrict the franchise, and cut Medicaid. Some are joining together to continue implementing measures outlined in the Paris Climate Accord even though the United States has pulled out. Others are declaring themselves sanctuary cities. They can do it because ours is a federal system that reserves broad powers to states, localities, and even school systems.

Now, with looming cutbacks in federal services and programs that are designed to give low-income people a path to the middle class, the states and cities will have to pick up the slack. But in New Mexico that will be no small task.

Everybody seems to know New Mexico is in trouble. The 2008 recession has not loosened its grip on the state after ten years. Our jobless rate is the highest in the country. National report cards regularly flunk us when it comes to child well-being, education, and crime. People who live outside New Mexico think that the popular television series *Breaking Bad* is a documentary, not a work of fiction.

But it's no laughing matter. As state legislators argue about how to balance the budget and prime the economic pump with declining revenues, our best young people are leaving the state. New Mexico's college enrollments are declining. And in the wake of a presidential election that portends cutbacks in federal spending, the future looks bleak given our dependence on the largesse of Washington.

Several years ago, former United States Senator Fred Harris edited a book published by UNM Press called *New Mexico 2050,* which projected present trends out into the future. If major policy changes are not attempted, the book's fourteen experts conclude, New Mexico will run out of water, see increased economic disparities, and experience dramatic declines in its standard of living, especially in the rural areas.

But things may not be as bleak as they seem.

There is something hopeful going on at the grassroots. In neighborhoods, classrooms, factories, and fire departments, on the banks of the Rio Grande and the slopes of the Jemez Mountains, a new group of unsung heroes is taking the bull by the horns. These folks are tired of waiting for help from on high, from Santa Fe or Washington, DC. They are developing new models for the health-care system in local clinics and on tribal lands. They're bringing back a new kind of agriculture and creating urban villages based on traditional settlements. They are teaching low-income families how to avoid payday lenders and accumulate assets. They are not afraid to venture outdoors, either. They have young people out in the field monitoring the flow of the Rio Grande, clearing forests, and taking wildlife issues to the real jungle—the New Mexico Legislature. In the process, they are developing new institutions, new leaders, and new career paths in natural resources and community health.

The people you will meet in this book are innovative educators, daring doctors, risk-takers, outraged neighborhood leaders, fighters, and dreamers. But they are also ordinary people—biology teachers, EMTs, asparagus farmers, seamstresses, struggling artists, and homebuilders.

Some would call these folks "social entrepreneurs." Others would call them leaders of a new, empowered citizen sector. I ran across many of them when I was in the New Mexico Legislature. Sometimes they would come asking for money or big reforms in the health-care or educational systems. Most often, they were turned away. But they were not deterred. They did it anyway.

The local projects and heroes profiled in this book are just a few of the hopeful forces at work in communities throughout New Mexico. You will note some obvious omissions, namely the abundant crop of breweries growing everywhere and a spate of small technology start-ups in Albuquerque, both sectors bolstered by tax incentives and economic development funds. The omissions are purposeful. First, these ventures are well covered in the local media. Secondly, I have chosen to focus on a different kind of economic development that is grounded in community development and social entrepreneurship, rather than simply wealth creation (don't worry, I'll explain later). Yet even within the field of "community development" I was not able to include myriad projects in early childhood, alternative education, solar and wind energy, the arts, and youth development. Some of these projects, like home-visiting programs, are well known. Others were simply too far afield for me to look at closely, given time and space restraints.

Here's a preview of what's to come.

Part One of *Another Way Forward* starts with an introduction to the guiding principles of successful grassroots entrepreneurs as they chart a path for community—not just economic—development. The second chapter is about a University of New Mexico doctor fed up with the rural/urban divide in health care and the lack of access to specialty care that thousands of New Mexicans with hepatitis C experience every day. To solve the problem, Sanjeev Arora came up with a simple technological solution—a disruptive innovation—that he hopes will touch a billion lives around the world by 2020. He is well on his way.

Chapter 3 is about a ragtag coalition of foodies, small farmers, and public health advocates who are creating new markets for New Mexico–grown fruits and vegetables and training a new generation of small farmers. These entrepreneurs are creating sustainable jobs in rural New Mexico, changing children's eating habits, and attacking obesity and diabetes, perennial New Mexico problems. Farmers' markets are revitalizing town squares throughout the state and partnerships with schools, clinics, and hospitals are beginning to take shape.

Chapter 4 describes the decades-long struggle of one traditional Albuquerque neighborhood to clean up a nearby toxic-waste site and develop affordable housing in a place they love. Today the Sawmill neighborhood is a vibrant community, based on traditional settlement patterns and a "big idea"—a land trust that keeps home prices low and assures a mixed-income community.

Part Two, Reinventing Health Care in New Mexico, features three examples of grassroots health reform and profiles primary-care doctors and CEOs who are unwilling to accept poor health outcomes in their communities. In clinics around the state, these visionaries are creating "wellness ecosystems," "health commons," and "medical homes" that put the patient—not the medical provider—at the center of the system. They draw on existing assets and strong traditions in low-income communities. And what they are doing does not stop at the barrio's boundary or on the road out of the pueblo. Dan Otero, CEO of Hidalgo Medical Services, speaks for them when he says, "our vision is fundamentally about changing health care delivery across the state and nation, not just in Hidalgo and Grant County."

Part Three, Reshuffling the Deck, describes the shift in health care to prevention and a team-based approach. It's a move that is creating new jobs, containing costs, and filling a need in rural areas. Throughout the state "promotoras," or community health workers, are helping people address social problems at the heart of chronic disease. In one community, fire department paramedics, usually charged with taking people to the emergency room, are now keeping them out—by helping them meet underlying needs like food and shelter. In another rural area, a mandolin player is creating innovative training programs and luring doctors, nurses, and dentists to places they never heard of.

Part Four spotlights a number of programs that train and empower young people to preserve New Mexico's best asset: the great outdoors. The Rocky Mountain Youth Corps is but one of many conservation programs providing opportunities for young adults to learn about natural resources, as they thin forests, and build trails. The Bosque Ecosystem Monitoring Program (BEMP) has students monitoring groundwater levels and doing real science up and down the Rio Grande. And the Wild Friends are learning about wildlife and civics through a unique program that every year takes them and their teachers to the New Mexico Legislature. The programs are a win-win, training students for jobs in national parks and natural resource agencies while building a sense of accomplishment and service among future leaders.

Part Five describes the efforts of two organizations, Prosperity Works and Southwest Creations Collaborative, which are helping families make the heavy lift out of poverty. One organization is adding support and childcare to the work environment. The other is teaching families how to build assets. Both are empowering parents to invest in their children and themselves.

Part Six highlights the efforts of a solitary high school teacher, dedicated to sending his promising students to college, thereby creating a critical mass of leaders who will transform low-income communities in New Mexico. Initially, Rio Grande High School teacher Alan Marks acted alone to organize trips for high school juniors to Stanford, Princeton, MIT, and Harvard. Now there are several groups dedicated to mentoring Hispanic and Native American students in their journey through higher education. And there's a vibrant charter school in the South Valley aimed at getting kids whose parents never went to college or high school into college—and keeping them there.

Part Seven showcases an unorthodox museum in Santa Fe, Meow Wolf. The museum's interactive experience is attracting thirty-five thousand visitors a month, and, after only a year, employs over one hundred people, most of them millennials. Founded in an old bowling alley far from the traditional arts district, the museum is attracting national attention and its founders are responding to requests to replicate the approach in other cities. It's a rare example of how a local resource—New Mexico's vast reserve of artistic talent and millennial energy—can be leveraged to drive non-traditional economic development.

This book was written in 2016–2017. With monumental changes afoot at a national level, the organizations herein will inevitably change, some of them shrinking in response to federal and state funding constraints, others growing in unforeseen directions. I have faith that they will rise to meet new challenges. Brad Knipper, coordinator at the Rocky Mountain Youth Corps, echoed the determination of most of the programs when he said, "No matter what, we're just going to keep showing up."

Throughout this book, I'll give you some tips on how you can keep showing up for this kind of grassroots development, both as an ordinary citizen and as a budding social entrepreneur. A box of ideas for what you can do is included in each chapter and an even bigger list appears at the end of the book. Each chapter ends with a list of resources you can use to replicate or support the projects described.

You have a role in mapping another way forward, too, whether by starting your own social enterprise, supporting those that already exist, or changing your living or eating habits in large or small ways.

Together, we can develop an alternative to the trickle down economic development that has left so many of us out and find another way forward. Bottoms Up!

PART ONE
Another Way Forward: Solutions from the Grassroots

"I am betting the healthy growth on the forest floor is more important than the rot in the canopy."

—David Brooks, A Nation of Healers,
New York Times, June 21, 2016

New York Times columnist and PBS commentator David Brooks visited some of the hardest hit states in the nation in the summer of 2016, including New Mexico. He visited New Day Shelter for runaway kids and the Children's Grief Center in Albuquerque, two grassroots projects, which he said were repairing the social fabric, and changing lives one by one.

These wonderful projects are not profiled in this book, but they are two of many in New Mexico that give us hope—and models for another way forward. Project ECHO, the Sawmill Community Land Trust, and the many local food projects highlighted in Part One are some of these. As the following introduction explains, they point the way to a different way of organizing larger systems in health care, housing and food production to address historic inequities, and forge promising new partnerships.

Chapter 1

Introduction:

Solutions From the Grassroots

For most of us, what lures us — or keeps us — in New Mexico is the idea that New Mexico is different from every other state in the nation. It is not "Californicated" or metroplexed, and in my Senate district in the North Valley of Albuquerque citizens have fought hard to keep it that way. The mass culture has not saturated parts of New Mexico. The Land of Enchantment is still small scale, based on personal and family ties, artsy, surprising, and decidedly not homogeneous.

The price we have paid for our unique culture has been a stagnating economy with a bad jobs market, low incomes, and not enough revenue to get us out of the ditch. Political leadership has not risen to the decades-long challenge.

"Economic development" has been the battle cry of almost every elected official in New Mexico, Republican or Democrat, since the 1980s. For years, no one in the legislature would dare dispute the conventional wisdom of recruiting large out-of-state companies like Intel, Tesla, Facebook, Eclipse, Siemens, Philips Semiconductor, Hewlett-Packard, or other huge corporations. Nor would they doubt that technology transfer from the state's national labs (Los Alamos National Laboratory and Sandia National Laboratory) could produce enough small enterprises to keep the economy humming when the state faced a downturn in the other sector New Mexico heavily depends on — energy production. Never mind that the state has never systematically studied how much the tax abatements, revenue bonds and training funds have cost — and how many permanent jobs they actually created.

The sustained slump in oil and gas prices, in addition to the precarious nature of coal mining and other extractive industries that rely on markets elsewhere, is forcing a reexamination of the traditional economic development strategy. Where are we going?

Traditionally, the major drivers of New Mexico's economy have been government (including the labs, defense installations, and the state bureaucracy) and extractive industries. Economic developers have told us that a major weakness is the lack of processing and manufacturing industries. The result has been countless tax incentives, revenue bonds, and exemptions from regulations for companies that have come and gone, sometimes leaving environmental degradation in their wake. Companies like Duke City Lumber in the Sawmill Neighborhood of Albuquerque once produced jobs, but they, like the semiconductor manufacturers that followed them, have threatened local communities instead of strengthening them.

Recently, the trend toward cultivating individual entrepreneurship is gaining steam. In Albuquerque, officials are creating a downtown innovation zone, a geographic answer to a deeper problem that has recently run afoul of high crime and homelessness in the area. Meanwhile, young people continue to leave the state drawn to jobs our faster-growing neighbors, Colorado, Arizona, and Texas.

But there is another way forward: community development. Community development is not simply the creation of wealth, which may go out of the state or into the pockets of larger entities without reinvestments in our people, our resources, or our infrastructure. Call me a Pollyanna, but for years I have dreamed of a type of development that does not increase dependency but, instead, rests on the ideals of equity, empowerment, and justice for all our diverse populations. Since the traditional approach has not worked, New Mexico is the perfect place to try out another way forward.

My premise is that the kind of development we want in New Mexico has more to do with community well-being, self-sufficiency, and human capital than simply the creation of wealth. With that in mind, I have selected a few grassroots projects that point the path to this new kind of development. There are many others, and someday with your help there will be a huge directory of even more projects.

A New Vision of Development

This type of development is broader than economic development, which primarily focuses on creating income and wealth. Sometimes called community development, this type of development:

- Levels the playing field and provides opportunities for low-income communities, locally owned businesses, and historically oppressed people who have not had a chance to contribute to the economy.

- Honors the place of New Mexico and stimulates a sense of stewardship for natural landscapes and historic communities.

- Puts public health and healthy communities first, stimulates prevention, and addresses disparities in health care between different regions and groups.

- Cultivates collaboration, networks, teams, and communities.

- Respects and draws upon New Mexico's unique cultures and tradition.

- Creates new jobs and career paths by rearranging existing systems and markets.

- Draws on existing assets put together in a new way.

- Creates a sense of engagement and optimism while empowering youth and ordinary citizens.

Not all of the projects highlighted in this book incorporate all of the attributes listed above. Most are works in progress and some have become long-standing community institutions. All of them were started by a stubborn individual or a small determined group unwilling to accept the status quo. Usually the leaders had a "big idea"—like a land trust or student science project—that solved a long-standing problem, and then they built an organization around it. They listened, spotted opportunities, made alliances, told their stories, and navigated the political system. They persevered, as one innovator remarked, with a "cockeyed sense of optimism."

The projects they built in medicine, local foods, affordable housing, service learning, art, education, and environmental stewardship are adding up to a new kind of community development that is more in keeping with New Mexico's culture and unique assets than typical economic development efforts. These non-profits and small businesses may not be as glamorous as the high-tech factory or the corporate branch office that we have been pursuing for years, but they are sustainable at the local level and, taken together, are creating alternatives to the state's current dismal economic trajectory. While most of them started with support from foundations and the state or federal government, many of them have moved on to become self-sufficient, with a steady revenue stream. Most have used readily available resources (land, community support, personal savings, or the unbounded energy of youth) and combined them in new configurations, with new partners and models that boost family income or improve community health.

You wouldn't know it from political campaigns or the evening news, but the smaller, non-profit sector of New Mexico's economy has always been significant, employing fifty thousand people, according to New Mexico Workforce Solutions data. But it has been neglected, even though its workers outnumber those in oil and gas and even the construction sector. The lack of state support has been unfortunate, because this approach offers a way out of poverty and toward a more equitable and healthy state at a far smaller investment than smokestacks and call centers.

But no matter. In recent decades citizens themselves have jump-started once-traditional occupations and brought together unlikely allies to revitalize small sectors of the economy, lift neighborhoods, and provide opportunities to find employment connected to nature or art.

Learning about these efforts has provided me with inspiration and hope at a time of dark political gridlock. And meeting the unsung heroes who have led these efforts has been a key part of my own way forward.

A word here about my bias: I have always been in love with change-makers, and I have even tried to be one in my own, political way. It is a tough, long road. Regarded as one of the New Mexico Senate's most liberal members during my sixteen years' tenure, I have always believed that government can provide opportunities for people to lift themselves out of poverty and protect them from the ravages of injustice. But I've lost faith in typical top-down government programs and gained new respect for communities and ordinary people who take risks and pioneer new types of public service.

I believe there are plenty of community leaders out there—not politicians or big money-makers, but true leaders, true citizens who will transform our state one community, one clinic, or one watershed at a time. **You** might even be one of them. I hope that this book will show you how it was done and give you some tools with which you can make lasting change, regardless of the headwinds coming from Washington, DC or Santa Fe, NM. There are boxes of ideas for ordinary citizens and emerging entrepreneurs throughout this book, and at the end of each chapter is a list of resources you can use to create your own projects or replicate those described here.

The first step is recognizing the guiding principles of successful grassroots social entrepreneurs and change-makers:

- **The Use of Existing Yet Overlooked Community Assets**
Grassroots leaders leverage land, cultural diversity, hard work, youthful enthusiasm, expertise—put together in new, innovative ways. One of these overlooked assets is the desire of so many to serve their communities. For the Rocky Mountain Youth Corps, profiled in Chapter 13, that asset is a supply of idle, unemployed young people, which it puts to work serving the community and restoring forests and parks. In Jemez Pueblo, the overlooked asset is cultural—a tradition of running now harnessed to combat diabetes, obesity, and other health problems. (Chapter 6)

- **Collaboration, Not Competition**
Social enterprises collaborate, rather than compete, against groups in the same economic space or within an enterprise to develop a sense of group entrepreneurship and team spirit. Meow Wolf, Santa Fe's innovative art collaborative described in Chapter 17, incorporates hundreds of young artists. While individual distinction is often the hallmark of traditional arts, Meow Wolf makers do not vie for individual recognition. The entire group shares the credit for its quirky creations. Likewise, the Agri-Cultura Network (Chapter 3) incorporates nine different farms that have found ways to market their produce together, without direct competition between themselves.

- **Partnerships**
Citizen start-ups often partner with larger institutions like hospitals or government agencies in public-private partnerships. Prosperity Works, the Albuquerque non-profit focused on building the assets of low-income families profiled in Chapter 14, partners regularly with local banks and community organizations. La Cosecha CSA (community-supported agriculture) partners with First Choice Community Healthcare to run cooking classes, and the Agri-Cultura Network is selling its produce to the Albuquerque Public Schools (Chapter 3). Also, as you will see in Chapter 12, data collected by students for the Bosque Ecosystem Monitoring Program (BEMP) is used by the Middle Rio Grande Conservancy District and the United States Fish and Wildlife Service.

- **Mentorships**
Both formal and informal mentors provide leadership training for team members, clients, and young people to transfer knowledge and ensure longevity of the enterprise. Alan Marks, the lone high school teacher who helped over a hundred low-income students from Albuquerque's South Valley get into college and later started the South Valley Academy, knows the value of mentoring. His story in Chapter 16 is a testament to it. In Southwestern New Mexico, Charlie Alfero's New Mexico Primary Care Training

Consortium is luring much-needed health professionals to a rural area with its innovative mentoring program (Chapter 10).

- **A Sense of Place**
  Leaders of grassroots organizations are keenly aware of and motivated by their local place and a desire to preserve it. And so are those who live, work and play nearby. Trust and purpose are most keenly felt close to home, far from the higher levels of government or corporate life. The Sawmill Community Land Trust, a remarkable neighborhood whose story is told in Chapter 4, was based on reclaiming a classic brown field to preserve a traditional neighborhood. Many of the agricultural projects described here are grounded in a love of the land, and the will to stay in one's hometown to make a living. The American Friends Service Committee, the Center of Southwest Culture's Cooperative Development Center of New Mexico (CODECE), and other organizations described in Chapter 3 are giving residents, both young and old, the tools to do it. The BEMP project, described in Chapter 12, is not just creating citizen scientists. It would not exist if it were not for the love of the Rio Grande's treasured riparian forest, the bosque. Like the Rocky Mountain Youth Corps (Chapter 13), BEMP is now creating a generation of stewards.

- **Sustainability, Not Growth for Growth's Sake**
  Sustainable development is not as rapid or glamorous as aggressive growth, but it creates satisfying, fulfilling jobs and new career paths. Small businesses and non-profits can start with assistance from foundations or government grants, prove themselves, and then generate revenue and results. These efforts are replicated in one form or another, creating new institutions and community wealth in different local communities. Southwest Creations Collaborative's small factory in Albuquerque is not a sexy start-up, but the goods it produces are selling. It has grown slowly over the years, providing stable employment and family support for about thirty low-income women. Now its families are brimming with new confidence and education—and the ranks of the middle class are growing, one family at a time (Chapter 15).

- **Passion and Fire in the Belly**
  Social innovators listen intently to their communities to understand how to solve long-standing problems. Once they do, they are ready to raise their voices, go out on a limb, advocate, nag, testify, and persevere for their projects. They are opportunists, spotting openings and allies. When they lose their fire, they prepare new leaders and move on. Some of the incredible heroes in this book—Debbie O'Malley, who spearheaded the Sawmill Land Trust (Chapter 4), and Carl Colonius, who started

the Rocky Mountain Youth Corps (Chapter 13)—have moved on to related endeavors. Others, like Bob DeFelice, who is trying to create a "wellness ecosystem" in the South Valley (Chapter 5) and Ona Porter, of Prosperity Works (Chapter 14), are still at it. They all deserve our thanks and support.

Perhaps the greatest common denominator of all the projects and leaders charting another way forward in this book is a faith that **one person can make a difference**, even in a system that seems stacked against those who are poor, sick, isolated, or uneducated. It underlies all their efforts and guides organizations even in tough times.

Cynicism is not a characteristic of the social entrepreneurs and change makers I interviewed for this book. But that does not mean that people like Debbie O'Malley (Chapter 4), Ona Porter (Chapter 14), Sanjeev Arora (Chapter 2), or Pam Roy (Chapter 3) are out of touch with the same political and economic realities that are driving many of us to despair about our country and our future. Mostly, they are too busy for that. They are navigating obstacles, listening to communities and coming up with solutions to nagging New Mexico problems— poverty, inequality, poor health outcomes, and a threatened natural environment. The times are demanding a more active, empowered citizen sector at ground level, right here where we live.

Maybe we should get busy too.

CHAPTER 2

Project ECHO:
*Disrupting the Medical System to Restore Hope to
Rural Patients and Joy to Burned-out Practitioners*

New Mexico isn't often at the forefront of systemic change. When I served in the legislature, I found that many of my colleagues were reluctant to adopt solutions until other states—preferably in the West—had tested them. The result is that we often overlook local heroes who have bold solutions to big problems.

But Dr. Sanjeev Arora, a University of New Mexico gastroenterologist who has steadily worked to bring specialty care to rural patients, is no longer overlooked. He is recognized internationally as a change-maker. His bold solution, Project ECHO, has received millions of dollars in funding from prestigious government and non-governmental organizations, including the Robert Wood Johnson Foundation, General Electric, the Ashoka Foundation, the Agency for Healthcare Research and Quality (AHRQ), and, yes, even the New Mexico Legislature.

The latest sign that Project ECHO (Extension for Community Healthcare Outcomes) is taking off comes from the United States Congress. In late 2016, both the House of Representatives and the Senate unanimously passed the ECHO Act to study how New Mexico's homegrown model of using technology to connect specialist physicians with primary-care providers in rural clinics could be brought to scale everywhere.

Sponsors and supporters of the bill, both Democrats and Republicans, lauded the program's success in addressing addiction, pain management, and chronic diseases using videoconferencing. Others are hailing it as a "disruptive innovation," a fundamental design shift that will change the way people deliver medical care around the world for decades to come. "We are on track for creating a new operating system," says Arora, who has set an ambitious goal: to touch one billion lives by 2025.

The Big Idea

In 2003 Sanjeev Arora was one frustrated doctor. His specialty is hepatitis C, a complex, chronic disease that, when left untreated, can lead to cirrhosis, liver failure, liver cancer, or death. He operated out of the University of New Mexico Health Sciences Center in Albuquerque, where only a fraction of the rural state's hepatitis C ("hep. C") patients could come. Even for patients with the resources to travel to Albuquerque, and lucky enough to get an appointment, there was an eight-month wait and hence a dramatic decrease in the likelihood of a cure—something very possible for hep. C patients with proper treatment.

"Why should there be a disparity in access to health care between rural and urban areas," Arora asked himself, "especially one with such dire consequences?" The problem was based in New Mexico's longstanding shortage of medical specialists, especially in its rural areas. The specialists in short supply are not just gastroenterologists and hematologists. They are psychiatrists, rheumatologists, endocrinologists, and others who could address New Mexico's elevated rates of chronic disease.

For hepatitis C patients especially—many of them in New Mexico's prisons—there was little hope. Even the few primary-care doctors outside the sphere of the state's one medical center were hard-pressed to understand the drug toxicities, the side effects of treatment (including depression), and comorbidities like substance use.

The solution, Arora said, just came to him as an idea during a meditation session.

At age forty-six, the Indian-born doctor had already achieved the pinnacle of medical—and material—success. He was named the Chief of Staff of the UNM Hospital; he was on the hospital board and served as the acting chair of the internal medicine department. Now the mild-mannered, polite physician was looking for something different.

As a child in India, Arora had followed his father, a leader in the World Health Organization's smallpox eradication efforts, and his mother, an OB/GYN doctor, on their rounds. He always knew he wanted to use his education and skills to serve those in need. "I was asking how I should serve, and ECHO emerged as an answer," Arora recalls. "A lot of people become experts, like I had, but when they die their experience goes in the toilet. But, teach people to fish, teach 100 people to fish—to treat hepatitis C, or addiction—then you can have an impact."

Arora's idea was to move the specialized medical knowledge to the patient rather than the patient to the knowledge, which is usually housed in an urban medical center. Using videoconferencing, he would run free mentoring sessions for remote community providers on how to treat hepatitis C. He assembled a number of specialists each week to advise the providers in local clinics on their specific cases. It is a format used in medical education, and it advances the flow of knowledge both ways—from the urban medical center to the rural clinic, and from the rural clinic to the urban medical center.

With the zeal of a crusader, he then set about recruiting providers in remote places, one by one. The specialists would help them manage their cases, patients with whom they already had a personal, continuing relationship. Doctors in five prisons and sixteen health clinics agreed. Soon, after starting with funding from the federal government and the Robert Wood Johnson Foundation, other funders came on board, including federal agencies outside of New Mexico like the United States Department of Veterans Affairs and the United States Department of Defense. By 2012 the project was being widely replicated in Arizona, Utah, and Washington. The number of diseases treated expanded from one, hepatitis C, to fifty-six other diseases, and the number of patients treated expanded exponentially.

A decade ago, in the early days of Project ECHO, I sat in on one of the program's teleclinics. A team of physicians, nurses, and specialists sat around a conference table in a medium-sized room located in one of the outbuildings at the UNM Health Sciences Center. A large screen carried video from three different clinics located around New Mexico (Las Vegas, Las Cruces, and Gallup), where doctors or nurse practitioners, some accompanied by their patients, had gathered to present cases to the Albuquerque group. There were questions about medications, adjustments, and the terrible side effects of interferon, a drug used to treat the disease. The doctors at the hub gave advice on depression and substance use as well, since those problems often accompany hepatitis C.

TeleECHO session on hepatitis C with Drs. Arora, Thornton and Deming consulting with rural providers

Photo courtesy of Project ECHO/ECHO Institute

What was clear to me was that—quite apart from the patients—both the experts in Albuquerque and those in the field were benefiting from listening to one another talk about what worked and what new treatments might be worth trying. For those who were able to break away from their overloaded schedule (no small task since the doctors' time is not reimbursed), it was a giant step forward.

In 2001 the Institute of Medicine reported that it took an average of seventeen years for new evidence to be incorporated into everyday health care practice.[1] But with interaction between the hepatitis C experts and those on the front line, new evidence-based practices took hold earlier. Patients began to get state-of-the-art treatment from providers they already trusted, and outcomes improved. The evidence was contained in a *New England Journal of Medicine* study published in 2011, which indicated that patients treated by Project ECHO had the same outcomes as those treated by the specialists themselves at UNM.[2]

"ECHO is allowing clinicians to reconnect with the reasons for being a doctor," says Arora. "It's about working to enhance your knowledge to develop yourself as a professional and to deliver the highest quality care for the right reasons. And it's about building a community to solve a major problem in our society."

For Arora, work of this kind is a joyful endeavor, and he believes joy is what everyone is after. His insight is that joy can best be achieved through service to others, and work itself can be joyful.

Sharing With Abandon: Building a Movement

It all sounded so corny. I had come to the Meta ECHO conference in Albuquerque in April of 2016 to hear about evidence, outcomes, and best practices. I did hear about those things, but I also heard about joy, sharing, respect, relationships, and cooperation, not competition and control. They are the principle values of what is increasingly called the ECHO "movement," and the approximately 100 staffers who now work for the program in Albuquerque say they are very much alive in everything the organization does.

The high-powered conference buzzed with excitement. There were TED-type talks by doctors from Ontario, pharmacists from the Fort Peck Reservation in Montana, community health workers in Albuquerque. There were workshops and poster contests on prison programs, diabetes, and chronic pain. Don Berwick, the well-known health-care reformer who popularized the phrase "the right care at the right time at the right place," spoke. All the while words like "inspire," "amplify," "educate," "celebrate," and "connect" flashed on nearby screens. I sat next to a doctor from Uruguay. With the help of Project ECHO, he was setting up a hub in Montevideo, Uruguay's capital, to consult with doctors in the rural areas on chronic diseases in that country.

Since 2003 ECHO's model has been used to assist primary-care providers in twenty-three different countries. Hepatitis C is no longer the only disease treated. There are fifty-six others, including tuberculosis in India, HIV in Africa, and Zika virus in Puerto Rico. In New Mexico, Project ECHO has turned toward one of the state's main health problems—drug and opioid addiction, which is rampant in northern New Mexico. In the past few years Project ECHO has worked with the federal government to train doctors to prescribe buprenorphine, also known as Suboxone. It is an antidote that can prevent overdoses, but there were only thirty-three clinicians who could use it in New Mexico. Now, thanks to ECHO and other advocates, there are five hundred. In addition, Dr. Miriam Komaromy has developed an ECHO method to assist rural providers with many types of behavioral-health problems, often using a team of mid-level providers and community health workers.

It's happening at an unbelievable pace, Arora said, not because there is some business formula to spread this knowledge. "We're just giving it away for free," he said. "We want to share with abandon, and build a system to pay it forward."

It is what ECHO calls "de-monopolizing" knowledge, and it makes change happen faster. It has other benefits, as well. Without sharing rapidly expanding medical knowledge, Arora says there is a great chance that disparities in treatment along geographic and economic lines will increase.

"How do we conceive of a world where half the people are dying and the others are benefiting from this knowledge?" he asks. "Is knowledge for sharing or for private gain?"

A Team-Based Approach

In order to share knowledge and mentor a wide variety of health-care workers, Project ECHO has expanded to train community health workers, physician assistants, social workers, nurse practitioners, and others to tackle chronic diseases like diabetes and obesity. The same technology (videoconferencing) is used, along with the same kind of case-based learning. The UNM office acts as a hub with rural primary-care clinics as the spokes. But the Albuquerque "experts" are no longer just doctors. They are nurses, dieticians, and community health workers who know that chronic disease does not always respond to a medical approach, but can best be addressed by social supports which allow patients to make a plan and care for themselves as well as they can.

I sat in on one ECHO teleconference for rural community health workers and their diabetic patients in April of 2014. Around the table in Albuquerque were two community health workers, two doctors, a diabetes specialist, an evaluator, and a Native American community health representative. One fifty-year-old female patient from Gallup was 5'1" and weighed 209 pounds. She had been prediabetic for nine years. The Albuquerque group asked the Gallup community health worker what the woman had eaten for lunch.

"A spam sandwich on white bread," came the answer. The reaction around the table was practical and focused on weight loss and how the woman might eat healthier foods in an area of the state that often lacks access to fresh vegetables and fruits. One suggestion was using some tricks from Weight Watchers, like walking around the building while interviewing the patient—a small step that could build confidence and spur change.

Next up was a more difficult case from Zuni Pueblo, which involved depression. Where to get help? The stigma of even seeking it in a small community was just too much for her patient, the community health worker said. Finally after much discussion, the community health representative, a veteran of tribal work, suggested talking to an elder or medicine man.

Managing chronic disease is a team sport at Project ECHO, and nowhere is this more evident than in the pilot project ECHO operated from 2013–2016 for "superutilizers," people who are repeatedly admitted to the hospital or emergency room for two or three conditions. These complex patients, many of them homeless or substance abusers, cost the Medicaid system dearly.[3]

ECHO assembled and trained five multidisciplinary teams in several communities to offer therapy and medication to treat patients' mental illness and substance use disorders, provide hands-on support in managing health problems and connect them with housing and services to stabilize their lives.

Data indicated that the ECHO Care program, funded by the Center for Medicare and Medicaid Services (CMS) and New Mexico Medicaid, was successful in reducing costs for HMOs, hospitals and the state, but it fell victim to Medicaid cuts in 2016.[4] Nevertheless, Arora remains convinced that the team-based approach is the best way to save lives and money.

"Never doubt the ability of a dedicated team to change the world," he says, paraphrasing noted anthropologist Margaret Mead.

A Billion Lives by 2025

Project ECHO's goal to touch a billion lives by 2025 is wildly ambitious by New Mexico standards, but the progress made by Dr. Sanjeev Arora, an unlikely social entrepreneur, has been rapid. His simple, innovative idea has taken off like wildfire, perhaps due to the conditions that gave rise to it: a sparsely populated state with one of the worst shortages of rural health-care professionals and one of the highest rates of chronic diseases. But there are other reasons for its success, including Arora's own leadership style.

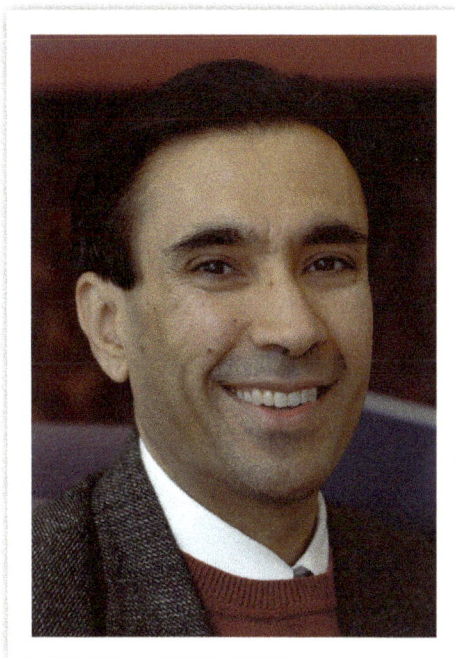

Dr. Sanjeev Arora, MD, director of Project ECHO (Extension for Community Healthcare Outcomes)

Photo courtesy of Project ECHO/ ECHO Institute

"You can just feel the values, the respect and dignity of the program," says Don Berwick, former CMS director and senior fellow at the Institute for Healthcare Improvement. Others, including policymakers at the state and national level, cite Arora's persistence and drive. Employees respond to his inspiration, mentorship, and collaborative nature— uncommon in the fast-paced medical field.

Making change in the health-care system—particularly at the pace Arora would like to see—is not easy. Currently the project is funded by foundations, and the participants are what Arora calls "a coalition of the willing." The key to further expansion is developing a funding system that reimburses clinicians who participate in ECHO clinics, perhaps through Medicaid, Medicare, or insurance plans.

Currently Arora says doctors are caught in a fee-for-service system that rewards them for ringing bells and triggering payment for procedures, not outcomes. This is not music to Arora's ears. But at least on the day I spoke with him, Arora was confident the project would reach its goal. In the past thirteen years, the project has gotten more and more publicity and support. President Obama recognized it early and Congress took it up in 2016. Medical centers in thirty states now serve as ECHO hubs. Eight hundred community health workers have been trained in New Mexico alone. The health-care workforce has multiplied. Despite some setbacks, there has been a convergence, and Dr. Arora is patient.

"When they are ready they will come," he said.

Principle Values of the ECHO Movement

1. **De-monopolization of Knowledge**
   - Engage in the free exchange of knowledge and expertise.
   - Enhance care by "Moving Knowledge instead of Patients." (Don Berwick)

2. **Mutual Respect**
   - Honor the contributions of all the different professions that contribute to the success of ECHO.

3. **Non-Exclusivity**
   - ECHO is not about competition. It's about cooperation.
   - The new knowledge and the new best practices we identify through knowledge sharing are not for ourselves but for everyone.

4. **Commitment to Innovation**
   - Incorporate new ideas and technologies into processes to disseminate knowledge and share best practices as fast as we can.
   - Innovate while maintaining fidelity to our principle values.

5. **Team-Based Care**
   - We are all in this together (doctors, nurses, physician assistants, nurse practitioners, community health workers, social workers, etc.)—a team of providers working together at maximum capacity to improve patients' lives.

6. **Mentorship**
   - Commitment to the mentoring relationship is essential because that's where knowledge transfer occurs.
   - It is how we expand resources and strengthen the health-care infrastructure of underserved communities.

7. **Commitment to Listening and Learning**
   - Be receptive to new knowledge created in the field by frontline community providers who are constantly discovering new best practices.
   - Recognize that the application of knowledge creates new knowledge that enriches everyone.

8. **Commitment to Serve**
   - Work hard for the greater good, always putting the welfare of patients and partners above our own.

9. **Joy of Work**

- ECHO is not just a knowledge network. It is also a social network that is supported by your positive and empathetic communication to all members of the ECHO team.

- Aggregate collective knowledge and expertise, to create and take advantage of opportunities and to improve patient care.

10. **Outcomes Research**

- Commit to data and community-based research to improve patient outcomes.

- Advance evidence-based medicine and help to discover new and emerging best practices.

In a Nutshell

Problem

Health disparities between rural and urban areas; high rates of hepatitis C; opioid addiction in rural New Mexico; the unavailability of specialized care in rural areas.

Big Idea

Moving specialized medical knowledge to patients in rural areas via teleconferencing; training mid-level medical professionals to tackle chronic disease.

Partners

Rural primary-care doctors and clinics; community health workers, physician's assistants, social workers, nurses.

What You Can Do

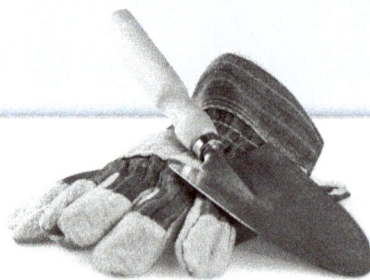

- If you are a patient in a rural area or have a chronic disease, ask if your provider works with Project ECHO and can make use of its expertise.

- If you are a health-care provider, doctor, community health worker, or nurse practitioner, contact Project ECHO and ask if you can join the movement. It's free.

- Share articles and links about Project ECHO with policy makers. Ask them to investigate whether this model might be a good approach to drug or other medical problems in your state. Lobby for funding from the legislature, Congress, and private foundations.

- If you are familiar with videoconferencing, webcasting, or other technological ways to connect people with ideas and knowledge, offer your services to your local clinic, senior center, or library. Organize an event to broadcast prevention tips and needed knowledge to specific audiences.

- Think about how you could incorporate the principle values of the ECHO Movement (see page 18) into your organization. How could you listen, learn, and share knowledge better? How are you maximizing teamwork and mentoring new leaders? Are you true to your core values but still incorporating new ideas? Are you having fun?

- What new networks could you create? A scholars network to share research findings that have policy solutions? A neighborhood Listserv that allows neighbors to share tips, transportation, tools? A Twitter feed, a Facebook page, or a special app with local treatment options for diabetes, asthma, or other chronic diseases?

Resources

Project ECHO
1 University of New Mexico • MSC07 4245 • Albuquerque, NM, 87131
505-750-3246 (ECHO) • echo@salud.unm.edu
http://echo.unm.edu/

CHAPTER 3

Planting the Seeds for Community Health and Viable Local Food Systems

There is no single inspirational leader like Sanjeev Arora, with his big, disruptive innovation, at the helm of the local food movement in New Mexico. Instead, a loose alliance of small farmers and public health advocates are beginning to shift the way we produce, buy, sell, and distribute food in New Mexico. These social entrepreneurs are reorganizing farmers into networks, hubs, and cooperatives ("co-ops") to market fresh organic food directly to consumers, and, more profitably, to institutions. They are training and mentoring young farmers, cultivating fallow land, and figuring out ways to feed hungry New Mexicans. They are creating new partnerships, collaborating, sharing knowledge, and inching their way toward a system capable of sustaining families at a reasonable level in the communities they love.

This kind of economic development might not ring the opening bell on Wall Street, but in New Mexico it is the kind of systemic change that fits our culture, increases incomes, decreases dependency, and boosts community.

––––––––––––––––

For centuries, New Mexico's traditional culture—its songs, its celebrations, even its style of dress—has been rooted in agriculture, but the decline of the family farm and the migration of thousands of young New Mexicans to the big cities and away from New Mexico have changed the landscape. The production and processing of agricultural products still is a significant portion (9 percent) of the gross state product, but, in spite of the trend toward organic fruits and vegetables, the market does not always work to create sustainable local enterprises for families who want to stay close to the land. And only rarely, very rarely, does New Mexico-grown food reach the plates of its citizens, who have been classified as some of the most "food insecure" (i.e., hungriest) in the nation.

Agriculture in New Mexico is now largely dairy farming, cattle ranching, and alfalfa growing. Only 0.5 percent of the thirteen million acres of agricultural land in New Mexico is devoted to growing fruit, nuts, and vegetables. Pecans are by far the biggest crop in this category, followed by onions, potatoes, and chile peppers, all mostly sold out of state (except chile peppers, of course). That leaves small farms, the primary producers of fruits and vegetables, at the back of the truck. Many farmers are facing hard times as incomes decline, water problems increase, and the growing season changes. The average age of a farmer in New Mexico is now sixty-one years. Agricultural labor and young people who want to go into the field are in short supply. Everywhere, farmers are wondering whether any of their children want the farm or whether they should sell out.[5]

Simultaneously, New Mexico faces another problem—one that could be solved by a regular supply of healthy food, especially fresh fruits and vegetables. The problem is the large proportion of citizens who live in food deserts (areas without access to basic foods), even though there are numerous farms and ranches nearby. Even if fresh foods were readily available, the inhabitants of these food deserts often cannot afford them. Instead they buy lower-priced food at convenience stores, subsisting on a junk-food diet that has contributed to the state's alarming rates of obesity (approximately 24 percent) and diabetes (almost 10 percent), two health issues that are particularly rampant in Native American and Hispanic communities.

Undaunted by these problems, a ragtag group of food entrepreneurs with a vision of healthy communities has come together over the past decade to leverage a growing public awareness of the importance of local food. They are training budding farmers in both urban and rural areas to grow crops with market appeal, form networks, and sell their bounty not just at seasonal farmers' markets, but to schools and other institutions all year round. They are creating food hubs, educating consumers, and pressing for policies that will make healthy food more affordable and available to those who need it most. In the process, they are building a more sustainable system for struggling farmers.

"A number of forces came together to create a spiral of awareness," said Robin Seydel, longtime manager of community development and civic advocacy for La Montañita Food Co-op. "People began to see the links between health, food, and a strong local economy." Seydel says that both the aftermath of the September 11 attacks and the subsequent economic recession played a role in spurring an interest in food security, self-sufficiency, and a different kind of economic development.

New Mexico is still in the early-adopter stage of this new kind of development, but there are signs in the South Valley of Albuquerque and elsewhere of a systems change. Foundations like W. K. Kellogg and institutions like Presbyterian Healthcare Services are weighing in. At the heart of the change is a group of young and not-so-young visionaries who are getting behind the plow and breaking some new ground.

Planting Seeds for the Next Generation

Don Bustos has a new invention. You might call it a weeder on wheels. It looks a little like one of the lowriders for which nearby Española is famous, and it allows him to sit—not kneel—between the rows of lettuce, asparagus, and blackberries that he's growing on his 3½ -acre farm near Santa Cruz. Bustos is well known to northern New Mexicans, particularly to fellow farmers whom he has helped over the decades by offering training, personal coaching, and on-site visits. I met him in the halls of the New Mexico Legislature in the mid-2000s when he was lobbying to protect the water rights of thousands of acequia[6] users in northern New Mexico. He had just become the director of a farmer-to-farmer training program sponsored by the American Friends Service Committee (AFSC), a Quaker service program that works on peace and development issues around the world. This was before he won a string of awards for his organic farming ability and even longer before he won the 2015 Leadership Award from the James Beard Foundation for efforts to include farmers of color in the national food movement. To me, he looked like your garden-variety ragtag farmer. I was wrong.

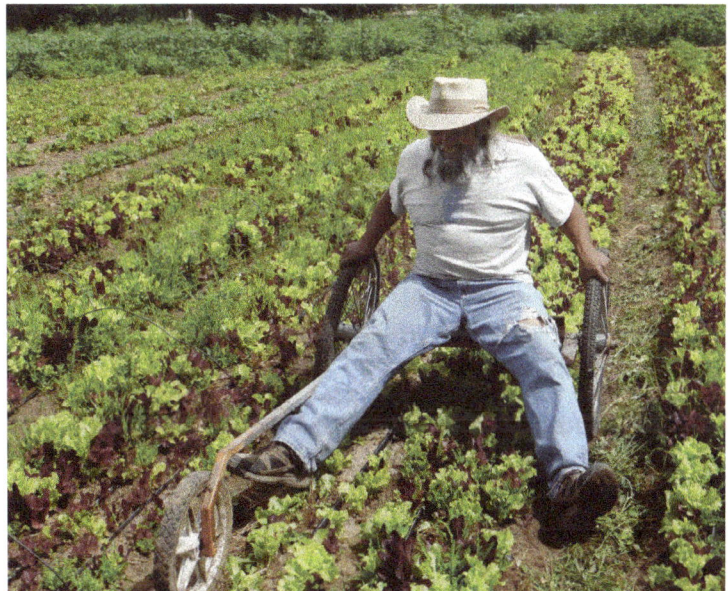

Don Bustos, former director of the American Friends Service Committee's Farmer-to-Farmer Program, weeds his lettuce field near Española, N.M. with a weeder on wheels.

"He's a key educator and farmer, one of the most important players in the state," says Robin Seydel. "He's a great organizer and has brought lots of money to Las Cruces and Española." Recently retired from AFSC, Don was involved in the Santa Fe Farmers' Market in the old days and later started the Agri-Cultura Network in Albuquerque's South Valley.

"I was just lucky to be there at the right time and the right place with the right idea," says Bustos, who is farming the same land that has been in his family since the days of Spanish land grants in the 1500s. One of those ideas was the use of hoop greenhouses to grow crops all year round. Another was replacing commodity crops (e.g., corn, pumpkin, squash) with high-value organic produce like the asparagus and blackberries that are now growing in Bustos's field.

Bustos rescued the family land from decline in the 1970s, often cleaning the overgrown ditches himself. His mother, Trinidad Valdez-Bustos, was a farmer, and the land had been passed down through the women of the family, all descendants of a nine-year-old girl who walked from Mexico to the furthest outreach of the Spanish empire at that time, what is now northern New Mexico. His heritage and determination to preserve the values of his community in the face of urban encroachment and mass culture have been what guided his efforts to teach young people to be as independent and self-sufficient as his ancestors. "When I think about the sacrifices our ancestors made to hang on to the land...it makes me want to do even more," says Bustos.

Bustos says there is a huge amount of interest from young people who are hungry for a sustainable livelihood. He's not surprised. The land and the water are there. An academic degree is not required. "What," he asks, "could be more empowering than working for yourself, feeding your family and your community?"

In twelve years, the AFSC under Bustos's leadership has trained 222 organic farmers, from Anthony, in the south, to Pecos, in the north. "We break it down for them," he says, working individually with the trainees, helping them develop a business plan, figure out when and what to plant, how to get grants for irrigation and equipment, and how to join with others to process and market their product. "They're brilliant," he says, "they want to do this, and the critical thinking skills they develop are transferable to any business."

Bustos said that he asks his trainees how much they want to earn each year. Bustos himself earns $65,000 from his 3½-acre farm and says he has seen farmers who earn much more from the same size field. "Most of the people I work with are not greedy. ...It's more of a lifestyle choice. They define success as being able to feed their families and communities." With average annual per-farm income a measly $9,500 in New Mexico (as of 2012), an increase to that level will boost the local economy considerably.

Pilar Trujillo of Chimayó is one young farmer trained by Bustos and the AFSC program. She shared a training spot with her mother, Marisella Trujillo, in 2015. Like many other rural New Mexicans, Marisella found herself in the position of keeping up a large parcel without the family and other helpers she once had. "Farming can be a brutal enterprise," Marisella says. "You can lose a crop so easily...you need young people to do this work—there is a lot of energy required."

Pilar and Marisella say that Don frequently visited their 5-acre farm and worked alongside them, sharing his skills and advice. "Most other farmers will not tell you their secrets," Marisella said. "But Don has defused the competitive impulse." Pilar, who also works with the New Mexico Acequia Association, said that the mother-daughter duo needed help "scaling up so we could keep up our confidence and skills—and pay our taxes." Bustos helped them switch to cash crops, build a hoop greenhouse, and use both acequia water and drip irrigation on their fields. Sustainable farming is fairly complex, involving timing, storage and transport of crops, and good business practices. "It's not just hoeing harder," says Marisella.

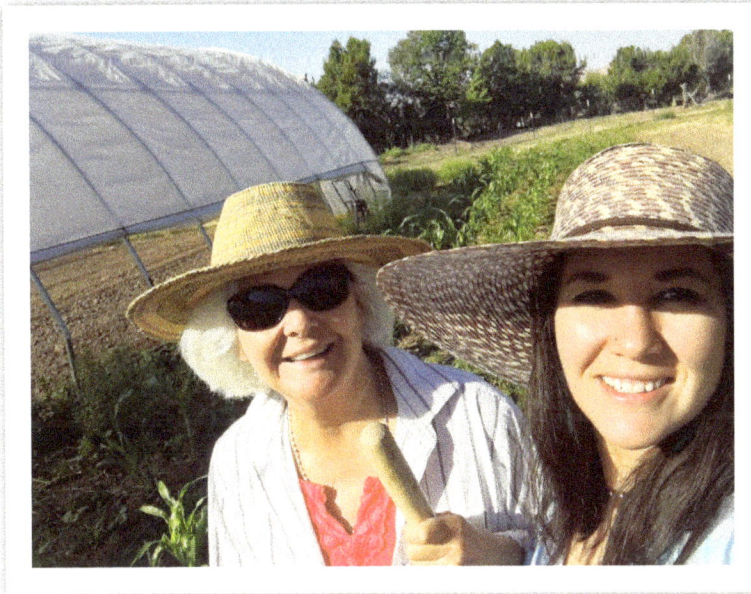

Marisella (l) and Pilar (r) Trujillo "scaled up" the family farm in Chimayo, N.M. with the help of the American Friends Service Committee's Don Bustos.

Photo courtesy of Pilar Trujillo

The Trujillo farm is linked into a co-op marketing organization established by the AFSC program, La Cosecha del Norte.[7] This co-op brings farmers together to market their wares, not just to the usual farmers' markets in the summer, but also to urban grocery stores, schools, and hospitals all year round. The community feeling created by the co-op is what makes it all worthwhile, according to

Marisella. "There's nothing more satisfying than helping other farmers, working and eating together afterwards."

Two other young farmers trained by the hands-on program are Bobo Armijo, twenty-three years old, and Donne Gonzales, twenty-two years old. The couple now manages AFSC's !Sostenga! Farm at the Northern New Mexico College in Española in addition to Donne's family farm in Chamisal. They work with Pilar Trujillo and several other trainees to grow cucumbers, lettuce, and several other crops on land near downtown Española and in the nearby greenhouse. They sell the food to Española schools. "We're proud of providing healthy organic veggies that we've harvested, washed and delivered ourselves to cute little kids," says Donne. The deliveries include a lettuce mix, carrots, radishes, red chile, garlic, and beans, which are used in the Frito pies popular with the kids.

Donne is happy to be working with the soil after a disillusioning experience in Albuquerque, where she had been going to cosmetology school. Her father had become ill, she sustained an arm injury, and then the school did not want her back. The training program was an opportunity to stay close to home. "Farming is very healing, too," she says. Donne had been hurt by the urban experience, but now she knows "the ground is beautiful—it gives back." Donne typifies many young people who want to stay in rural areas but have no way to make a living, says Pilar Trujillo. Donne and Bobo are fortunate to still have land and water, and, with the right skills, they can stay and build a future in their community.

There are many other farmer-training projects in New Mexico, including New Mexico State University's Cooperative Extension Service's Grow the Growers program, La Montañita's Veteran Farmer Project,

Bobo Armijo (l) and Donne Gonzales (r), young managers of La Sostenga Farm at the Northern New Mexico College in Espanola, N.M.

and the Rio Grande Community Farm's program in Albuquerque's North Valley. The projects' entrepreneurial training does not end at the farm gate. Rather, it has led to the formation of a network of regional hubs that connect community-based growers to new produce markets, like schools and hospitals. It has also taught them how to engage with decision- makers in the New Mexico Legislature and the United States Department of Agriculture (USDA) in order to secure funds and promote more progressive policies.

Loans and grants for greenhouses and farm equipment are an important piece of the puzzle. "You have to learn how to farm the USDA," says Bustos, who learned over the years how to testify before committees in Congress and the state capitol, how to find common ground — and be persistent. It has not always been easy for a self-avowed "hell-raiser," but, gradually, Bustos says, "we're starting to get a chair at the policy table."

In 2009 the AFSC program launched a farmer-to-farmer training program in the South Valley of Albuquerque with a USDA grant. It has since spread to four counties, resulting in scores of new farmers, technical support for hundreds of others, and the formation of two farmer co-ops: La Cosecha del Norte in Española and Sol y Tierra Growers in Anthony. A new codirector, Sayrah Namaste, co-created and managed the training program. She says AFSC's role is to start the ball rolling and eventually walk away. In 2017, for example, the efforts in the north were turned over to the New Mexico Acequia Association. "We want to incubate a model and turn it over to local leadership," she says.

The incubation efforts have been particularly successful in Albuquerque's South Valley, one of the poorest parts of the metro area. The training project there resulted in ten new organic farmers, a dozen new farm sites on previously fallow land, eight passive solar cold frames, and the flourishing Agri-Cultura Network farmer co-operative. The nine-farm member group uses the South Valley Economic Development Center to wash and process fruits and vegetables, which are then delivered to schools, mobile markets, restaurants, cooking classes, and local clinics. A unique part of the Agri-Cultura Network is La Cosecha, an innovative community-supported agriculture (CSA) project with a public health twist. "The South Valley is blowing up," says Bustos, smiling.

In more-remote areas of the state, the Center of Southwest Culture's Cooperative Development Center of New Mexico (CODECE) works with a network of nineteen cooperatives, linking organic farms to markets and developing cultural tourism projects that can increase family income in rural areas. The center has linked one co-op in Pecos to the nearby Glorieta Camps, which runs summer camps that need food for their campers. In Rio Arriba County, it has matched Medanales Co-op to the Ghost Ranch Education and Retreat Center, and co-ops on Isleta Pueblo have been matched to the Indian Pueblo Cultural Center's restaurant and catering services in Albuquerque.

"There's no capital in these little villages, but there is land and water," says Arturo Sandoval, founder and executive director of the Center. Sandoval estimates it takes only about $3,000 to get a rural agricultural co-op up and running. His organization goes door-to-door in small villages like Gallinas and Ramah to get things started, and then helps with a small amount of seed money.

"The model is predicated on historical realities," he says. "Native American communities own the water rights and the land, and small Hispanic communities are next in line for senior water rights." If farmers can be persuaded to switch from alfalfa to vegetables they can garner $35,000 per crop per acre instead of $7,000, says Sandoval.

CODECE also helps communities develop recreational and cultural attractions like matanzas (pig roasts), traditional music, weaving demonstrations, natural herbs, wild foods, and other traditional experiences. They also offer horseback rides and bike excursions through the mountains. "It takes a critical mass and maybe five years to see an economic benefit," he says. His goal is between $3 million and $5 million per year in sustainable income for rural communities.

Connecting the Dots From Farm to Table
"Educate, coordinate and make it happen."

—Jedrek Lamb, general manager, Agri-Cultura Network

The downtown farmers' market in Albuquerque comes alive early, with farmers from up and down the mid-Rio Grande valley setting up their booths and arranging their produce as the sun begins to rise. By 9 a.m. the music has begun, the crafters have arrived, and children are running amok in the park. The aisles are packed with customers talking to growers, asking where this cucumber came from or how to cook squash blossoms. In between there might be a stop to check out today's empanadas from the Bosque Baking Company. The scene is typical of the seventy-plus farmers' markets throughout the state and has it come to symbolize trendy, revitalized communities. And with $8 million in annual sales, it signals that customers are willing to pay more for local organic food.

Farmers' markets are not the only way farmers have of avoiding the middleman and selling their food directly to consumers. Over the past decade, more than a score of CSA groups have begun selling food boxes (or bags) on a weekly or monthly basis to subscribers who sign up and pay a fixed price at the start of the growing season to receive

Mesquite honey and othe local specialty foods are on sale at the Belen Farmers Market.

Photo by Abby Feldman

produce from a nearby farm. The subscribers are, in effect, shareholders with a stake in the local farm. The CSA model allows the farmer to collect seed money from members up front to ease cash flow at the start of the season and ensure a reliable stream of customers. Growers and shareholders connect, often at local distribution points or on visits to the local farm, which many offer. There's a feeling that "we're in this together."

"CSAs are a great marketing tool for farmers, and all sorts of fascinating hybrids and forms have developed to bring consumers and farmers together," says Robin Seydel, who recently retired from La Montañita Food Co-op. Two of the largest CSAs in New Mexico give a hint at the different variations of the CSA model. Monte Skarsgard has one of the largest of the small farm operations in the Albuquerque area, with 40 acres in the South Valley, a warehouse, a fleet of ten delivery trucks, and thirteen hundred members. But he started small, as an intern on California and Washington farms. Skarsgard, who hails from the North Valley, started his operation in 2003 on 6 acres at the Los Poblanos farm in the North Valley. At first, it was just him and his truck. After operating two farms for several years, in 2013 he moved all of his operations to the South Valley.

By 2016, after years of operating under a traditional CSA model, Skarsgard moved to a hybrid operation with on-line ordering, pay-as-you-go, and mix-and-match options. His offerings have also expanded to include more than local organic produce. Meats, fruits from Arizona, breads and bakery items, and much more can be part of the boxes if the customer desires. The average cost is about $50 per week, and same-day home delivery is now offered in certain areas (in Albuquerque delivery is $5, free for orders of $75 or more). About ten thousand Skarsgard Farm boxes are delivered throughout the state each week, he says. Skarsgard has recently partnered with MoGro to deliver to Indian reservations and pueblos.

The year-round business operation is geared to consumer convenience. "It was a big leap to go to on-line ordering and same-day delivery," Skarsgard says, "But it is the future." Although popular with millennials, most people are unfamiliar with buying food online in the US. With the growth of Amazon grocery delivery, Blue Apron, and other internet-based food-ordering systems, that will change.

Skarsgard is proud of the growing scale of his business and says that it's only when organic food operations become really big that the paradigm will change. "We've been fortunate that the CSA model has worked for us, but overall the needle really hasn't moved. ...When you compare all the food sales at farmers' markets and CSAs, it's a drop in the bucket compared to yearly sales at one Whole Foods grocery store."[8]

La Cosecha is the Agri-Cultura Network's CSA, and it operates very differently. La Cosecha provides weekly bags of produce to members during the twenty-week growing season, but there's a twist. One-half of the four hundred shareholders pay full price (about $30 per week for a full share or $600 for a season); the other half—low-income South Valley families—receive drastically discounted shares.

Anzia Bennett, an effusive young woman eager to share her vision, joined La Cosecha in 2012 to develop this model, which was initially subsidized by the W. K. Kellogg Foundation. She has overseen its growth from twenty families to four hundred in 2016, honing the model as it grew. Families with young children who qualify for the USDA's Supplemental Nutrition Assistance Program (SNAP, also known as the food stamp program) can now buy a large weekly bag of fresh organic vegetables for $6, or a smaller bag for $3. It's a good price for lettuce, garlic, squash, cucumbers, kale, turnips, radishes, chile peppers, or whatever is in season. And it is a price that families in one of the poorest areas of the city can afford.

"We're selling food to those who can afford it and getting food to those who need it," says Jedrek Lamb, general manager of the Agri-Cultura Network, which is now a farmer-owned cooperative. Last year Agri-Cultura Network produced $100,000 worth of farm products grown in the South Valley, selling 80 percent to La Cosecha. "We're trying to survive, to feed our own people and develop capacity for the future." Lamb, who manages the network of twelve farms, often has his hands full. "It's tricky balancing supply and demand," he says, but he keeps his eye on the big picture: "educate, coordinate and make it happen."

That has been the operating manual for Anzia Bennett, who has developed partnerships between La Cosecha and local organizations to develop mobile farmers' markets, cooking classes, and educational materials about healthy eating. Bennett's energy, resourcefulness, and dedication to food access are well known in the neighborhood. "She comes from a tradition where the first 'no' doesn't stop her and the second 'no' doesn't either," says one South Valley activist. She has now moved on from La Cosecha, but she remains active in the local food movement through her new venture, Three Sisters Kitchen, a culinary incubator.

Partners and Policies

Developing partners all along the food chain—and beyond—is a necessity for anyone trying to sustain, grow, and increase revenue from local organic farms. One stumbling block for many small farmers has been getting produce to market. It's more perishable than typical products, and it's grown in remote areas. Transportation, storage, and processing are big issues. Over the past decade, new co-ops and food hubs have sprung up to deal with these issues. The pioneer was La Montañita Food Co-op, a consumer cooperative owned by over sixteen thousand New Mexico families with $41 million in sales at six grocery stores in Albuquerque, Santa Fe, and Gallup in 2016.

At first the co-op rented one refrigerated truck, which it used to pick up produce from farms from Southern Colorado to the Mesilla Valley. The truck delivered the fruits of the fields to their own stores, as well as to Whole Foods, Raleys, Los Poblanos Organics, and Cid's in Taos. Beneficial Farms helped to coordinate. In 2007 the co-op, a champion of local foods for forty years, opened a warehouse in Albuquerque, which it quickly outgrew. The co-op now operates a 17,000-square-foot Cooperative Distribution Center in Albuquerque on Menaul Boulevard NW (complete with cooler), which serves the 300-mile-radius "food shed" around it with three trucks that run seven days per week during the growing season. In 2016 over $10.5 million in locally and regionally produced food passed through the warehouse. La Montañita has invested $1.5 million over the past decade to become the state's first food hub. Others have followed, including the South Valley Economic Development Center.

Along the way, La Montañita has helped hundreds of small organic farmers navigate the system, scale up production, and locate markets. In 2011 it started a grassroots investing and microlending program called the La Montañita Fund, which offers "nurture capital" loans at affordable rates to farmers, ranchers, value-added producers, and other food businesses that might not qualify for conventional loans.

There are others—from both inside and outside of the food business—beginning to partner to bring fresh produce directly to customers who have lacked access in the past. The result is not just more sales for local farms, but improvements in public health as well.

Rick Schnieders retired to Santa Fe from a career with the food industry giant, Sysco Corporation. He soon learned that about twenty rural and tribal communities in New Mexico had lost grocery stores. He had always been interested in nutrition, and he knew about distribution, so he started a conversation about how to get foods to food deserts, where Native Americans and other rural residents shop where they can—at convenience stores.

MoGro mobile grocery was born in 2008 with funding from the Johns Hopkins Center for American Indian Health, the Notah Begay III (NB3) Foundation, and the W. K. Kellogg Foundation. Initially, the mobile grocery store delivered fresh fruit and vegetables in a 33-foot refrigerated trailer that Schnieders called a "beer truck" for its resemblance to Budweiser trucks. It became well known in New Mexico pueblos and rural communities. A 50-foot store on wheels replaced the original vehicle, and families were able to enter from the rear and shop like they do in a traditional grocery store, searching through bins and removing items from freezers.

The trucks served nine communities, including the Jemez, San Felipe, and Santo Domingo pueblos. MoGro employees offered recipes, cooking classes, and exercise programs as well, to provide a more holistic approach. "Our objective was never to sell groceries, that's just a vehicle to provide healthy alternatives," said Schnieders, who funded many of MoGro's activities out of family funds. "Our objective is to have some small positive impact on the health of the population we serve, an impact on diseases like diabetes and heart disease, those things that are attributable to diet."

Difficulty with trailers and trucks prompted Schnieders to change MoGro's model to a CSA (Community Supported Agriculture) service, where food boxes are ordered online and delivered by Skarsgard Farm trucks. In 2016 between 600 and 800 families got MoGro food boxes each month. Many of the families are pueblo members; others are clients of La Clinica, a primary health clinic in Santa Fe. All are low income, with many qualifying for SNAP and others for the WIC (Women Infants and Children) program. Thanks

MoGro, a mobile grocery store, partners with Skarsgard Farms and uses a CSA (Community Supported Agriculture) model to deliver food boxes to rural and Native American communities.

Photo courtesy of MoGro.

to the efforts of Farm to Table and others, the benefits can be used to drastically reduce the price of the local food. MoGro is still adapting to changing circumstances and is now affiliated with the Santa Fe Community Foundation and funded with USDA Food Insecurity Nutrition Incentive (FINI) Grant Program funds. MoGro has formed an alliance with Skarsgard Farms, which has a fleet of trucks. Volunteers cover some rural deliveries, and food boxes are also dropped off at community schools, housing, and arts projects.

Another mobile food delivery service is a partnership between Agri-Cultura Network, La Cosecha, Bernalillo County, and Presbyterian Healthcare Services. It is the Healthy Here Mobile Farmers' Market, which travels every week to two of the poorest neighborhoods in Albuquerque—the International District and the South Valley. The collaborative project is funded by the Racial and Ethnic Approaches to Community Health (REACH) grant from the Centers for Disease Control (CDC), which Presbyterian was awarded in 2014.

Healthy Here Mobile Farmers Market sets up shop at First Choice Community Healthcare in Albuquerque's South Valley during the summer in partnership with Agri-Cultura Network, La Cosecha, Bernalillo County and Presbyterian Healthcare Services. Clinic patients can use SNAP and WIC coupons for discounted fresh foods.

Presbyterian is using the $2.9 million grant to address health disparities experienced by Hispanics and Native Americans who live in these neighborhoods, where health outcomes are poor. The life expectancy in the neighborhoods surrounding one of the food distribution sites in the South Valley, for example, is thirteen to fifteen years shorter than other areas of the city. The program, which also includes a monthly cooking demonstration and exercise classes at the First Choice Community Healthcare Center (a federally qualified health center, or FQHC), aims to reach forty thousand people. "Healthcare is now shifting to influence health in the community...and we are acknowledging that big institutions like Presbyterian have a role in connecting the community to different types of resources, and investing in infrastructure," says Leigh Caswell, director of the Presbyterian Healthcare Services Center for Community Health.

The infrastructure in which Presbyterian is investing is not roads and buildings. It is farmer training, community gardens, demonstration kitchens, nutrition education, and the direct purchase of produce from the Agri-Cultura Network. And it is food from that co-operative that appears on the tables of the mobile markets set up in front of clinics and in the bags of free produce distributed to mothers who go to cooking classes. Anzia Bennett, previously of La Cosecha, has been a key partner. Part of the hospital's investment was required by the 2010 Affordable Health Care Act (ACA)—and part is from the REACH grant. But Caswell says it will continue since healthy eating is a priority of the Bernalillo County Community Health Council and her own institution. "For a long time we've made the assumption that poor people don't care about where their food comes from," says Caswell. "It's not true. They are not always happy with what they are eating—but we haven't supported them and made it possible to make better choices."

Supporting mothers and their children has become a priority for the coalition of groups working together to improve health and prevent the spread of prevalent conditions like obesity and diabetes in the South Valley. Parents bringing their young children to First Choice Community Healthcare are prime customers at the farmers' market set up in front of the main entrance. Neighbors, clinic employees, and anyone who qualifies can get double the value of their food stamps, and there are myriad recipes available too. On the day I visited, Tatiana Falcon Rodriguez, a staffer at Presbyterian's Healthy Here program, pointed out a blue stripe that had been painted around the clinic to create a low-cost walking trail. Meanwhile, the Street Food Institute, a training ground for nascent food service entrepreneurs (also supported by Presbyterian) has pulled its food truck up nearby. It is dispensing tasty samples of healthy tacos, stews, and other dishes.

The Street Food Institute has also supplied guest chefs for the bilingual cooking demonstrations held once a month at the clinic in partnership with the project and the Korimi Early Childhood Cooperative of daycare workers, which brings a steady stream of working women and children from the area. At the cooking classes, and others that Presbyterian supports in the public schools through Kids Cook! program, parents learn how to put the local produce into food that children will eat. "People have to know how to cook, not just to taste, to make local food sustainable," says Mary Meyer, director of Kids Cook!

Caswell says it's all about partnerships, working with different groups through the county community health council, Agri-Cultura Network, and many others to create a culture of health. The synergy from these combined efforts is beginning to affect behaviors.

"I see mothers, some of my patients learning from each other, sharing tips," says Dr. Will Kaufman, a primary care doctor at First Choice Community Healthcare. "It's working on health in a very different way—beyond what a 10-15 minute clinic visit can provide." Caswell adds, "You can't just put it on an individual to change his or her behavior. You have to create the proper environment, connect them to the resources they need and support them."

It's all about partnerships like the one between these three women powerhouses: Anzia Bennett of La Cosecha (l) Michelle Melendez of First Choice Community Healthcare (c) and Leigh Caswell of Presbyterian Center for Community Health (r).

Since 2006 Caswell and a cadre of food activists, mostly under the banner of the Santa Fe-based Farm to Table New Mexico, have been working to crack a big nut in the food arena. Procurement of local food for use in public institutions like schools could be a game changer for small organic farms—and for the health of young children, who have become increasingly obese and inactive. The massive purchasing power of institutions could redirect millions of dollars into increased local sales and revenue, translating into a jumpstart for local economies. But how to convince schools to change their USDA habits and start serving salad instead of the artificial cheese and other heavily subsidized commodities from the federal government?

Pam Roy, a long-time activist with Farm to Table New Mexico, along with advocates from the AFSC and the New Mexico Food & Agriculture Policy Council, approached me and other legislators in the mid-2000s to join a budding national movement to get state and federal funding for schools to purchase local crops. As anyone who is familiar with her persistence knows, Pam Roy is not someone you can turn down easily, particularly since she is always accompanied by a basket of fresh food—just for you.

In 2007 I responded with a small ($85,000) recurring appropriation for my senate district's schools in the North Valley of Albuquerque. The pilot program drew on the success that Don Bustos had found in supplying lettuce out of his Española hoop greenhouses to the Santa Fe Public Schools on a regular basis. A coalition of partners from Albuquerque Public Schools, the Department of Agriculture, local farmers, and nutrition advocates soon formed—and the ball started rolling. Almost every year since, bills to fund food purchases statewide have been introduced with varied success. By 2016 over $600,000 had been appropriated, although much more was requested.

Critics of farm-to-school programs contend that small farmers are not capable of producing and transporting crops to schools and other institutions on a regular basis even if the funding was there. "The biggest hurdle is that farmers have to compete with Sysco and other large distributors," says Roy. As efforts to ramp up production of local crops to meet demand intensify, advocates like Delicious New Mexico are pushing hospitals, prisons, and other large institutions to become bulk buyers.

Procurement changes have been just one item on the growing menu of policy recommendations for the local food advocates, who have become accustomed to lobbying each year for the all-important farm bill on the national level as well as for local initiatives. In 2006 education and nutrition advocates joined the group to get the New Mexico Public Education Department to curtail the sale of junk foods in schools, which was often used to support athletic programs.

Thanks to the efforts of the New Mexico Farmers' Marketing Association, New Mexico became an early adopter of several innovative farmers' market programs that have provided access to foods for those who need it most: young families, low-income seniors, and food stamp recipients. In the late 1990s, New Mexico started allowing the use of electronic benefit transfer (EBT) cards at farmers' markets as well

Pam Roy has been a local food activist for decades with New Mexico Farm to Table and the NM Food and Agriculture Policy Council, among other organizations.

as grocery stores, becoming the model for a national program. In the early 2000s, the administration of the program improved and more people started using their EBT cards. Then, in 2007, New Mexico became one of the first states to implement the WIC (Women, Infants and Children) Farmers' Market Nutrition program, allowing nursing mothers and their families to use WIC coupons at farmers' markets. Advocates got the state to add money to the national program, which leveraged even more federal funds.

Seeing a food gap for seniors as well as for children, in 2007 these advocates got the federal government to include southwest states in a Senior Farmers' Market Nutrition Program, which gives low-income seniors a $25 voucher at farmers' markets and leverages about $500,000 in state and federal funding—all of which works its way back to local farmers.[9]

An even bigger boon to the local economy has been the Double Up Food Bucks program that started in 2014 to double the value of SNAP benefits (food stamps) used by recipients to buy food. If a shopper uses $20 in SNAP benefits, for example, she gets an extra $20 in market tokens to buy fresh fruits and vegetables. The subsidy can be used at farm stands, CSAs, and mobile farmers' markets like those operated by MoGro and La Cosecha. A growing number of retail groceries, led by La Montañita, are accepting the tokens as well. It has had a significant impact on broadening sales to a group that can't afford the high prices of organic produce. New Mexico takes credit for being the first state in the nation to use state as well as federal funds to support this program, and it has promoted it heavily in news releases and advertising. In 2016 Double Up was projected to stimulate an average of $1.2 million annual local food sales.[10] It is a victory for local food advocates who fought off efforts to cut the program in the wake of a tight state budget in 2016.

To the west, local food and public health advocates lobbied the Navajo Nation Council for a 2 percent junk food tax and a 5 percent tax break on locally grown fruits and vegetables. The Diné Community Advocacy Alliance and the Diné Food Sovereignty Alliance worked throughout 2014 and got the council's support, but the Navajo Tribal Chairman vetoed the measure. Finally, in April 2015, the Healthy Diné Nation Act of 2014 took effect, making the Navajo Nation the second area in the United States (after Berkeley, CA) to implement the change, which is squarely aimed at reducing high rates of obesity and diabetes caused by a junk food diet.

Skeptics are worried that the measure is misplaced, since there are few grocery stores where fresh food is available on the reservation. Virtually the whole of the Navajo Nation has been declared a food desert, and families often travel to towns bordering the reservation (where the tax is not in effect) to buy food.

Making It Happen

Creating a vibrant local food economy is no small task. Despite the potential for rural jobs and more robust local markets, economic developers have focused on attracting high-tech industries like Facebook by offering tax credits and revenue bonds. Supporting the small vegetable or fruit farmer close to home does not seem to be as sexy as the long-awaited technology transfer from New Mexico's national labs.

But as entrepreneurs like Don Bustos, Anzia Bennett, Rick Schnieders and Monte Skarsgard are demonstrating, there is revenue to be made and opportunities to be seized. Obstacles abound, but you must "educate, coordinate and make it happen," as Jedrek Lamb of the Agri-Cultura Network says.

The can-do attitude has set the pace as these new players in a larger agricultural economy continue to spot opportunities, craft solutions, and build partnerships. Their efforts are already bearing fruit in increased farm income and production. The synergy created in the South Valley by Presbyterian, First Choice, Agri-Cultura, and other organizations is creating a new, holistic model to address community health needs. "There's a lot of innovation going on in this state. We're leveraging funds, and working together," says Pam Roy.

But are these efforts sustainable? The local food sector is still a miniscule part of the state's economy, and there are those who believe it will take much larger farms to create jobs and sustainable family income. Currently, the non-profits spearheading these developments are dependent on foundation funding and government grants.

Two local foundations that have joined the effort, the Thornburg Foundation and the McCune Charitable Foundation, are optimistic that all the activity is leading to a sustainable systems change beyond grant money. "We're increasing our self-reliance," says Anzia Bennett. "Every year we are savvier. Our operations are tighter and we are developing more fee-for-service lines that produce revenue."

Micaela Fischer, previously of the Thornburg Foundation, says that it will not take that much to put small farmers in New Mexico over the top. As Bustos and others have shown, $65,000 per year in income is very doable using existing land and resources. "Add that up for the two thousand or so farms which report growing fruits and vegetables, and we could be talking about an additional $120 million in sales," she says.[11] Some experts say that the multiplier effect is much greater for locally produced crops, with $1 spent on local farmer's produce stimulating $4 in spin-off spending.[12]

For New Mexico's fiercely independent, creative people, the beauty of it is that you can do it your own way—like Don Bustos, in keeping with the stubborn New Mexico determination to protect the land and water, or like Monte Skarsgard, with a more urban vision of web-based sales and à-la-carte food boxes.

All the talk about scaling up, making operations profitable or even self-sustaining, must be seen in a larger context, many of those interviewed for this chapter said. "It's not fair to look to non-profits and small mom-and-pop operations to create a sustainable market," says Leigh Caswell. Caswell and others point to the years of subsidies received by big agriculture.

"We didn't get here overnight," says Rick Schnieders. "We're fighting a system that is getting millions in subsidies, but we'll keep trying, we'll keep changing based on cockeyed optimism."

In a Nutshell

Problems

- Decline of the family farm
- Food deserts
- Hunger
- Unhealthy diets and chronic diseases

Big Ideas

- Cooperative farmers' marketing programs and food hubs
- Training for young organic farmers
- Direct-to-consumer marketing through farmers' markets and CSAs
- Procurement of locally produced food by public and large private institutions
- Co-location of farmers' markets, cooking classes, and primary healthcare clinics
- Double Up Food Bucks and vouchers for vulnerable populations at farmers' markets
- Junk food taxes

Partners

Non-profit training programs, farmers' marketing associations, food co-ops, CSAs (community-supported agriculture), local clinics and health care insurance companies, foundations, public health advocates, food hubs and incubators, universities, local farms.

What You Can Do

- Shop at farmers' markets, join a CSA.

- Offer your vacant land for use as a community garden or a training station for budding farmers.

- Connect the purchasing department of your school or institution to the Agri-Cultura Network or a local farmers' organization; convince them to buy local.

- Eat at restaurants that pride themselves on locally sourced food.

- Contribute to non-profits and foundations that support local agriculture.

- Lobby your representatives at the state, local, and federal levels to fund voucher programs like Double Up Food Bucks at farmers' markets. This is especially powerful if you are a senior, a nursing mother, or part of a vulnerable population that would benefit.

- Organize a cooking class for kids at the local school. Kids Cook! in Albuquerque or Cooking with Kids in Santa Fe will help.

- Join a food co-op and shop there.

- If you are a realtor, public official, or insurance agent, publicize the location and times of local farmers' markets in mailings to your customers.

- Eat healthy. Tend your garden. Share your produce. Keep and share the seeds.

Resources

The American Friends Service Committee New Mexico
2047 Tapia Blvd. SW
Albuquerque, NM 87105
505-842-7343
https://www.afsc.org/office/albuquerque-nm. To download *Farming for a Sustainable Community: A Training Manual* by Don Bustos (in Spanish or English) go to https://www.afsc.org/program/new-mexico-farmer-farmer-training program/

Farm to Table New Mexico
518 Old Santa Fe Trail, Suite 1
Santa Fe, NM 87505
505-983-3047
http://www.farmtotablenm.org/

For *Success Stories from the Field: NM Guide to Business & Financial Resources for Food System Entrepreneurs* ($15) go to http://www.farmtotablenm.org/resources/publications/

For *The Power of Public Procurement: An Action Plan for Healthier Farms and People in New Mexico* go to http://www.farmtotablenm.org/wp-content/uploads/2014/12/The-Power-of-Public-Procurement-Executive-Summary-Final-10-28.pdf

New Mexico Acequia Association
806 Early St., Suite 203 B
Santa Fe, NM 87505
505-995-9644
http://lasacequias.org/

Agri-Cultura Network
South Valley Economic Development
318 Isleta Blvd. SW, Suite 202
Albuquerque, NM 87105
505-217-2461
http://agri-cultura.org

Delicious New Mexico
South Valley Economic Development Center
318 Isleta Blvd. SW
Albuquerque, NM 87105
505-877-0373
http://www.deliciousnm.org/

La Montañita Food Co-op
901 Menaul Blvd. NW
Albuquerque, NM 87107
Administration: 505-217-2001
Distribution: 505-217-2010
http://laMontañita.coop/

New Mexico Farmers' Marketing Association
731 Montez Pl.
Santa Fe, NM 87501
505-983-4010
http://farmersmarketsnm.org

MoGro
3435 Stanford Dr. NE
Albuquerque, NM 87107
505-216-8611
http://www.mogro.net/

Presbyterian Healthcare Services-Community Health
https://www.phs.org/community/committed-to-community-health/Pages/community-hcalth-program-highlights.aspx

Mid-Region Council of Governments
809 Copper Ave. NW
Albuquerque, NM 87102
505-247-1750
www.mrcog-nm.gov/local-food

La Cosecha
South Valley Economic
Development Center
318 Isleta Blvd. SW, Suite 202
Albuquerque, NM 87105
505-217-2461
http://lacosechacsa.org

The Diné Policy Institute
Diné College
For the *Diné Food Sovereignty Report* (April, 2014) go to www.dinecollege.edu/institutes/DPI/Docs/dpi-food-sovereignty-report.pdf

Skarsgard Farms
3435 Stanford Dr. NE
Albuquerque, NM 87107
505-681-4060
www.skarsgardfarms.com

The Cooperative Development Center of New Mexico (CODECE)
Center of Southwest Culture
505 Marquette Ave. NW
Suite 1610
Albuquerque, NM 87102
505-247-2729
http://cooperativedevelopmentcenter.org/

Grow the Growers
Farm Business Training
New Mexico State University
Bernalillo County
Extension Office
1510 Menaul Blvd. NW
Albuquerque, NM 87107
505-243-1386
http://aces.nmsu.edu/county/bernalillo/farmranch/farm-business-training-.html

Veteran Farmer Program
La Montañita Co-op
901 Menaul Blvd. NW
Albuquerque, NM 87107
505-217-2001
http://laMontañita.coop/vfp/

Rio Grande Community Farm
1701 Montaño Rd. NW
Albuquerque, NM 87107
505-916-1078
http://riograndefarm.org/

Kids Cook!
7900 Lorraine Ct. NE Suite E
Albuquerque, NM 87113
505-821-5552
http://www.kidscook.us

Cooking with Kids
P.O. Box 6113
Santa Fe, NM 87502
505-438-0098
www.cookingwithkids.net

CHAPTER 4

Preserving Traditional Communities:
How Neighborhood Hell-Raisers
Became Innovative Housing Developers

It takes a village, they say. Collaboration was the hallmark of the efforts of local food and public health advocates in the previous chapter. It was also a remarkable trait of the residents of one traditional Hispanic neighborhood with dreams of creating its own urban village within Albuquerque. Together these citizen activists struggled to eliminate pollution and create affordable housing in their neighborhood, which reflected their culture and made the best use the one asset that remained, their land. Like the members of Jemez Pueblo, another traditional community you will visit, the residents of the Sawmill Neighborhood stuck together against outside forces and came up with an innovative solution. Along the way they found partners and branched out into new endeavors that are now creating jobs and a path to self-sufficiency.

With 20 percent of New Mexico's population living near the poverty line, finding affordable housing is a major problem, especially in cities like Santa Fe and Albuquerque. Pricey new infill developments with refurbished old houses—or sparkly new ones—are making it hard for the children of aging residents to stay in the area. Housing prices are up—not as high as in other states—but still out of reach for many.

The Department of Housing and Urban Development declares that housing costs should consume no more than 30 percent of a family's monthly income. At that rate, minimum wage earners cannot afford decent housing anywhere in New Mexico.[13] Even families with two breadwinners have trouble.

But not everywhere. Not in the Sawmill district of Albuquerque.

Just north of Old Town, an apple orchard grows in what was once a wasteland of sawdust, formaldehyde, and other industrial pollutants. It is surrounded by an innovative housing project, envisioned and constructed from the ground up by the local community. Nearby, in a thriving mix of shops and apartments, a glass blower fires up his kiln and a local caterer loads trays of tacos into her food truck for delivery to a concert scheduled for later that night. It's all happening on a once forlorn tract of land between one of the city's major freeways and Albuquerque's original plaza.

The story of the Sawmill Neighborhood's redevelopment is a story important to all New Mexicans. It's about restoring community, repairing environmental damage, and empowering ordinary citizens to shape their own destiny. Sawmill residents stuck together over decades to get funding, fight city hall, preserve their history, and protect a prime asset—their community. In the process, they have created affordable housing for generations to come. The Sawmill Community Land Trust is now one of the largest land trusts in the country and a model for community developers.

"This all started because of the sawdust."

Max Ramirez, now eighty-four years old, does not look much like a hell-raiser. He wears thick, large glasses and doesn't get out to the golf course as often as he once did. He has eighteen grandchildren and twenty-seven great grandchildren, and he recently lost his wife Rita, a neighborhood stalwart in her own right. But still, there are glimmers. He's worried about all the traffic from the nearby Starbucks, and he doubts that the city will do much about it. He can't believe the problems with the local police, and he shakes his head when we talk about national politics.

Ramirez still lives on the same street where he was raised in a house made of the discarded scraps from the nearby lumber mill. His father—and hundreds of others from rural New Mexico—worked at the mill. Ramirez did too, helping his father pack the milled lumber into freight trains. He remembers a big lagoon in the area where log riders guided the floating logs into the shop and then into the waiting saw. He still loves his neighborhood, which was once a farming community complete with orchards and fields irrigated by an acequia. Back then residents of the old Spanish-speaking community attended church at San Felipe de Neri (said to be the second-oldest church in the United States), cleaned out the ditches every spring, and celebrated Las Posadas on Christmas.

The neighborhood got its name from the huge sawmill owned by the American Lumber Company. It began operating at the turn of the last century, employing fifteen hundred people at its peak. By 1908 it was

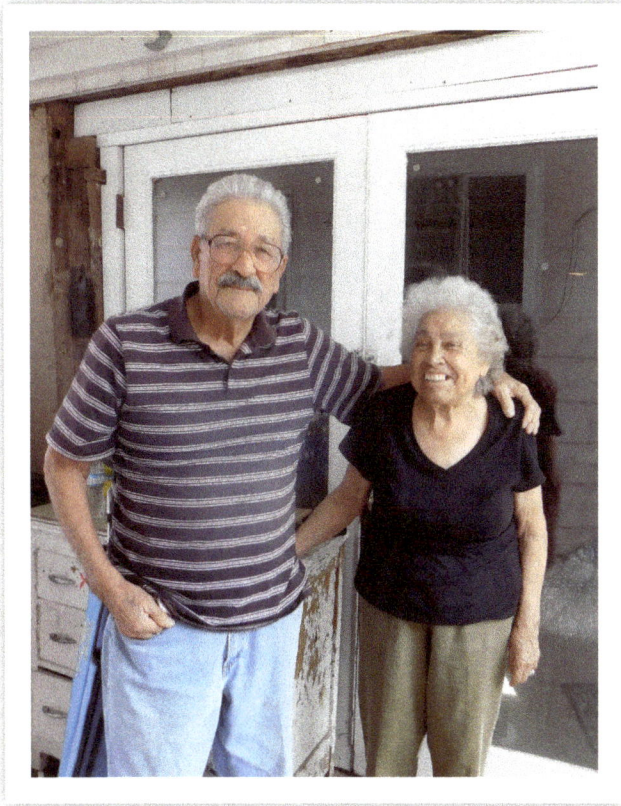

Max and Rita Ramirez started organizing their neighborhood in the 1980s, overcoming a local polluter and starting a community land trust that now provides affordable housing in the Sawmill area of Albuquerque.

the largest sawmill in the nation. Job seekers came from all over New Mexico and the world, with immigrants from Poland, Germany, and other European countries marrying into local families, soon adopting Spanish as their native tongue.

Duke City Lumber, the successor to American Lumber, operated the sawmill until the early 1980s, when it relocated to northern New Mexico. It sold off part of its one-square-mile site to other industries, including Praeger Partners, for a power plant. In the 1970s Ponderosa Products, a spin-off factory, began to convert the waste sawdust into sheets of particle board, discarding the waste products—glue, form-aldehyde, nitrates, toluene, and other toxic substances—into a nearby pit. Elsewhere on the site, Praeger was contaminating the soil with asbestos.

By the mid-1980s it was impossible to hold the outdoor celebrations the community relished. There was too much "snow" in the air. The snow was a fine, sticky substance that coated car windshields and seemed to increase at night. Neighborhood residents were beginning to complain of respiratory illnesses.

For Max Ramirez and his wife, the last straw was when they awoke one morning and looked at their bed and saw the outline of their bodies traced in sawdust. "Our bodies were painted on the sheets," recalled Rita. Max went over to Ponderosa Products and spoke to its owner, Ed Stewart. "He told me, 'You're going to eat my dust,' and I said, 'No, I'm going to fight.'"

That's when Max, later described by friends as "an old *pachuco* from the bad old days with heart," started calling the city to get the company to stop polluting the area. "I used to go there, raise hell with these people…and they said I was a dumb troublemaker."[14] Soon there were more troublemakers. The SouthWest Organizing Project (SWOP), a door-to-door group making its first venture into the environmental justice field, had members in the area, including organizer Teresa Juarez. In 1985 the Sawmill Advisory Council (SAC), a new organization spearheaded by SWOP, started to press the city and state to enforce environmental regulations. The factory was forced to install air pollution control equipment and clean up groundwater contamination. But the process was contentious. At one point, the plant's owner threatened to sue the community if it publicly released an air quality study detailing the health effects of the pollution.

But the community persevered with a focus on children's health. Along the way, SAC identified political allies. It worked through the city council to force concessions from Ponderosa Products and get funding to upgrade the neighborhood with basic amenities like curbs and gutters. Although nearby neighborhoods were redeveloping, the Sawmill barrio had been left behind.

SAC tackled the larger problem with gusto, incorporating as a non-profit, holding meetings in a little house behind Max and Rita's, raising money through enchilada dinners, organizing a youth component that worked with local artists, and helping AmeriCorps volunteers dig into local history and culture. The result was an intergenerational burst of energy that scored small victories—a better Wells Park Community Center nearby, a string of inspiring murals on local buildings once covered with graffiti, an afterschool program, and a new principal at the local elementary school.

"It showed us that you can take some stuff back, and it encouraged us to do more," Debbie O'Malley recalled. A local resident, O'Malley had gotten a SAC flyer on her doorstep and was drafted into the group as vice president at the first meeting she attended. At the time, she was raising two young daughters and remodeling her house in the neighborhood. Her family was from the area. Her father and uncles worked in the mill and her great-great-grandfather, Major Melchior Werner, had been a prominent Old Town businessman who had come to New Mexico from Germany in the 1800s. She had a background as a secretary and a bookkeeper. She had a solid connection to the area, and, more important in 1989, she was the only one with a computer.

Debbie O'Malley, now a Bernalillo County Commissioner, got her start with the Sawmill Advisory Council soliciting donations for an enchilada fundraiser. She became a savvy community organizer, fundraiser and director of a community development corporation that got things moving.

Photo courtesy of Neri Holguin

She was immediately put in charge of an enchilada fundraiser and solicited donations from local restaurants. In only a few years she would become the leader of the effort.

When the 35-acre Duke City Lumber property came up for sale in the mid-1990s, O'Malley and others were fearful of another industrial polluter moving into the area. Fighting polluters was getting old. If the zoning could be changed from manufacturing, perhaps the area could be protected. SAC mobilized the Sawmill and an adjoining area, the Wells Park Neighborhood, to get the city to revise an outdated sector development plan—a process that led to even greater participation and cohesion.

Emboldened by community support, SAC leaders went further, deciding that the only way to truly control their destiny was to own the land and develop it themselves. Their first choice was affordable housing for the community's children and grandchildren who, they knew from past settlement patterns, would someday want to move back to the area. In the Sawmill Neighborhood and other gentrifying neighborhoods downtown, that possibility was receding. Home prices would just be too high.

To assist in their efforts, the group contacted the Center for Community Change in Washington, DC, which helped them form a community development corporation (CDC) and begin generating funding to acquire property. Design Workshop, based in Denver, led days of workshops to develop a master plan. Children, elders, and local architects joined in the sessions, which stretched over days. The CDC helped the city assemble $1.5 million from state capital outlay grants, city general obligation bonds, and Community Development Block Grant funds, and, in 1995, the city bought the site. The group then began negotiation with the city to develop the twenty-seven acres of the industrial wasteland and retain ownership of the land.

The New Mexico constitution does not permit the city to simply turn over land to a corporation (either for-profit or non-profit), and the city said the newly formed Sawmill CDC did not have enough experience in the building process to respond to any request for proposal (RFP) for the construction of a mixed-use land trust. To overcome the obstacle and prove itself capable, the Sawmill CDC built seven homes in the area in cooperation with Neighborhood Housing Services, a local non-profit.

Arbolera de Vida Is Born

Planning for the housing development continued for several years, and it was now informed by real-life experience in building and marketing affordable housing. Debbie O'Malley and others became convinced that affordability was a tricky business. The problem with the houses they had just built (costing $81,000 for a three-bedroom house), recalled Dory Wegrzyn, one of the troupe of planners involved, was that while the original purchasing costs were subsidized, making it easier for the buyer to afford, it was a one-time deal. When the original buyer sold, the house zoomed up to market value, making it unattainable to community members.[15]

"We were educating ourselves," says Debbie O'Malley, "and we became convinced that a community land trust, where a community non-profit owned the land in trust for the community, was the only way to preserve permanent affordability." Under the model they ultimately adopted, houses would be geared to families and seniors who were at or below 80 percent of median income. They would be constructed on land owned by the trust, which would lease the land to the buyers for a minimum of ninety-nine years (with the option to renew by heirs or assignees). In other words, the houses would be owned by the buyer, but not the ground. As a condition of the ground lease, homeowners would agree to certain resale restrictions—limiting the return to the seller to 30 percent of the appreciation, thus preserving affordability for others.

The concept was new, and not everyone was enthusiastic.[16] But in New Mexico the idea of common ownership of land is not entirely foreign. "People here have a history of land grants and are used to owning land collectively," says Debbie O'Malley. "We have a strong connection to place and to the land."

Finally, in 1997, a memorandum of understanding was signed with the City of Albuquerque and an RFP was issued. In addition to calling for a community land trust, it defined the central features of the mixed-income development to include a public plaza, commercial/industrial space to create jobs and provide neighborhood services. The new housing would fit in with the existing neighborhood, with porches, sidewalks, and ample space for public gatherings. It would be laid out on an east-west axis, allowing for south-facing windows and solar exposure. The vision that had emerged from a decade's worth of enchilada dinners, flyers, community meetings in Max Ramirez's little house, T-shirts, and endless design charrettes was becoming a reality.

In August of 1999, the City of Albuquerque awarded a contract to develop the project to the Sawmill Community Land Trust (SCLT). The new project would be called *Arbolera de Vida* ("orchard of life"), a name suggested by the neighborhood's resident philosophers, Tomas and Consuelo Atencio. The Trust would manage all construction, sales, resales, and rentals—a daunting prospect for most community organizers. Yet by 2001, nineteen homes (townhouses and detached dwellings) in Phase I were sold. Streets were landscaped, and a new central plaza was built, which later won an award from the Society of Landscape Architects. Most of the buyers earned between 50 to 60 percent of median income.

"Developers make it sound so complicated," says O'Malley, "but it's as easy as balancing a checkbook." O'Malley had become the go-to person among a team which largely consisted of neighborhood women—Jesse Sais, from the Wells Park Neighborhood Association, Dory Wegrzyn, Rita Gonzales, Betsy Najjar, and later Connie Chavez, and Robbie Ann Muhammad. "We threw our feet in the fire and stuck together like glue...and the neighbors kept going," says O'Malley.

The group's task soon became an educational one. First-time homebuyers knew little about mortgages, upkeep, insurance, and other details. They had to be educated on what ownership meant and on the unique opportunities and responsibilities of living in a land trust. In an effort to create a sense of stewardship and draw on a sense of place, the history of the Sawmill became a part of the training.

"We were trying to create a community, not just sell houses," says Connie Chavez, who became the Trust's executive director during a later phase of the development.

O'Malley and Chavez say that the whole group developed a rhythm and a faith that it was all doable, even as others were saying it wasn't. "It takes intent and determination to put all the pieces together," O'Malley says. "The whole thing was a chance to learn about yourself and others. It was a growth opportunity."

By 2002, O'Malley was running out of gas. For years, her strength in assembling funds and working with elected officials had moved the organization forward, but by then she knew it was time to leave. But O'Malley did not go away completely. Buoyed by her success, she ran for the Albuquerque City Council in 2003 and was elected, becoming a key ally of the project, positioned to access even more funding. In 2007 she passed a measure to create a city Workforce Housing Trust Fund, funded by general obligation bonds. The bonds are on the ballot every two years. They provide $10 million for land acquisition, low interest loans, and other support for affordable housing citywide.

Even the Railroad Tracks Didn't Stop Them

Ken Balizer, a former planner with the City of Albuquerque who was also attracted to the trust ethic, replaced O'Malley as executive director later in 2002. He and the group were eager to extend the development east and build a loft-style apartment building, but a new problem arose. The site was crisscrossed by railroad tracks used to transport lumber from the old plant to market. In order to proceed, the tracks had to be moved—an almost insurmountable bureaucratic challenge that involved the group's old opponent, Ponderosa Products. Ponderosa Products had closed in 2000 and was in foreclosure. A 7-acre parcel that included the tracks and the abandoned factory was for sale—along with the remains of decades of pollution. It seemed almost unthinkable, but what if the trust were to buy it and implement a remediation plan?

With the help of community allies it was not undoable. To help the trust buy the property, the New Mexico Community Development Loan Fund made the largest loan in its history. The Enterprise Social Investment Corporation joined in the risk sharing for a total loan package of $1.2 million.[17] In one fell swoop, SCLT moved out from under city control, says Balizer. "We no longer had to say, 'Mother may I.'" Instead, over the next several years the trust proceeded to work with lenders and developers to build several innovative low-income apartment buildings, including the Sawmill Lofts and Artisan Village, and they built more stand-alone houses on the original trust land. Along the way, they added a forty-six-unit senior housing development called Villa Nueva, complete with clubhouse, orchard, and community garden.

When I was a state senator, I joined in the community celebration to mark the demolition of the old Ponderosa Products factory. All the partners were there. It was one of the greatest neighborhood events I ever attended. I am proud to have helped them along the way.

Ponderosa Products had been a source of pollution in the Sawmill area of Albuquerque until the neighborhood organized to buy the land, tear it down and develop a housing project.

Photo by Erica Jett, courtesy of the Sawmill Community Land Trust.

The Sawmill Lofts, completed in July 2006, was a low-income housing tax credit project in which the trust contracted with a developer to build affordable live-work units designed for artists who wanted to be part of a community lifestyle. Designed by Dekker/Perich/Sabatini architects, the Lofts included a large commons area for meetings and parties and a playground. It was an immediate hit.

Connie Chavez, who became the Trust's third executive director, continued the momentum toward a style of mixed-use affordable devel-

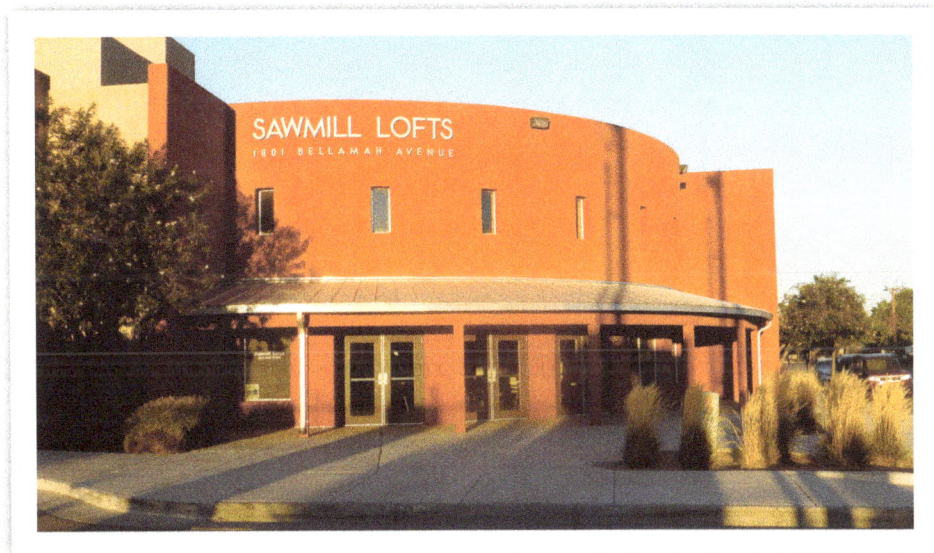

Connie Chavez, became the third executive director of Sawmill Community Land Trust and partnered with a developer on Sawmill Village, which incorporates businesses, a brewery, live-work spaces and apartments.

opment, which included retail and more live-work opportunities. Looking for something that would pay for itself without the burden of doing everything from renting to advertising, she leased the recently acquired land to another developer with infill experience in Portland, Oregon.

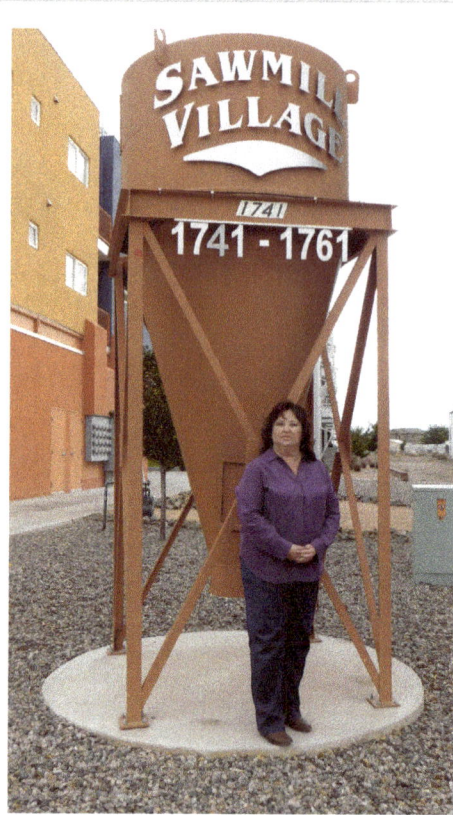

Chad Rennaker, owner of PacifiCap Properties Group, had used tax credits to build low-income housing before, and he was searching for a site in Albuquerque when he turned off the freeway onto Rio Grande Boulevard. He saw the newly cleared land and called the number on the nearby real estate sign. It was the beginning of a partnership between Chavez and Rennaker that built Sawmill Village, which now includes the "Mix," a twenty-unit apartment building that sports the Ponderosa Brewery, a coffee shop, and small fitness center on the ground floor; the Mix II, another apartment building; the two Artisan apartment buildings, which also feature shops and studios on the ground level; and Madera Crossing. The newest of these, Madera Crossing, has its own wastewater treatment system, which is tied into reclamation of an old detention pond for an urban refuge.

Rennaker says he was not familiar with land trusts, but had worked with low-income tax credits. Rennaker says the community component is unique, and he has come to appreciate it. When we talked, Rennaker was facing a community meeting with the neighborhood over the prospect of locating a Flamenco Academy, a charter school, on another piece of trust property. "I'm looking forward to it," he said, an unusual attitude for a developer. "The questions are so good and most of the people are so appreciative. It feels like a celebration of what we're doing together."

Rennaker is also the owner of the Ponderosa Brewery, which occupies a large part of the commercial area at the front of the Sawmill Village. He also owns a brewery in the Lents neighborhood of Portland. True to Sawmill style, the Ponderosa is family-friendly, with a children's area and an outdoor patio that is the scene of daytime meetings as well as nighttime drinking.

One of the offices in the nearby Artisan complex is occupied by the New Mexico Water Collaborative, a non-profit dedicated to water conservation. The director, Yvette Tovar, is working hard to contain her excitement about just finishing the Mill Pond Refuge, a project she has been working on for more than a year for the Sawmill Community Land Trust.

The project will recycle two thousand gallons of wastewater from Madera Crossing and divert it underground to provide drip irrigation for the banks of a 1½-acre detention pond. The now barren, empty pond will be revegetated with riparian landscaping and will include a

Ponderosa Brewery, owned by Chad Rennaker, is part of Sawmill Village.

walking trail, benches, and a pedestrian bridge. Rennaker was the first to jump on board, she said, with City Councilor Ike Benton and now County Commissioner Debbie O'Malley promising capital outlay funds. The project will not only serve the hundreds of residents of the land trust, but the surrounding neighborhoods as well.

"Our projects are all about collaboration," says Tovar. "We want to set a precedent for a zero–water footprint with no ground water pumped." The innovative approach, which required cooperation from permitting agencies, continues the Sawmill Community Land Trust's tradition of stewardship. The stewardship concept—applied to both resources and property—is something that is still taught to buyers who have never owned homes before. Even renters learn what Balizer calls a land trust ethic. "There needs to be a kind of stair step, to get in the door with an apartment," said Ken Balizer. "That's a big deal for some people who will go on to be homeowners."

Sawmill Today

The garage door fronting Rashan Jones's art glass studio is always open, and everyone passing by can see Rashan using a torch to fire and shape molten glass into objects. Rashan is a more recent convert to the Sawmill Community Land Trust. He serves on the board of the Trust and he loves to talk about the Artisan neighborhood, where he knows all the dogs. Jones has rented his shop/studio for three years and considers the neighborhood ideal for creatives. "It affords me the opportunity to do anything I want," he says.

Even before Sawmill Village was complete, Jones sensed something good. He moved in before the Ponderosa bar was open, when there was less pedestrian activity. The bottom line: he was eager to be a part of a community.

Although Jones doesn't have an apartment in the Artisan, others are operating out of live-work houses nearby. Judith Phillips is a landscaper and author who moved to her home from Vegita, NM, in 2013, attracted by the neighborhood's proximity to Old Town. She was one of the first owners of a live-work home on trust land. Her studio is on the ground level, as are the work areas for a nearby jeweler, hairstylist, and caterer. Because she was not a first-time homeowner, Phillips was not eligible for a subsidy and pays $824 per month—a fair price, she believes.

Rashan Jones' art glass studio in Sawmill Village is part of the live-work ambiance of Sawmill Village.

Kristina Leeder, a younger woman, lives nearby and has a small catering business. Her food truck is parked outside her 1,634-square-foot home, which she bought in 2008 with almost no down payment. She qualified for a $44,000 subsidy, making the $159,000 home cost $115,000—a price she could afford. She's proud to be a part of the trust, and until she became overwhelmed with a new baby and five other children, she was on the board of Artisan Village.

"There's a whole range of ages here, very diverse, very interesting people, and a walkable neighborhood," says Judith Phillips.

Lessons Learned: It's Doable

It has taken over three decades of organizing, deal making, and building, but Sawmill Community Land Trust and its neighborhood founders have proven that a well-organized community can defend its homeland and control its destiny. Sawmill hung on to its dream of a new kind of urban village and put its land and other assets—including the skills, connections and perseverance of its leaders—to work to reach it. The trust is now developing affordable housing projects in the Barelas section of Albuquerque. Residents anticipate a charter school focused on flamenco on a vacant piece of the Trust's land, as well as a proposed arts market to be developed by the nearby Hotel Albuquerque. The emphasis on traditional art and culture is not foreign to the area, as it was an important aspect of the original organizing effort. Several other charter schools are located nearby.

What did it take to succeed? "It takes intention and a determination to overcome obstacles and put all the pieces together. You have to believe it's doable," says Debbie O'Malley. "I learned by throwing my feet in the fire, and what a learning experience it was."

Once the project got started, O'Malley said that the group had to keep innovating, keep selling, keep networking, and keep getting revenue. That took perseverance and work, but one new leader took over from the other when the inevitable burnout struck.

Still, it takes an infusion of energy and enthusiasm to keep the original idea

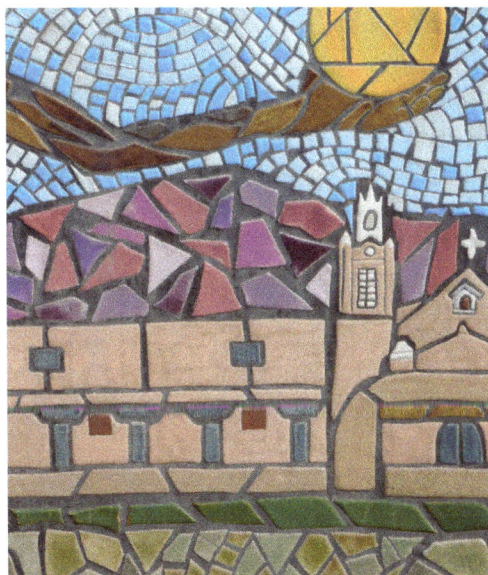

A detail from a mosaic created by one of Sawmill's myriad youth projects includes area landmarks: the local Catholic Church, mountains and adobe buildings.

alive and not let the project become just another housing development. For the past few years, the SCLT has had multiple directors and some have worried about its future, but the basic structure is there, and that helps, says Balizer. And, in New Mexico, the idea of stewardship and love of a particular place—along with its land, its history, and its past—does not disappear easily.

Yvette Tovar may not be familiar with the genesis of the Sawmill Community Land Trust years ago, but the energy and faith of Tovar, who in 2016 was installing the Mill Pond Refuge, is reminiscent of the environmental urgency of the original Sawmill Advisory Committee. She is pushing officials, residents, and everyone else in earshot for a zero–water footprint for all the housing developments—and she is succeeding. She is forging new partnerships and demonstrating that low-income people can be interested in the environment, as well as survival. It's a message that would make Sawmill's founders smile.

"We're in a crisis," she says, looking out from her Artisan office over the dry, empty drainage pond soon to be reclaimed. "But we have solutions. There are things we can do. We love the state, and we have a responsibility to leave it in better shape. It's doable."

A single-family home in Arbolera de Vida

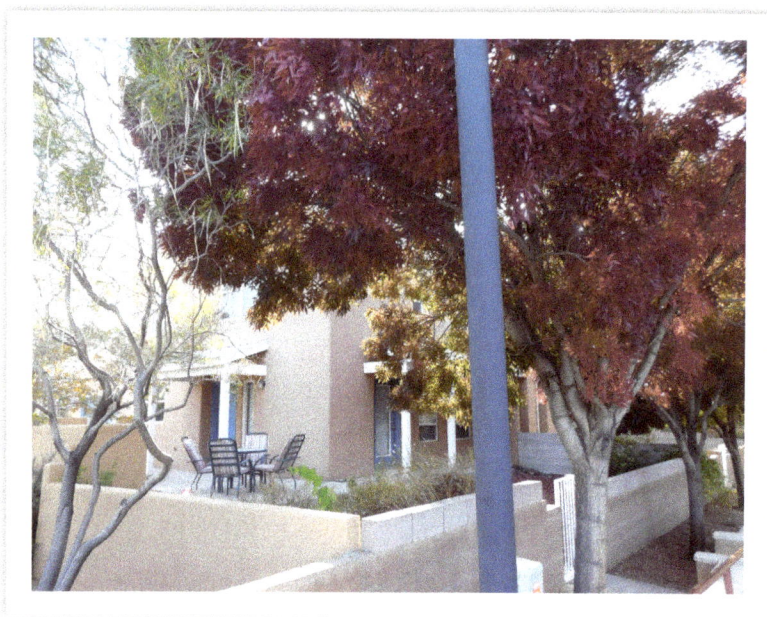

In a Nutshell

Problems

- Air and groundwater pollution contaminating an old low-income Hispanic neighborhood in Albuquerque

- Lack of affordable housing in the area due to gentrification

- The loss of community in an urbanizing area

Solution

- A community land trust to keep legal control and provide affordable housing

Partners

Neighborhood associations, City of Albuquerque, State of New Mexico Community Development Block Grant program, SouthWest Organizing Project, developers, local public and charter schools, a water collaborative, national and local foundations, elected officials, land use consultants, art centers and museums, a local hotel, banks and mortgage companies, UNM School of Architecture, volunteers and local residents.

What You Can Do

- Need to move? Check out apartment, loft, senior, or single-family living at the Sawmill Community Land Trust. Visit with its housing counselors to see whether your income qualifies you for a reduced price or whether a live-work space is right for you.

- Contribute to the Sawmill Community Land Trust. It is a non-profit. If you are part of a corporation, school, or business, consider sponsorship opportunities.

- Visit the Artisan Village, shop, have a cup of coffee at a local coffee shop or a beer at the Ponderosa Brewery.

- Attend a Sawmill Community meeting at the Lofts to see democratic decision-making in action.

- See if there is a housing trust or a land trust in your town and support it. Use the resources on the next page to investigate whether you could start a trust.

- Think about your own neighborhood and what kind of collective activity might be helpful to seniors, parents with young children, people with disabilities or those without transportation. Don't wait for a crisis.

- Defend your own turf against pollution. Work with the city and local agencies to create parks, trails, pedestrian-friendly streets, public transportation, and appropriate development.

Resources

Shelterforce
60 S. Fullerton Ave., #202
Montclair, NJ 07042
973-509-1600
www.shelterforce.org

Center for Community Change
1536 U Street NW
Washington, DC 20009
202-339-9300
http://www.communitychange.org/

National Housing Trust
1101 30th St, NW
Washington, DC 20007
202-333-8931
http://www.nationalhousingtrust.org/ice.php

Sawmill Community Land Trust
990 18th St. NW
Albuquerque, NM 87104
505-764-0359
http://www.sawmillclt.org

SouthWest Organizing Project
211 10th St. SW
Albuquerque, NM 87102
505-247-8832
www/swop.net

Lincoln Institute of Land Policy
113 Brattle Street
Cambridge, MA 02138-3400
Phone: 617-661-3016 or 800-LAND-USE (800-526-3873)
www.lincolninst.edu

Grounded Solutions Network
P.O. Box 42255
Portland, OR 97242
503-493-1000
www.cltnetwork.org

PART TWO
Reinventing Health Care in New Mexico

"Our vision is fundamentally about changing health care delivery across the state and nation, not just in Hidalgo and Grant Counties."

—Dan Otero, CEO, Hidalgo Medical Services

For years, good health care has been out of reach for a high proportion of New Mexicans, either because it costs too much or because it is simply unavailable in rural areas where there were few medical providers. Until the implementation of the Affordable Care Act ("Obamacare"), over one-fifth of our population did not have health insurance. Most small employers couldn't afford to offer it. And when there was no insurance there was usually no treatment, except in high-cost hospital emergency rooms, where patients would go when their problems became severe. Chronic diseases went untreated, and the incidence of diabetes, obesity, alcoholism, and drug addiction climbed. Medical and insurance costs also rose, partially to cover the cost of indigent and uncompensated care.

The Affordable Care Act had a big impact on New Mexico. Implementation began in 2011. Medicaid was expanded to cover almost 300,000 more patients, bringing the state's total to 760,000. Almost 40,000 more got coverage through the health insurance exchange. With the help of federal grants, primary health-care clinics ramped up to meet the increased demand. Programs to train the health-care workforce multiplied.

The Affordable Care Act, which may be rolled back in the coming years, focuses mostly on increased health-insurance coverage. But some of its measures are aimed at an underlying challenge: rearranging the delivery system to stem costs and improve quality. The high cost of medical care in the United States and our mediocre health statistics compared to other countries has long troubled health-care reformers. They want to make the shift from high-cost medical procedures to prevention.

That is like turning a battleship around. Even so, an intrepid group of health-care reformers keeps turning.

In New Mexico, long before the Affordable Care Act, most of the population was already covered by public insurance programs—Medicaid, Medicare, Indian Health Service, TRICARE, federal or state employee policies. Change would have to start there. Health maintenance organizations (HMOs) and private insurance, which contract with the state to operate the public programs and hire medical providers to deliver services, would have to comply. If the new programs were effective, the HMOs would adopt them for commercial policies as well.

In 2014 New Mexico launched Centennial Care, a reformed Medicaid program, which aimed at many of the same goals as Obamacare: more integrated care, case management of the most at-risk members, use of nonmedical providers, and payment for outcomes, rather than procedures. In 2017, the state is rolling out Centennial Care 2.0.

Implementation of the new program has been difficult, but all around the state, visionary leaders with a talent for spotting opportunities and building organizations are crafting solutions to New Mexico's long standing health-care problems from the ground up. By doing so, they are boosting local economic development and creating new opportunities and career paths for young people.

You will read about some of these innovative programs in the following chapters.

- Near the boot heel of New Mexico, in the far southwest corner of the state, a mandolin player with a PowerPoint presentation created one of the state's first medical homes, and he is now recruiting dentists and primary-care doctors to underserved rural areas.

- In Santa Fe, a fireman with a degree in the classics from St. John's College has created a community paramedicine program where firefighters help the most frequent users of the local emergency room.

- In Albuquerque, a CEO in the South Valley is on a mission to create a wellness ecosystem in a low-income area with some of the poorest health outcomes in the state.

- In Jemez Pueblo, public-health advocates are mobilizing the community's assets to prevent disease, using the outdoors as their fitness center and opening the doors of their clinic to non-tribal members. Elsewhere, communities are mobilizing, coordinating previously separate efforts, and beginning to prove that these new models can save money and improve lives.

- Everywhere around the state community health workers, navigators, and community health representatives are focused on underlying patient problems—the social determinants of health. In doing so, they are beginning to reduce costs all around.

A common denominator of these efforts is that they put the patient—not the medical provider—at the center of the system. They draw on existing community assets to address the social roots of many medical problems—and help patients help themselves with proper nutrition, access to better housing, education and training programs. Ultimately, the new programs will be paid for based on the well-being of their patients—moving the incentive from multiple treatments to prevention of illness.

This kind of change is "transformative," says Dr. Art Kaufman, "and it saves money." Kaufman, the University of New Mexico's vice chancellor for community medicine, says that we are now in a transition period. Many of the programs are struggling. He agrees with Institute for Healthcare Improvement founder Don Berwick's description: "We have one foot on the dock and the other in the boat." HMOs and Medicaid are not yet willing to fully reimburse programs for some of the innovative services. But Kaufman and others believe the ship has sailed and it's not coming back. And as federal reimbursements for treatments once paid for by Medicaid shrink under the new federal administration, the HMOs will begin to come onboard.

Kaufman says that the HMOs ultimately will change from a fee-for-service system to a capitated one where providers will be given a per member payment and allowed to arrange treatment as they see fit. Then, the use of community health workers, team-based care, and mid-level professionals will make sense.

Regardless of what happens to the other parts of the Affordable Care Act, Kaufman believes this shift will happen in more and more networks—with better outcomes for the patient. The costs of the current uncoordinated, procedure-driven system are simply unsustainable.

Berwick calls it a boat, but Kaufman says it's a train, and he says "the train has already left the station."

Meanwhile, the visionaries you will meet here are driving it, taking detours if needed, and charting new directions. The home base for many of these reformers is a primary health-care clinic.

In most of rural New Mexico, and in parts of the state's urban centers, community-based health-care clinics offer the best chance for affordable health care. Since the 1970s, New Mexico's clinics have been on the front line, providing primary care at 160 sites for patients who have no regular doctor or who are not covered by insurance. The clinics' sliding fee scale and their local boards of directors (with patient members) has kept them at a human, community scale. Many of their 340,000 patients are covered by Medicaid.

Now, the clinics are providing innovative solutions to problems that have social as well as medical roots by using a team-based approach and nonmedical professionals. One (First Choice Community Healthcare) offers access to healthy, organic food. Another (Hidalgo Medical Services) provides mentorship and training opportunities for the next generation of health-care providers. Yet another (Jemez Comprehensive Health Center) offers an array of physical fitness programs to prevent disease—and not just treat it after the fact.

All of them are driving economic development in the communities that need it most, creating direct and indirect jobs and driving the purchase of local goods and services.

We begin our journey in the South Valley of Albuquerque, visiting a clinic operated by First Choice Community Healthcare, which has clinics in four New Mexico counties.

CHAPTER 5

Reaching Beyond the Clinic Walls:
First Choice Community Healthcare

"Health begins where we live, work, learn and play."

—Dr. Will Kaufman, director, Community Health and Wellness,
First Choice Community Healthcare

O n the last Saturday of every month, the kitchen area at the
First Choice Community Health Center in Albuquerque's
South Valley is filled with mothers and grandmothers of all
ages, many with children in tow. They are eating up the samples of the
healthy dishes prepared by visiting chefs, learning how to substitute
healthy ingredients, and sharing shopping tips. Some are scribbling
notes and listening to Dr. Will Kaufman, a primary-care doctor at the
clinic, explain the role of sugar in diabetes—in Spanish and English.
Many are drawing the little boxes Kaufman uses to illustrate the role
of insulin in the chronic disease.

Diabetes is one of the nagging health problems in this low-income,
minority, and immigrant area. The overall rate is three- to four-times
higher than the rest of the state. Half of all the children are overweight
or obese, and neighborhoods adjacent to the health center have a life
span that is between thirteen to seventeen years shorter. [18]

The area's poor health—in comparison to the rest of the state—comes
despite the best efforts of doctors and nurses. The disparity is based on
nonmedical factors: the lack of good jobs, a low graduation rate at the
local high school, and a shortage of healthy foods and safe places to
exercise. Those problems add up to chronic stress, and sometimes even
violence.

Dr. Will Kaufman, director of Community Health and Wellness at First Choice Community Healthcare, explains diabetes. It goes down easier at Saturday morning cooking classes co-sponsored by the South Valley clinic and community groups.

To address what the experts call these "social determinants of health," First Choice has teamed up with La Cosecha, a community-supported agriculture (CSA) group, the New Mexico Early Childhood Alliance, and the Korimi Early Childhood Cooperative of daycare workers. Presbyterian Healthcare Services and Blue Cross/Blue Shield are also partners. Between thirty to sixty people attend the classes each month, taking home a free grocery bag of local, organic food. Some of the mothers walk there; others are patients at the clinic.

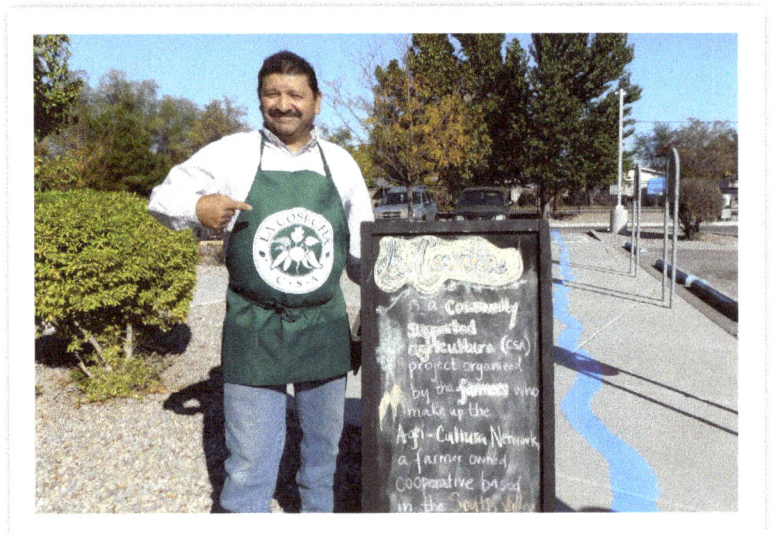

Not every cooking class has a "barker" like Ramon Dorado, of Koremi, to welcome participants to the healthy gathering, sponsored by La Cosecha, the Agri-Cultura Network, and local health-care providers. The wavy line on the sidewalk is a painted exercise trail used by visitors to the clinic.

"It's working on health in a very different kind of way," says Kaufman. "They are learning from each other, sharing tips...it's so much more effective than a ten-minute office visit." In that short period, or even in a series of visits, Kaufman said, doctors don't always get to connect with patients on an effective plan that fits their lifestyle.

Often patients will come back in three months without any change—and that's three important months lost in the course of their disease. "Our tools are mismatched to our needs," Kaufman said.

That's why he was so excited to join First Choice four years ago where they were aiming upstream—at some of the causes of poor health. "They were stating out loud that they were going to address the social determinants of health," he said. He credits the approach to Bob DeFelice, the CEO of First Choice since 1999.

A Man on a Mission

Bob DeFelice sits in a small, unassuming office in the portable structure dedicated to the administration of what is now one of the largest providers of primary care in New Mexico. He keeps pointing outside his window, toward a cluster of nearby houses. As he talks about the organization he has led for almost twenty years, his hands fly and his eyes twinkle. When he says "out there" I realize he's talking about the community outside the window, outside the walls of the forty-four-year-old clinic.

DeFelice's neat mustache is gray now, testimony to just how long DeFelice has been at it, attending almost every meeting concerning public health or primary care at the state legislature, at the forefront of coalitions designed to increase access through a nurse advice hotline, or protecting uninsured patients. Trained in both public health and busi-

Bob DeFelice, CEO of First Choice Community Healthcare, is a man on a mission to create a wellness ecosystem in the South Valley.

Photo courtesy of First Choice Community Healthcare

ness, DeFelice started his work on the Navajo Nation's reservation in the early 1970s, where he was inspired by the legendary Annie Dodge Wauneka, who first introduced the idea of disease to the Navajos and facilitated the Many Farms Project.[19] There, he watched community health representatives from the Indian Health Service help patients, even delivering hay for them in the winter. Later, he traveled the state with Presbyterian Medical Services, and was called in on an early rescue mission to refine the business practices of a developing clinic in the South Valley called the Family Health Center, later First Choice. He has always been guided by the idea that a primary care clinic is a business. "A compassionate business, he says, "but a business." But like other clinics in New Mexico, First Choice did not start that way.

A Clinic in a Rectory, a Matanza, and Fifty Cases of Beer

The first clinic operated by what is now First Choice opened in 1972 in the rectory of the St. Francis Xavier Church in the South Broadway area of Albuquerque. The clinic grew out of a community process, led by activists including Richard Moore of the Black Berets and doctors like Suzanne and Ham Brown, two pediatricians who had been seeing patients at the University of New Mexico Hospital. The barrio, the activists pointed out, had no health facilities that low-income residents could trust or travel to easily. Over thirty doctors volunteered for the cause, but it would take more than good will to serve the South Valley.

To prove the need to the elected officials who controlled the purse strings, a study was undertaken. More important, recalls former Bernalillo County Attorney Joe Diaz, was a huge *matanza* (pig roast). The community feast—a South Valley tradition—was a great success, in part because of the donation of fifty cases of beer by well-known liquor distributor George Maloof. Both federal and state officials attended and ate the *chicharrón* (fried pork rinds) and roasted pork. Shortly thereafter, in 1974, government money began to flow. The Family Health Center (*El Centro Familiar*) was created off of Isleta Boulevard, south of Arenal Boulevard.

Over forty years later, First Choice operates eight different health clinics (and one school-based clinic at Rio Grande High School) in three counties (Bernalillo, Santa Fe, and Valencia), serving over fifty thousand patients with 425 employees and an annual operating budget of $35 million. Approximately eighty of the employees are medical providers, many of them from the communities they serve. A Federally Qualified Health Center (FQHC), First Choice provides dental and behavioral health services as well as primary medical care. It is the state's largest WIC (Women Infants, and Children) site, and one of the largest providers of Suboxone, used to treat opioid addition. It is a major teaching site as well, with thirteen family-practice residents and clinical rotations for physician assistants and nurse practitioners, many of whom decide to stay in New Mexico, some at First Choice.

Like other FQHCs, First Choice has long served clients who need it with a sliding fee scale and discounted prescription drugs. Since the implementation of the Affordable Care Act, more patients are covered by Medicaid (50 percent) and other insurance through the New Mexico Health Insurance Exchange. Still, about 17 percent are uninsured, many of them immigrants. The number is sure to grow if the Affordable Care Act is repealed or cut back.

Throughout the 1990s and 2000s, the clinic pioneered a health-commons approach, "colocating" dental and social services in its clinics. The facilities themselves expanded and modernized. The hallmark of the health commons is a "warm handoff" of patients from one type of practitioner to another. It is a holistic, multidisciplinary approach that makes life easier for patients, who get more coordinated care. In response to patient demand, more behavioral-health services were added. Later, First Choice was designated as a patient-centered medical home, which allows even more coordination. It also allows First Choice to focus on chronic diseases like diabetes and hypertension, using patient care facilitators and community health workers to coach and educate patients.

Linda Baca and Veronica Torres are two of these facilitators in the South Valley office. They are often on the phone or visiting with patients who are struggling to adjust their blood sugar, teaching them how to inject insulin or reminding them about the benefits of exercise and healthy eating. On Monday, Tuesday, and Wednesday at 6:30 a.m. they walk with a group of patients at a nearby community center. Some can't afford insulin, they say. Others can't read or write, and don't understand directions on pill bottles.

"There are a lot of success stories," Linda Baca says. "In two years one of our patients, Ronald, lost 20 pounds and his [blood sugar] count went from 12.1 down to 5.6. He's no longer diabetic." Baca and Torres say patients develop a sense of trust in them and tell them things they don't share with others.

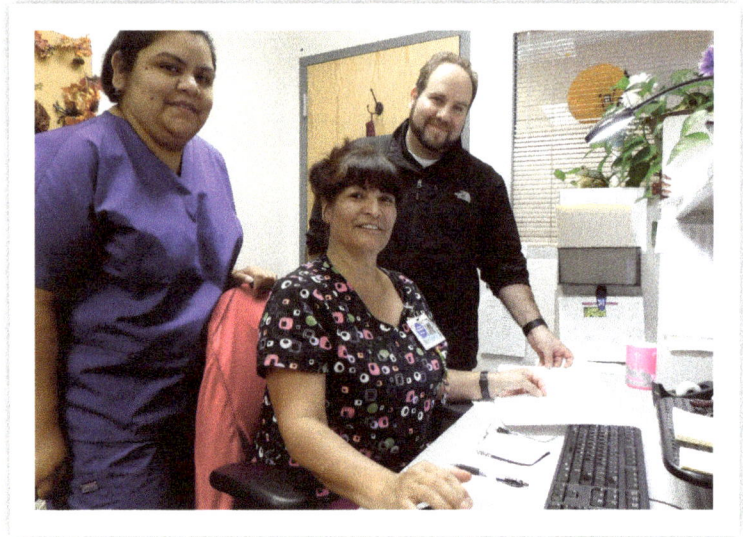

Patient Care Facilitators Veronica Torres (l) and Linda Baca (c) help patients manage chronic diseases like diabetes, in consultation with their doctor, Dr. Will Kaufman (r). A coordinated plan for social, as well as medical factors, is the key to improved outcomes.

Most important, the facilitators help patients develop a plan—and keep them on track. For more complex social needs, First Choice refers patients to community health workers who are hooked into a network of social, as well as medical, agencies. It is all a part of a more coordinated plan. "It's important to address the chaos in patients' lives in order to focus on chronic illness," says Bob DeFelice. "Not too many patients have just one problem."

To screen patients for social needs that may be affecting their health, First Choice developed and piloted WellRX, an eleven-question survey administered to patients that asks about adequate food, shelter, transportation, employment, and other factors. Patients are now screened at each visit, and if they answer "yes" to any of the questions they are referred to either a facilitator or a community health worker for help. About half of the patients screened positive for at least one area of social need, and 63 percent had multiple needs.

Community health workers, stationed at the clinic, follow up, searching for resources like food banks, helping patients fill out job applications, and accompanying them to apply for benefits.

I visited with one of the First Choice's community health workers, Jorge Monroy-Sosa, as he prepared to visit one of his clients, a man who had sustained a traumatic brain injury in a motorcycle accident. Jorge noticed that, although the man had arrived on a bicycle, he seemed to constantly veer to the left as he walked, increasing the risk of accidents. Monroy-Sosa discovered the man lived in a trailer with no food or decent clothing. Now he meets him periodically, bringing him a food box and clothing from a rescue mission. Other encounters are brief. Jorge can sometimes just arrange for physical therapy or make sure that a client's utilities have not been shut off. Then he may never see the client again. "We do a little of everything...I can jump in or send them to someone who can help," he says.

Doctors were skeptical of the approach at first, but as a larger team assumed the burden they could not carry alone, they began to see changes. The Well RX pilot has been published in the *Journal of the American Board of Family Medicine*, and the screening tool has now been adopted by other clinics operated by University of New Mexico and Hidalgo Medical Services (in southeast New Mexico).

"Our big idea here is to convince the managed care organizations (MCOs) who serve Medicaid patients that they ought to pay for this since it both improves outcomes and saves money," said Will Kaufman, who is now the First Choice Director of Community Health and Wellness.

Although some MCOs like Molina Health Care are believers, Kaufman and other proponents of the approach aren't there yet. Medicaid cuts may delay the process, but they are determined to prove the model they've built will work.

"We Are Inspired by a Bold Vision"

Even with the new approach, Bob DeFelice and his team were not satisfied that their organization was fulfilling its mission. "While we provide the highest level of care and access, we find our community is not getting well. The reason is that access to high-quality care is only one piece of the puzzle of wellness. Addressing the social determinants of health is key," DeFelice told a legislative committee meeting at the clinic in the summer of 2016.

DeFelice says that it's things like nutrition, adequate housing, healthy lifestyles, safety, and education that most affect health. Medical care only affects health outcomes about 10 percent of the time. To increase the wellness of a community, DeFelice says you must "partner up" with innovators in education, agriculture, and fitness, and he has a bold vision to do so.

"I hope our legacy will be that we've shown people how they can work together and maximize their collective resources to impact the wellness of communities. One person can't do it alone, and it's not just health care that's going to increase the wellness of communities. It's jobs, education and all the other pieces," he says

In the next five to seven years, First Choice will expand its South Valley campus to become a "wellness ecosystem," which will include a 5,000-square-foot food hub, a 4-acre community farm and solar greenhouse, as well as a farm-to-table restaurant that will provide local food for adjacent facilities. Nearby, a 6,000-square-foot early childhood development center will prepare sixty toddlers for kindergarten, and a 30,000-square-foot charter high school, the Health Leadership High School, will be home to 440 students. The site will also include a 15,000-square-foot workforce-training center to train and retrain unemployed residents, along with a 15,000-square-foot wellness center to provide fitness and health education for anyone from the area. The nearby national Valle de Oro Urban Wildlife Refuge, the nation's first urban wildlife refuge, will operate a satellite at the expanded 20-acre site, which will ultimately include a pond and hiking trails.

The bold vision of a "commons with a heart" was developed through a series of community workshops. Local residents, already involved with First Choice as board members, patients, or employees, wanted something in keeping with local tradition, so a plaza will be the center-piece of the $25 million project.

Money for the project will come from grants, partnerships, donations, and revenue generated by the businesses that will be located on the expanded campus. First Choice is well on its way. In 2010 it started acquiring adjacent land, and it has won several prestigious national grants from the Robert Wood Johnson, Kresge, de Beaumont, and Colorado Health foundations, as well as support from local partners like Blue Cross/Blue Shield, Presbyterian Healthcare, Wells Fargo, and Public Service Company of New Mexico.

One funder is especially enthusiastic about the holistic approach. "First Choice gets that health is more than pills and procedures," says Brian Castrucci, chief program and strategic officer of the de Beaumont Foundation, which specializes in public health.

First Choice was recently (2016) awarded a $1 million grant for infra-structure from the Economic Development Administration (EDA), and it is working to access new tax credits for FQHCs. "Each part of the economic model will be self-sustaining, and their interactions will increase family income, the most important step to improve health," says DeFelice.

Michelle Melendez, former First Choice development director, says that First Choice is simply creating a "platform for enterprises" in an area that desperately needs the economic development. Over time the platform will pay off and, as the businesses develop, they will create 481 direct and indirect jobs paying a projected $77 million in sala-ries in the first ten years. The activity will inject $135 million over a ten-year period into the local economy, according to an independent economic analysis.

In spite of the economic benefits, DeFelice still finds resistance. "They ask me for a product—a widget," he says. "But healthcare is not like that...it's complex."

Healthcare may not be a widget, but since the 2008 recession it has been the only segment of the state's economy that has continued to grow and provide job opportunities. Why not build on it? Unlike manufacturing or call centers, health-care services are based on in-state patients. The skills used are transferable from clinic to hospital to nursing facility to medical labs. And the jobs are more stable than call centers or manufacturing.

Building Toward a Robust Health-Care Economy

A robust health-care economy will require a new kind of medical and paraprofessional training. First Choice is already a major training site for UNM medical school residents, dentists, nurse practitioners, and physician assistants. It is a National Health Service Corps site, where medical and dental residents from other states can get partial repayment for their weighty student loans. Most of the residents select the clinic for its integrated model and are willing to accept lower salaries (about $40,000 per year less) for the exceptional mentoring and learning opportunities available there.

In order to develop a better pipeline, First Choice has championed a charter high school in Albuquerque focused on other health careers. It is called the Health Leadership High School. Housed in a temporary office building near Albuquerque's airport, it is focused on students who drop or flunk out of local high schools. But it is by no means a traditional vocational school. In 2017 the school graduated its first class, 44 students, and it aims to enroll 440 students by the time it is fully built on the new First Choice campus.

Whether it is math, science, or other subjects, everything that is taught at Health Leadership High School is taught through the lens of community health. "We want our students to understand what a healthy lifestyle is both personally and for the community," says the school's principal, Blanca Lopez.

"It's very much a school that asks the public health questions about root causes of illness," says Melendez, who was active in the school's founding. "We're trying to get them to see how the food system and early childhood development can determine health."

The school's curriculum is project-based, with the projects designed with the input of community partners—often other health-care businesses like the University of New Mexico Hospital. Students form teams to do research on topics like shaken baby syndrome or the treatment of opioid addictions and then make presentations to community members, business leaders, and health-care professionals. Students must also complete service projects. Last year, one student team produced age-appropriate books and reading materials for the waiting room at the children's clinic at UNM Hospital. Another team presented health-based entertainment for patients in waiting rooms.

The school feeds students into health programs at the Community College of New Mexico (CCNM) and counsels students on their chosen career pathways, maybe as a fitness trainer at a gym or a licensed practical nurse. Graduates receive a "certificate with currency," which, while not a license, means something to First Choice and the other members of the community board of directors, who say that the caliber of students emerging from the private for-profit training schools is often poor.

"We need problem solvers," says Melendez, previously director of First Choice training. In the new environment, it won't be enough to work in isolation, to just draw blood or take blood pressure readings. Even entry-level jobs involve the soft skills of listening, interviewing, working with clients, and understanding the system.

In a Nutshell

Problem

- High rates of chronic disease and poor health in the South Valley of Albuquerque, based largely on social factors like the lack of jobs, safe neighborhoods, access to healthy food, and exercise opportunities

Big Ideas

- A "Wellness Ecosystem" that incorporates medical care with education, jobs, healthy food, and exercise
- The use of community health workers to address the social determinants of health and help navigate patients through the system
- A "Health Commons" to centralize the delivery of medical and social services

Partners

Patients, health-care providers, community health workers, community board of directors, community coalition of daycare workers, a local agricultural network, a county health council, a charter health high school, an interagency "pathways" program to help coordinate care for local residents, a national wildlife preserve, the UNM Medical School, several health insurance companies, national and local foundations, state, local, and federal governments.

What You Can Do

- Attend a meeting of your county's community health council to understand health problems in your neighborhood and what you can do as a volunteer, donor, or partner.

- Volunteer at the Health Leadership High School to be on a community panel reviewing the work of these emerging healthcare workers.

- Enroll in one of the clinic's prevention programs or come to a cooking class or a farmers' market during the growing season.

- Make a tax-deductible contribution to First Choice; play golf at one of its fund-raising tournaments.

- If you are a medical student, check out the First Choice residency program.

- Write a letter to your Congressperson, United States Senator, or state legislator supporting adequate funding for primary care clinics and Medicaid.

- Find ways for your church or fraternal organization to partner with First Choice through sponsorships or in-kind donations.

- Not happy with the medical care you or your family members receive? Check out First Choice and if you like what you see, make it your medical home.

Resources

First Choice Community Healthcare
Administrative Offices
2001 N. Centro Familiar SW
Albuquerque, NM 87105
505-873-7400
http://www.fcch.com/

New Mexico Primary Care Association
4206 Louisiana Blvd. NE
Albuquerque, NM 87109
505-880-8882
http://www.nmpca.org

Center for Primary Care
Harvard Medical School
https://primarycare.hms.harvard.edu/

The de Beaumont Foundation
7501 Wisconsin Ave. Suite 1310 E
Bethesda, MD 20814
301-961-5800
www.debeaumont.org

Health Leadership High School
1900 Randolph Rd. SE
Albuquerque, NM 87106
505-750-4547
http://healthleadershiphighschool.org

CHAPTER 6
Using Tradition to Build a Healthy Community in Jemez Pueblo

"It's a strength-based approach. We look at cultural strengths, natural resources and values in the pueblo, and try to use those to foster the health of individuals and the community."
— Kristyn Yepa, public health manager, Jemez Pueblo

At first glance there is a big difference between the South Valley of Albuquerque where First Choice Community Healthcare is trying to create a wellness ecosystem and the self-contained Pueblo of Jemez, seventy miles to the northwest. However, both communities are drawing on their own assets to promote healthy behavior. The assets are found in each area's unique culture, and native languages (Spanish and Towa) convey the appropriate messages. For both, the focus is on wellness, not just sickness.

———————

I knew they would come. Any minute they would round the bend on Highway 4, stretching from one end of San Diego Canyon, with its steep red cliffs, to the other. Some might straggle along and others sprint, but the runners from Jemez Pueblo would not fail to come. It was Pueblo Independence Day, and they would be headed toward the Jemez State Monument for a day-long celebration of the day in 1680 when runners from several of the state's nineteen pueblos carried knotted yucca cords to communicate the date of the successful uprising against the Spanish.

And there they were—a few young men and women in the lead and then a score of children, teenagers, followed by a back-up chain of SUVs and trucks bearing mothers, grandmothers, and supporters with water and provisions.

Running is a tradition that goes deep within Jemez Pueblo. Footraces are a part of feast days at Walatowa, the traditional name for the pueblo, which is located fifty miles northwest of Albuquerque, bordering the rural checkerboard expanse that includes a patchwork of Native American settlements, federal, and state land. At an elevation of 5,600 feet, the air is rare, something that may have helped native sons Al Waquie and Steve Gachupin become two of the best high-altitude and long-distance runners in the world.

"It's who we are," says Steve Moya, a health advocate and part of the ten-member Fitness Innovate Training Team (FITT). "Running is a good balance of the spiritual and the physical and it's at the core of everything," adds Daniel Madalena.

And it's not just for hardcore athletes. Daniel Madalena, Steve Moya, Cornell Magdalena, and Brandon Pecos, FITT members, do their best to get everyone involved. There are turkey trots, warrior dashes, resilience runs, triple-fit duathalons, fifty-yard tire throws, and uphill farmers' walks (carrying buckets of water). There is something for everyone in the 3,500-member pueblo, from ordinary fitness buffs to those who have been referred by the medical staff of the Jemez Com-

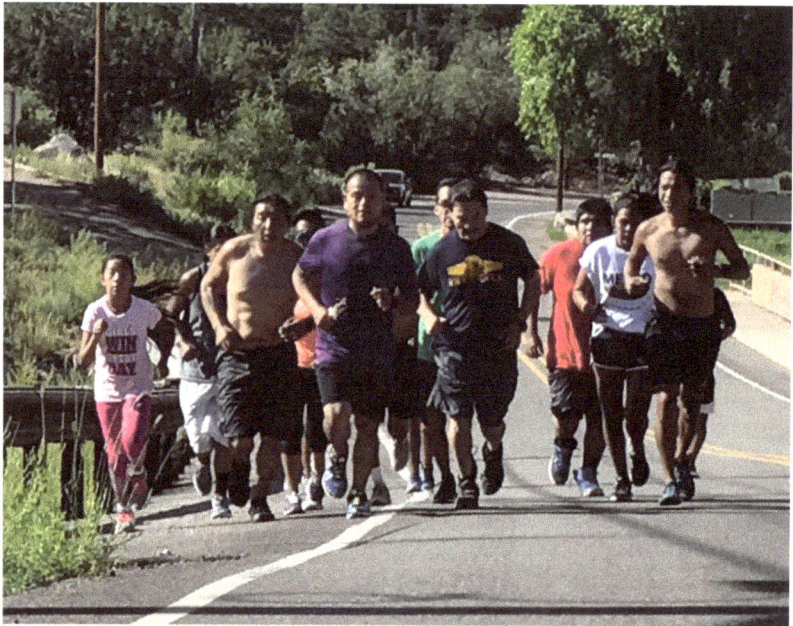

Jemez Pueblo's tradition of running can be traced back to the Pueblo Revolt in 1680. Today it is harnessed by the Pueblo's Fitness Innovate Training Team for public health. Here Jemez runners complete the last leg of a ten-mile ceremonial run to the Jemez Historic Site.

Photo by T.S. Last @Albuquerque Journal. Reprinted with permission.

prehensive Health Clinic or one of the pueblo's community health representatives. Most popular are the all-ages fun runs and walks along the prescription trail network built a few years ago with funding from the Centers for Disease Control (CDC) to encourage walking, biking, and hiking. It was an effort to address the alarming rates of obesity in the pueblo (68.6 percent of people between five and fourteen years old and 93.5 percent of people between twenty-five and forty-four years old were overweight or obese in 2009) and the high rate of diabetes.[20] Many of the free events draw from 60–250 people. They are part of a deliberate strategy to mobilize the community using the tradition of running. To reinforce the practice, the FITT team has produced a documentary about the life of six-time Pike's Peak Marathon winner, Steve Gachupin.[21]

Other communities in rural and urban parts of New Mexico are realizing that providing access to trails can help address obesity-related diseases like diabetes and heart ailments. In Cuba, NM, sixty miles from Jemez, the Step Into Cuba Alliance, along with the Nacimiento Community Foundation, has built a trail network that offers opportunities for walking and hiking. There are now walking clubs and volunteers who maintain the trails. A new section of the national Continental Divide Trail is planned. In Taos County, the Taos Land Trust is creating a prescription parks and trails program. The efforts to maximize opportunities for healthy outdoor recreation are almost endless in New Mexico, yet, according to a study by Headwaters Economics, Hispanics and low-income residents use trails about half as frequently as other residents.[22]

"Our fitness center is out there in the mountains," says Cornell Magdalena. "The mountains await us, to put forth our footprint and connect with nature." The outdoor approach was born out of a realization that Kristyn Yepa, the manager of public health, had a few years ago. "The medical model was not working for us." In ten years, she says, there has been very little success in affecting the pueblo's long-elevated diabetes rate. One good attempt was a $1 million Communities Putting Prevention to Work (CPPW) grant that in 2010 brought Health and Human Services Secretary Kathleen Sebelius to the pueblo to distribute bicycles and kick off a physical education program for elementary students. Although the program created a generation of biking enthusiasts and started a gardening project, it was not completely successful, Yepa feels, because it did not fully utilize the social context.

"We have to look at culture and language, the practices and relationships that make Jemez Jemez," she says. "We have to look at ways we were self-sufficient and reintroduce historic practices like agriculture and running."

A Medical Home for More than Pueblo Members

The Jemez Comprehensive Health Center, as the name implies, is more than a regular Indian Health Service facility. It is a state-of-the-art rural primary-care center based in family practice, but also incorporating dental, optometric, radiology, behavioral health, and pharmacy services. It employs 130 people—including Kristyn Yepa and the FITT team, and it is integrated with the tribe's human services department and its array of social and senior services. The clinic's approximately 2,100 patients wait for the doctor or nurse in a beautiful waiting room with flagstone floors below and a wooden, viga-supported ceiling above. Patients sometimes bring salsa or oven bread to sell or share. Despite the clean lines and the high tech electronic records system there is a distinctive Native American feel.

It's a "hybrid" model, explained Dr. David Tempest, the clinic's medical director for six years. The clinic is funded by both the Indian Health Service (IHS) and HRSA (Health Resources and Services Administration), which typically funds rural primary-health clinics. But it's operated by the tribe under the "638" program, which allows the tribe and not IHS to call the shots. "That has made all the difference," says Tempest.

"Jemez is pretty progressive," he added.

One of the most progressive moves the administration made in 2013 was to open the clinic—previously for members only—to the larger rural community, including the village of Jemez Springs where medical care was only available one and a half hours away in Albuquerque. The Jemez clinic is one of the few Native American facilities nationwide to swing open its doors, and it has had a big impact on the isolated area.

"Every non-native person who comes here has said, 'Wow,'" Tempest said. "They are surprised and impressed by the full services we offer." Like other rural primary-care clinics, the Jemez clinic charges on a sliding scale, offers lower prices on prescription drugs, and accepts Medicaid and private insurance. It was designated in 2013 as a medical home in recognition of its electronic records and integrated approach.

But the Jemez clinic is different because the main community it serves—the pueblo—is contained just outside its doors and connected by a web of employees and long-time patients. Five community health representatives, Towa-speaking patient advocates and educators, link chronically ill patients to the clinic. They do monthly home visits with members who are over age sixty-five, deliver medications, and help people who have been recently discharged from the hospital. It's nothing new to Jemez and other New Mexico tribes. Communi-

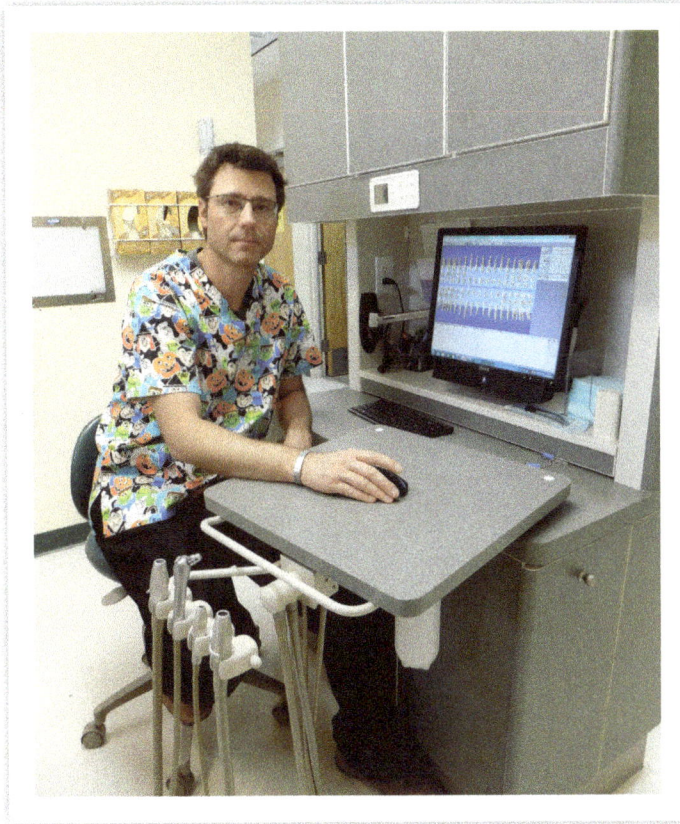

Dental care is part of the medical home at the Jemez Health and Human Services Comprehensive Health Center, which is open to the surrounding rural residents. Dr. James Strosheim is the dentist.

ty health representatives were the precursors of community health workers, now used in urban areas. Because they were usually isolated and already offered multiple services, native health facilities were "ahead of the game," said Tempest.

Moving From a Food Desert to Food Sovereignty

The bulletin board at the entrance to the Jemez Comprehensive Health Center was overflowing with announcements, notices, and calendar items on the day I visited. Among them was an invitation from the Jemez Public Health Department to several upcoming grocery-shopping trips to three different stores (Walmart, Albertson's, and Smith's) located in Rio Rancho, an hour away. The goal of the trip was to learn how to read labels and become a smart shopper. Another flyer advertised the upcoming visit of MoGro, a mobile food distribution service that visits the clinic regularly, offering food boxes at $10 for a box of twenty organic fruits and vegetables. For food-stamp recipients, the cost is half. Orders could be placed online or with clinic staff.

The information is valuable to those who live in a food desert, with few places to shop for food other than convenience stores. Although Jemez is only an hour and a half from Albuquerque, transportation can be a problem. Technically, Jemez is a food desert, even though the pueblo is surrounded by fields once farmed by families to produce the tribe's prized red chiles and corn.

"I used to see men from the pueblo with wagons laden down with tools or carrying buckets, making their way down to their fields by the river," says Eileen Shendo. "Now everybody is too busy, or texting. We've lost that kind of healthy outdoor lifestyle."

Shendo is one of a group of young people reviving agriculture in Jemez Pueblo. Eileen Shendo and Towana Yepa have been through a training program sponsored by the American Friends Service Committee (Chapter 3). Along with Justin Casiquito and Dale Tafoya they are starting a small business, the StrictlyRoots Greenhouse.

The venture will operate a 30-by-100-foot hoop greenhouse all year round, and supply organic foods to local schools and social-service programs. The greenhouse will be located behind the San Diego Riverside Charter School. In October 2016 the greenhouse kit lay in a large canvas bag at the side of the site, and the enthusiastic young woman was eager to get it up. She is no stranger to hoop greenhouses (there are two others on the nearby community garden), and she knows they are the key to producing a steady stream of crops for customers.

Red chile is a Jemez tradition. Here, Eileen Shendo, a young farmer trained by an American Friends Service Committee program, tends to the harvest in a hoop greenhouse. The chile, and other crops, will feed elementary school children at the San Diego Riverside Charter School.

Shendo says the business will incorporate an agricultural curriculum with hands-on opportunities for elementary students, like her own children. The instruction will be in Towa, the unique language of Jemez. The group has been key in revitalizing farmers' markets in the Jemez Valley, and it understands the importance of cooperating with other farmers—native and non-native.

Shendo's group is already farming multiple fields. Five families from the pueblo have allowed it to use their land allotments, and Shendo says they are seeking more partners of all kinds. Water and land use are key issues for Native American tribes. Tribal nations like Jemez Pueblo have senior water rights, meaning that in times of shortage they have the first claim on water coming from rivers like the Jemez River. But farmers in the Jemez Valley have had a tradition of cooperation, which Shendo hopes to build on with an ethic that strives to protect natural resources for everyone.

The group's efforts are squarely in line with the Jemez clinic's focus on "food sovereignty." It is a term that reflects the tribe's status as a sovereign nation, as well as a drive toward the self-sufficiency that traditionally characterized all of the pueblos. The pueblo operates a community garden, Kristyn Yepa explained, an effort that grew out of

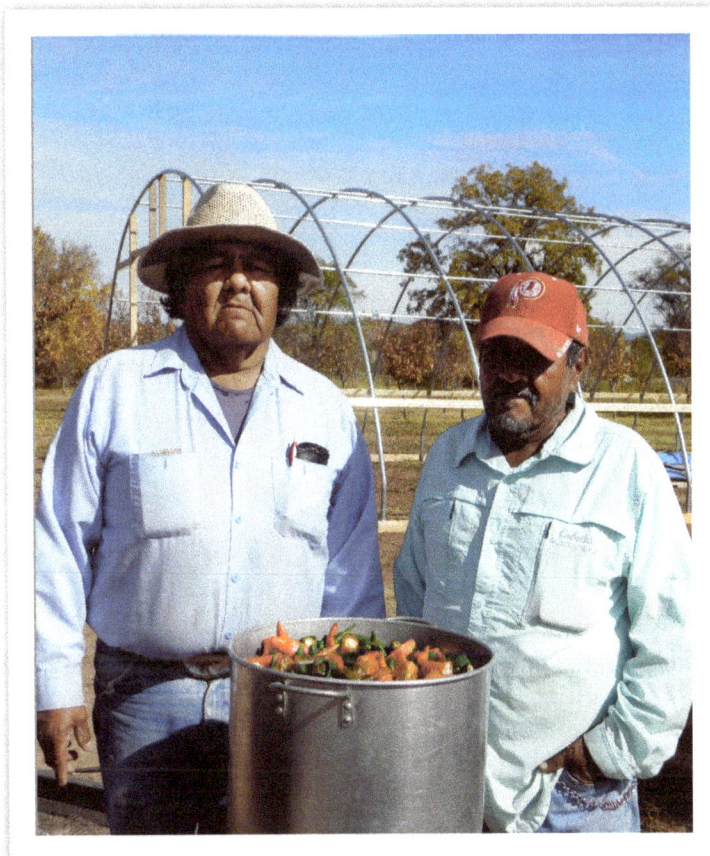

Martin Loretto (l), chief farmer at Jemez Pueblo, and his associate take a break from constructing a hoop greenhouse to show off their chile harvest.

the CDC grant linking food with the prevention of chronic disease. Along with the garden, two greenhouses on the 7-acre site provide food to the pueblo's senior programs and two Jemez charter schools— Walatowa High School and San Diego Riverside. She says Shendo's business is collaborating with the New Mexico Public Education Department to provide food for the larger Jemez Valley High School and utilize a commercial kitchen there to process produce.

At the same time the pueblo has started a 4-H chapter and is working with the New Mexico Livestock Association and the pueblo's Natural Resources Department to bring back ranching since most ranchers (and farmers) are retiring. Creating new career paths for pueblo young people is part of the plan.

"We are trying to integrate farming into the medical home," says Yepa. And she is looking at the economic potential as well. "We look at ways we were self-sufficient in the past and promote that."

Martin Loretto, who works with Eileen Shendo and others at the community farm, is proud of the pueblo's efforts. He and his three workers have just erected another hoop greenhouse and are harvesting a crop of red chiles. It's been a tough year for grasshoppers, though. "We learn from our ancestors, but we are not born knowing everything. It's just trial and error," says Loretto, who is the chief farmer. But he says the bottom line is that "this is beneficial to people."

In a Nutshell

Problems

- Inaccessible health care for rural residents surrounding the pueblo
- High rates of obesity and diabetes among pueblo members

Big Ideas

- Open the pueblo's tribally operated health center to residents of the surrounding area
- FITT, a fitness program emphasizing running, a traditional practice
- Agricultural ventures to support "food sovereignty"

Partners

Health Resources Services Administration (HRSA), Centers for Disease Control (CDC), tribal administration, local farmers organizations.

What You Can Do

- Support Indian sovereignty, including the right of tribes to operate their own health clinics under the 638 program.
- If you live near a pueblo, participate in its runs or walks. Many pueblos and tribes have these activities. If you are in the Jemez area, sign up with the Jemez Comprehensive Health Center's fitness program.
- Look for native-grown produce, including red chile from Jemez Pueblo, at farmers' markets, and buy some.
- If you live in Sandoval County, near Jemez Pueblo, you can get primary care and dental services on a sliding payment scale at the Jemez Comprehensive Health Center.

Resources

Jemez Pueblo
Governor's Office
PO Box 100
Jemez Pueblo, NM 87024
575-834-7359

Jemez Health and Human Services
PO Box 70
110 Sheep Springs Way
Jemez Pueblo, NM 87024
575-834-7517

Jemez Comprehensive Health Center
110 Sheep Springs Way
Jemez Pueblo, NM 87024
575-834-7413

Jemez Fitness Center
4531 HWY 4
Jemez Pueblo, NM 87024
575-834-7059

CHAPTER 7

A Model for Rural Health Care
Takes Root in Old Mining District

ealth equity is a term used by health-care reformers of all
stripes. Bob De Felice, of First Choice Community Health-
care, worries about the poor outcomes for patients in the
low-income South Valley of Albuquerque. Sanjeev Arora, of Project
ECHO, and the folks at Hidalgo Medical Services see a different kind
of health-care "disparity" based on geography. Rural patients don't get
the care they need. Specialists and providers of all stripes are in short
supply in places like Grant and Hidalgo counties in southwestern
New Mexico. And when patients do get care it is often fragmented,
with providers spread out over the rural landscape and spotty electronic medical records.

Hidalgo Medical Services (HMS) has been a pioneer in rural health care
for over thirty years. It is addressing these inequities head on. As the
chair of the legislature's health and human services committee during
the late 1990s and 2000s, I regularly led legislators down to Silver City
to hear about the latest innovation adopted by the remote primary-care
clinic. *Medical homes* and *community health workers*—these terms are
now on the lips of health-care insiders nationwide. They have become
familiar practices at First Choice Community Healthcare—in an urban
setting. But they got an early start in southwestern New Mexico, where
the residents are used to making do with what they have, depending on
each other, and defending their rural lifestyle.

With health-care costs still rising nationally and the numbers of
uninsured sure to rise if the Affordable Care Act is defunded, HMS's
grassroots solutions are even more relevant.

It's right there on the wall of HMS's contemporary new clinic on Pope Street in Silver City: the mission statement with its promise of comprehensive, affordable, and integrated personal and community health. And HMS makes another promise to boot—to provide affordable education for health care professionals.

The building features local tiles, Mondrian-style windows, and earth tones based on copper, gold, and the other minerals that made Grant County famous. And it is a living testimony to the idea of *integrated care*. Patients—eighteen thousand of them at last count—are served by a team of providers that includes doctors, physician's assistants, dentists, counselors, nurses, community health workers, even a chiropractor—all located in the same place. The health professionals are not hidden away in offices somewhere behind the examination rooms, but clustered in accessible, open offices called pods, which facilitates dialogue between them. Before construction of the 30,000-square-foot building began in 2012, Dr. Darrick Nelson, HMS Chief Medical Officer, toured many practices in search of something that would fit the needs of the local community. He wanted the building to live up to the clinic's reputation as a health commons (one-stop medical and social services shop). He also wanted it to showcase the idea of a patient-centered medical home where ongoing relationships are fostered, lifelong care for entire families is provided, and everything is coordinated both inside and outside of the clinic.

Nelson was assisted by students from University of New Mexico Architecture School, who held community meetings and offered ideas for the latest clinic in the HMS network. "I knew what I didn't want, more than what I did want," Nelson recalls.

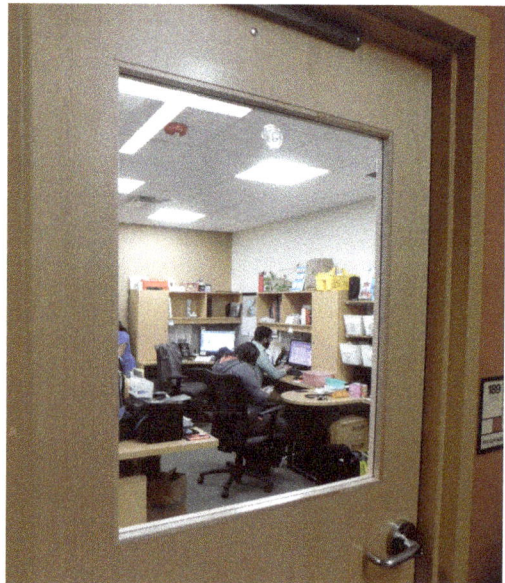

Doctors, nurses and other members of Hidalgo Medical Services integrated teams are purposely clustered together into pods, where information is shared and treatment plans coordinated.

Four years later (2017), natural light filters into the clinic's spacious lobby where clusters of patients sit in several different small waiting areas. It's quiet. Somehow, the assembly line seems to have slowed here, even though, as I found out on a tour of the facility, there is a lot going on. The first floor houses two pods where providers share common office areas. A few doorways down are offices offering family support, a key offering of the HMS clinics, provided by promotoras, also known as community health workers. Short hallways connect the pods to twenty-two exam rooms, ten dental operatories, a digital radiography machine, a bone density meter, and a urology lab. To save time and money, as much as possible is done on site, not in faraway labs miles away.

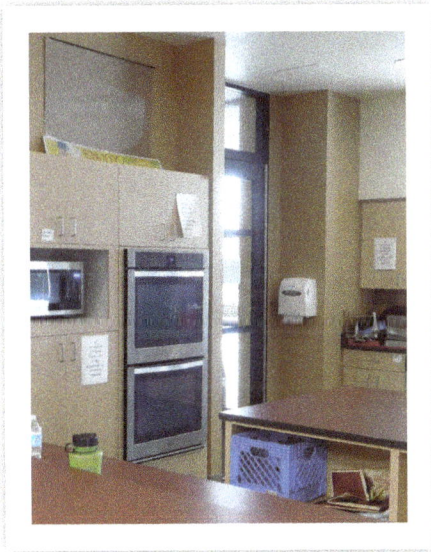

HMS offers modern loft apartments to lure medical residents to rural New Mexico.

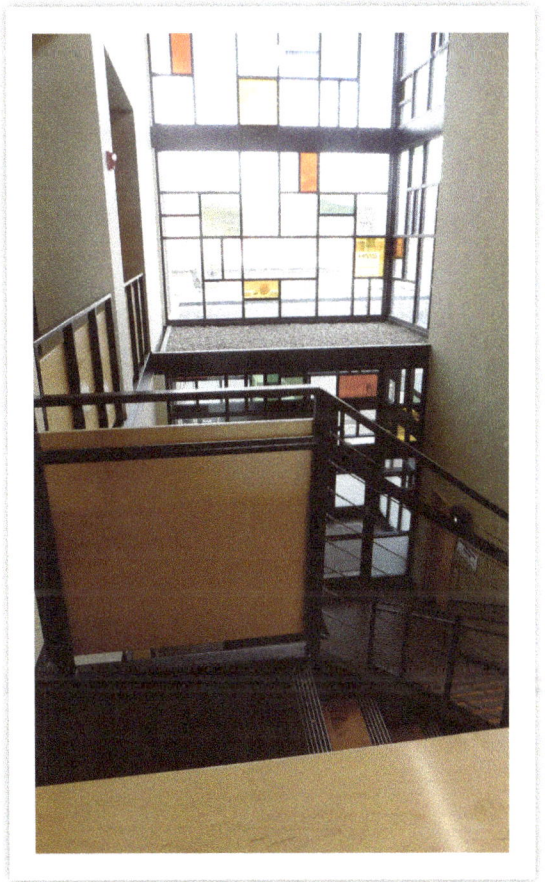

Across the lobby, there's a spacious conference room, used by community groups including the HMS Board (composed largely of patients). It is used for medical resident education, a source of particular pride for Nelson, who, along with Charlie Alfero, HMS founder, was instrumental is starting the first rural family residency program at HMS. Project ECHO often links specialists at the university in Albuquerque with HMS health professionals via teleconference there, and, Nelson says, "We host between sixty to eighty different flavors of learner."

On the second floor, nine mental health offices offer patients and their families individual and group counseling. The clinic took over the provision of behavioral-health services in 2015 after La Frontera, an Arizona company, left the state in the latest of a long line of disputes that behavioral-health providers have had with New Mexico's Medicaid program. Patient privacy was paramount in the design and access to the counseling suites, given the stigma that mental health issues can carry in a small community. The focus on behavioral health is an important feature. These kinds of services are in critically short supply in rural New Mexico, where economic booms and busts make fertile fields for drug and alcohol abuse, as well as domestic violence.

Nelson was giving me an inspection tour in early 2017, and he had finally come to his favorite part of the tour. Opening the door to one of three loft-style apartments that HMS provides for medical residents, he broke into a broad smile, which came straight through despite Nelson's military background and scientific training. The apartments were designed to lure residents to train in Silver City, far from the big cities lining the state's Rio Grande

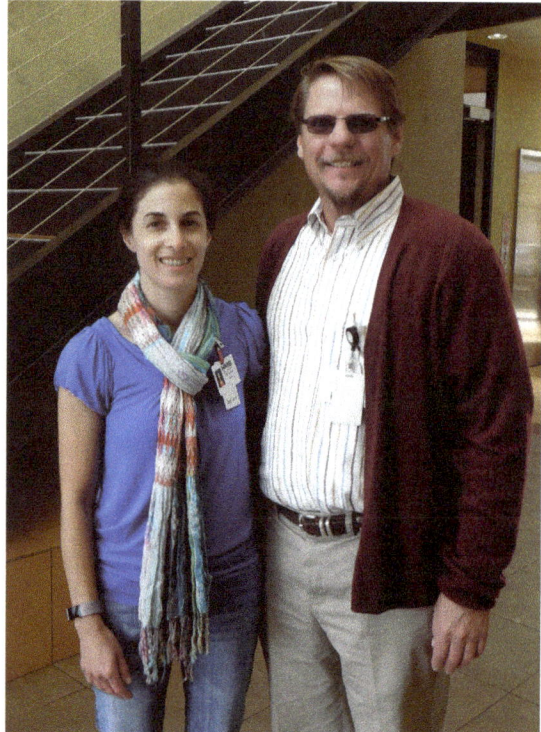

Dr. Rachel Sonne (l), a primary care doctor at Hidalgo Medical Services and Dr. Darrick Nelson (r), HMS Chief Medical Officer, in the Silver City clinic

corridor. And the apartments are working, part of a larger program at HMS to attract and retain rural doctors and dentists (see Chapter 10). In the past few years hundreds of applicants have applied for the two residency slots open each year. Even better, says Nelson, the doctors who trained there have not gone on to big cities but to places like Anthony, NM, Page, AZ, northwest Arkansas, and Silver City itself.

One who stayed is Rachel Sonne, now a primary-care doctor working in the Bayard HMS clinic. Sonne came to Silver City for its rural, outdoor lifestyle. So did Nelson, who was itching to get back to his rural roots (he is the son of a miner from Arizona) after a stint in the United States Army, and then at Texas A & M in Corpus Christi.

Resurrected From a Hard-Scrabble Grave

In 1979 the local hospital in Lordsburg, which is located in the "boot heel" of New Mexico, one of the remotest areas of the state, closed down. By 1983, the last doctor had left town and the community was unable to recruit another one. Area residents had to drive to Tucson (152 miles west), Las Cruces (60 miles east), Silver City (45 miles north), or Albuquerque (300 miles north) for health care. But in 1995 a volunteer board worked with Charlie Alfero, then part of the UNM School of Medicine's rural outreach program, to create what ultimately became HMS. In those days, Alfero regularly commuted between Albuquerque and Hidalgo County, where Lordsburg is located, a six-hundred-mile round trip.

At first, four family physicians rotated in from Silver City and the clinic was open two days per week. In the fall of 1996, HMS was able to add a full-time nurse practitioner to its staff, and for the first time in thirteen years, the community had a clinic that was open every day. The next year, with the help of the county and University of New Mexico Office of Rural Outreach (now the Office of Community Health), HMS hired a full-time family physician. Then the next year, it hired a part-time dentist. HMS was on a roll. The community was galvanized behind it. With broad public support, but few health professionals, HMS enlisted members of the community itself to act as promotoras—health promoters. They were some of the state's first community health workers, and they extended the reach of the clinic to ranches and small outlying communities where they helped patients with diabetes and other chronic diseases. Even before the policy wonks came up with the plan to intervene to address the social and environmental determinants of health, community members knew that they had to help one another. The mines had closed and the stage-coaches and railroads had deserted the poor, isolated area.

Today HMS has an annual budget of $18 million, employs 215 people at thirteen sites (including three high-school-based clinics) in Grant,

Hidalgo, Luna, and Catron counties. Thirty of these employees are medical professionals. Federal funding from the Health Resources and Services Administration (HRSA) makes up about 15 percent of the budget of the non-profit, with patient revenues from private insurance, Medicaid, and Medicare accounting for the bulk of its revenue. For those with limited ability to pay, the Federally Qualified Health Center (FQHC), like others in New Mexico, offers a sliding fee scale based on income. A basic office visit is $20. Before the expansion of Medicaid that came with the Affordable Care Act (or ACA, also known as Obamacare), about 20 percent of patients had no insurance. The number dropped to 9 percent after the expansion.

Any changes in Obamacare that reduce reimbursements from either Medicaid or Medicare will be a threat to the clinic, which primarily serves low-income patients. In 2010, during the first round of funding for the ACA, HMS benefitted handsomely from a grant to build the new facility in Silver City—part of the new law's drive to bolster rural health. The local college, Western New Mexico University, also received a grant to train more nurses. For Silver City, the attention was not an accident. In 2009 then-Senator Jeff Bingaman, a member of the Senate Committee on Health, Education, Labor and Pensions, wrote the section of the law on rural healthcare and workforce development. Bingaman is from Silver City and knows the hard-to-serve area well.

Huddles and Warm Handoffs

Rearranging the medical delivery system to focus on patients, prevent illness, and ultimately control costs, took a back seat to increasing the number of people with insurance in the ACA, but it was not omitted altogether. With an innovative approach already established prior to the enactment of the ACA, HMS was able to capture the federal ACA funding that had been allocated for this purpose to expand the health commons it had established early in its clinics. Members of the New Mexico Legislature and others were impressed, and committees often traveled there to hear about the medical home and its patient-centered design, complete with electronic medical records, a wrap-around approach, and community involvement.

"I love the model that we use," said Dr. Rachel Sonne, one of the medical residents attracted to HMS who stayed on to become a family doctor there. "We're a team—medical assistants, community health workers, me, sometimes a physician's assistant. We huddle together before seeing patients and compare notes. It's not an in-and-out-the-door kind of thing. I try to focus on one prevention thing each visit." One week it is making sure patients are screened for colorectal cancer, another it is flu shots. And Sonne says she does four hours of computer work at the end of the day to record everything.

"We don't have clearly delineated scopes of practices here," she said. "We are too small and too understaffed." But not everybody does everything. Often there is a warm handoff of a patient from a family doctor to a psychologist, whose office is upstairs, or to a promotora down the hall. This is different from a referral to an unknown specialist who must start from ground zero with a patient, collecting records and sometimes duplicating tests. Follow-up appointments at HMS are relatively quick, and when patients have them they show up.

But both Sonne and Nelson said there is a basic problem. The clinic is reimbursed for its services based on the number of patient visits. Each visit must be for one thing only, and services like the four hours at the computer that Sonne spends every day to document cases is not included.

"There are lots of things that are not reimbursed," she says.

In spite of the rhetoric about health improvement and outcomes, the whole system is geared around quantity, not quality, Nelson says. "But there are only so many patients that you can put through the chute on any given day," he says.

A primary-care doctor like Dr. Sonne is expected to have about 4,200 encounters (patient visits) per year, Nelson explains. It's the Medicare standard, but it's almost humanly impossible. Instead, he has reduced the number of encounters required to 3,100 but increased their length, rewarding his doctors with bonuses for the number of electronic prescriptions, screenings, and other quality measures. Doing so has cost HMS, but federal funding to rural clinics has provided a cushion. And he is proud of the quality care—and positive outcomes—HMS provides.

Federal programs like Medicare and Medicaid are moving toward reimbursements to teams that take responsibility for a group of patients and, in the new world, payment will be based on outcomes, not the number of visits or procedures. But the new world isn't coming quickly, and innovative clinics like HMS and First Choice, which provide an array of services targeted to the needs of their unique communities, may be ahead of their time. But they are providing a path that others can follow. In 2013 the New Mexico Legislature recognized HMS as "an effective community based model, which brings coordinated care to the neediest patients."[23]

In a Nutshell

Problems

- Fragmented care
- Lack of medical providers due to geographic isolation

Big Ideas

- A medical home and health commons
- A residency program geared to retain rural providers
- Housing for medical residents

Partners

University of New Mexico's Health Extension Rural Offices (HEROs) and BA/MD programs, Western New Mexico University, Burrell College of Osteopathic Medicine, Grant County Community Health Council, promotoras (community health workers), libraries, elected officials, teams of providers, Project ECHO, New Mexico Department of Health, Gila Regional Hospital, New Mexico Primary Care Consortium, Health Resources and Services Administration (HRSA), Arizona School of Dentistry and Oral Health, the GRADs program, the First Born program.

What You Can Do

- If you live in the southwestern New Mexico, contribute by getting involved with Hidalgo Medical Services as a volunteer, board member, donor, or partner.

- Attend a meeting of a county community health council near you to understand more of your area's health problems. The Grant County Community Health Council is not the only one. There are many in New Mexico.

- Participate in the many health promotion activities sponsored by Hidalgo Medical Services and other primary-care clinics— family fundays, health fairs, exercise classes, and various screenings.

- If you have a young family, check out HMS family support services including parenting classes, the First Born home visiting program in Hidalgo County, graduation celebrations, and child safety seat rodeos. The First Born Program is also in Los Alamos.

- If you are a medical student, check out the possibility of a residency at Hidalgo Medical Services.

Resources

Hidalgo Medical Services (HMS)
https://www.hms-nm.org
Toll Free: 888-271-3596
24/7 Mental Health Crisis Line: 855-422-4334

Lordsburg HMS Community Health Clinic
520 E. DeMoss St.
Lordsburg, NM 88045
575-542-8384

Silver City HMS Community Health Clinic
1007 N. Pope St.
Silver City, NM 88061
575-388-1511

Grant County Community Health Council
c/o Gila Regional Medical Center
1313 E. 32nd St.
Silver City, NM 88061
575-388-1198 ext. 22
http://www.grmc.org/Community/Grant-County-Community-Health-Council.aspx

PART THREE
Reshuffling the Deck:
A New Kind of Healthcare
Workforce for New Mexico

*"The shift to prevention has enormous implications
for our future workforce."*

—Victor Rubin, Policy Link

Clinics like Hidalgo Medical Services, First Choice Community Healthcare, and Jemez Comprehensive Health Center play key roles in rearranging an outdated delivery system to put patients first, address inequities, and ultimately cut costs. But things are happening outside the clinic walls as well. A new health-care workforce is taking shape based on shifts in the delivery system. Already the single fastest-growing sector in New Mexico's economy, new health-care opportunities and careers focused on prevention and coordinated care are emerging in both rural and urban areas.

"Houston, we have a problem," Charlie Alfero, the founder and first CEO of Hidalgo Medical Services, declared on the new web site of the New Mexico Primary Care Training Consortium. The problem that he was highlighting is grounded in New Mexico's shortage of health-care practitioners—doctors, nurses, dentists, psychiatrists—in vast expanses of our frontier state. The Health Resources and Services Administration (HRSA) has designated thirty-two of New Mexico's thirty-three counties as professional shortage areas. For years policymakers have tried to attract doctors and dentists from outside the state with loan forgiveness, tuition remission, tax breaks, and other incentives. For the most part it has not worked. Nowhere is the problem more serious than in the shortage of primary-care doctors. Some say we need over three hundred more, just to keep up with the influx of new patients unleashed by the Affordable Care Act.

Yet traditional medical training turns out far more specialists than primary-care doctors, who earn far less than their counterparts in specialty practices, like dermatology or orthopedics, and have trouble paying for medical school. The current residency program is skewed against the rural areas. And the lack of rural docs—of all types—means a lack of potential economic development, since each doctor who comes to town hires eighteen folks directly and indirectly and generates $1 million in economic activity.

The current medical system has another adverse effect. Procedures and pharmaceutical products are reimbursed at the highest rates—and continue to eat up available funding—even though there's a mounting body of evidence that it's the low-tech, high-touch community services that improve health outcomes—and create local jobs.

A caring corps of approximately one thousand community health workers spread throughout the state is beginning to change the equation. The promotoras, as they are called in the southern part of the state, and the community health representatives, as they are called on the Indian reservations, don't have higher degrees for the most part. But they speak the language, know the problems, and come from the communities they serve. And they get remarkable results. Programs are springing up to train these new members of the health-care team in community colleges and high schools. If we play our cards right, a huge number of high school graduates with good hearts but slim prospects for other good jobs in their own communities will gain employment, which can lead to careers in the health-care field—the only area of steady growth in New Mexico since the Great Recession.

Another group waiting to join the new health-care team is already trained in emergency medicine. It is composed of the hundreds of emergency medical technicians (EMTs) now working in fire departments and ambulance companies around the state. These first responders are called to put out structural fires less and less often. The vast majority of 911 calls they receive are medical ones—and most are not serious enough to warrant a costly trip to the emergency room. In hundreds of communities around the country—and now in Santa Fe— EMTs are becoming community paramedics, working with hospitals and social-service agencies to locate "frequent flyers" who overuse emergency rooms. And they are beginning to address the underlying needs of residents with chronic conditions and behavioral-health problems.

Repurposing an underutilized workforce, or retraining those willing to work at the top of their capacity, is another way to get more bang for the health-care buck and provide appropriate care for those who are isolated or lack resources. It also creates new jobs.

More and more, these new types of health-care professionals are working within an interdisciplinary team charged with tackling complex health problems from many different directions. "Healthcare wants to go to a team-based approach," says Brad Moran, a pharmacist working with Project ECHO in Montana. "The conventional approach is not working."

Reshuffling the health-care deck will never be easy. Practitioners who jealously guard their scopes of practice and those who won't venture out of their organization's silo often stand in the way. But there are pioneers in New Mexico who have developed pilot programs that have attracted national attention. The following three chapters are their stories.

CHAPTER 8

Community Health Workers:
Solving Patients' Problems,
Developing New Career Pathways

"Community health workers are transforming
 health care in New Mexico."

—Joaquin Baca, director, Office of Health Equity,
New Mexico Department of Health

When Daniel Mejia injured his spinal cord in an ATV accident in 2014, it was more than a medical problem. It was a catastrophe with what seemed like insurmountable social, financial, and psychological dimensions. A Rio Grande High School graduate, Daniel had come to the United States from Chihuahua, Mexico, in 2001. He was without legal papers and had no health insurance or money to pay for medications or therapy. He was in deep debt to the hospital and the ambulance company. His single mother already had her hands full with a job and Daniel's younger brother. Now paraplegic, he would need a full-time caregiver at least until he adapted to a new lifestyle.

He was, in short, a tough case. How could doctors—or anyone—address his medical problems without confronting his dire personal situation?

Enter Margarita Perez, an efficient, Spanish-speaking community health worker (CHW) with First Choice Community Healthcare in Albuquerque's South Valley. Within months, Perez had gotten Daniel a laptop and an electric wheelchair at a bargain-basement price, negotiated down his medical debt by 45 percent, and gotten the ambulance company to forgo payment entirely. She's working with the Immigrant Rights Center in Albuquerque to get him legal status, which will allow him to qualify for Medicaid so that he can pay for doctor's visits and medication.

Perez is a new type of community health worker, embedded in a clinic, serving as the navigator between medical providers and patients. Other community health workers in Albuquerque work for social service agencies and managed care organizations. Sometimes they are called "promotoras" or "promotoras de salud," sometimes "community health representatives (CHRs)," "navigators," or "health educators." All address the social determinants of health—the social and environmental factors like education, income, neighborhood safety, or availability of healthy food that impact peoples' health. These factors are more important in an individual's continuing health than medical procedures, studies have found.

"This was a challenge to find resources, but luckily New Mexico has a lot of non-profits that support the community. It's just a question of bugging them," Perez says, holding up a fat notebook marked "Resources."

Perez says that she is helped by a local network called Pathways,[24] which links social workers, CHWs and medical providers. Members meet every month to exchange referrals, share information on how to overcome systemic barriers and get training on topics like domestic violence or depression.

Depression is a likely outcome for those with serious, lifelong injuries.

But Daniel says, "I try to stay positive and move forward, no matter what life throws at me." He now is a student at Community College of New Mexico (CCNM) and thinking of social work as a career. He's involved with United Spinal, a rehab group at the University of New Mexico (UNM), and he's accomplished a lot on his own.

"Daniel is very committed to helping himself," Perez told me, as Daniel listened to us talk. "I knew there was a choice," he added, "and sitting in bed, depressed won't get you anywhere." Daniel says his accident actually motivated him and Perez provided the guidance.

Community Health Worker Margarita Perez helps Daniel Mejia fill out paperwork at the First Choice Community Healthcare Center in Albuquerque's South Valley.

A Long Tradition of Non-Medical, Community-Based Care

New Mexico has had a long tradition of using non-medical workers like Perez to serve indigenous communities. Community health representatives fanned out to help isolated Navajos on their sprawling reservation and worked in pueblos lining the Rio Grande as early as the 1950s. *Curanderas* (herbalists), *parteras* (midwives), and *doulas* (pre- and post-natal aides) are part of Hispanic tradition.

No one is more familiar with this tradition than Sylvia Sapien, a former police officer and single mom from Las Cruces who, in over two decades, has trained approximately six hundred promotoras (community health educators) on New Mexico's southern border. Promotoras were the first versions of today's community health worker.

The idea came from Juarez, Sapien says, from a program called Madres a Madres. In 1991 she went to check out the program started in the 1970s in a little blue house owned by La Senora La Vega. It was a volunteer program at first focused on family planning. "The whole dining room table was filled with contraceptives," she remembers. They had promotoras who had HIV themselves working the bars. They used the concept that the people who had that behavior were the best ones to help those with the disease get treatment.

The New Mexico Office of Border Health promoted the idea of using promotoras in public health programs, and in 1992 La Clinica de Familia in Las Cruces started the first program, which served migrants from Mexico who lived in colonias, ad hoc semirural settlements near the border built with no water and sewer and fewer services. The program is still alive today, with scores of promotoras working in thirty-eight colonias, sometimes going out to the onion fields, more often knocking on doors in town. Sapien is the former director of La Clinica's promotora program.

"I tell them to be feisty, flexible and watch out for goats," she says, as she recounted some of the odd situations that promotoras find themselves in when they make home visits. "Never park in the driveway, always on the street—an angry husband can block you in, and you don't want to get involved with a domestic dispute," she advises her trainees.

Although Sapien's promotoras are trained in various diseases and work out of a clinic, they are still what she calls "the generalist promotora." They get the word out about where to sign up for benefits, opportunities to go back to school, or where to get windows that don't allow so much air in. If a patient misses an appointment at the clinic, it triggers a visit. If one is discharged from the hospital, promotoras follow up. They monitor medications, call on support from churches and relatives. They go into a house, open the cupboards and see what's in there, sometimes translating the labels on cans for their clients.

"It's not just a referral or a phone call," Sapien says, "It's developing a relationship that allows clients to tell you what they won't tell the doctor. It's all about trust."

One day a few years ago I followed one of Sapien's promotoras, Darlene Mayes, as she checked on two of her clients: a teenage mother with a newborn, and a fifty-five-year-old disabled woman who had called La Clinica threatening suicide. The former hairdresser had been "trapped in her mobile home alone," where she was taking care of her estranged husband who had experienced a stroke. After Darlene helped her untangle several different problems, she began riding her three-wheeler to and from the nearby Walmart, tending to her own needs. Darlene says it took months.

"If you go into a house and all you do is fill out forms, soon they won't open the door," Darlene said, differentiating her approach from agency caseworkers or HMO care coordinators.

A Very Exciting Time

By 2014, after almost two decades of advocacy by community health workers who had organized the New Mexico Community Health Worker Association, state government and HMOs began to recognize the value of these lay health workers (that is, health workers without specialized medical degrees). Initially organized at UNM in 1995 under the aegis of the New Mexico Prenatal Care Network,

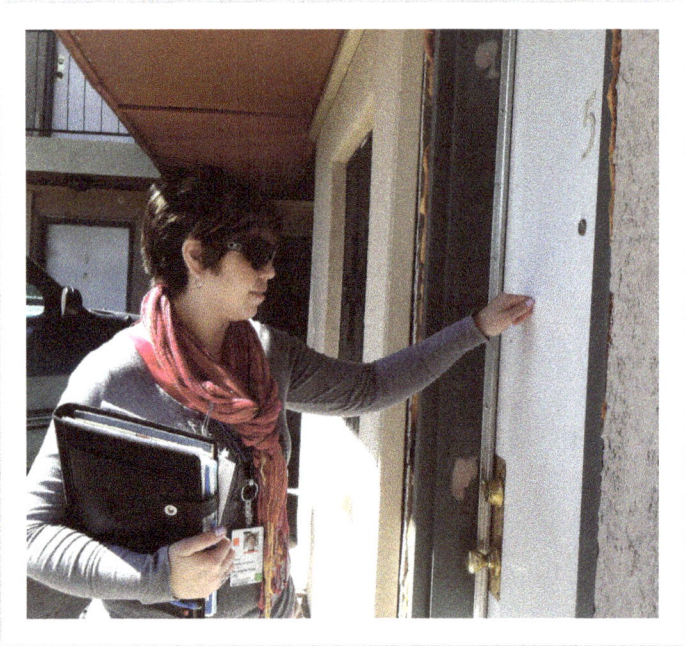

ECHO Project Community Heath Worker Vanessa Oldhorn knocks on doors in the Southeast Heights of Albuquerque, looking to keep high-risk patients on track and out of the emergency room.

initial training programs focused on maternal and child health. But the efforts of CHWs soon expanded. They began helping patients with costly chronic diseases like diabetes adhere to their treatment regimes and take their medicine. They were locating frequent utilizers of the emergency room and people who were constantly readmitted to hospitals. And they were hooking up patients with primary care doctors and Medicaid.

Looking to contain costs and serve the influx of patients under the Affordable Care Act, New Mexico's reformulated Medicaid program, Centennial Care, mandated the use of CHWs in some programs in 2013.

"With shortages of doctors, nurses, and dentists in thirty-two out of thirty-three counties, the Governor (Susana Martinez) recognizes that these folks are gold," former New Mexico Department of Health (NMDOH) Secretary Rhetta Ward told me. "They know their communities and they spend time with patients…they improve outcomes at a very reasonable cost."

"This is a very exciting time," she said.

That year (2014) the New Mexico Legislature passed a voluntary certification program for community health workers, aimed at beefing up training of the non-medical group and ultimately qualifying them for Medicaid reimbursement.

Unlike most groups responding to new requirements from the state, CHWs for the most part embraced the opportunity to learn about blood pressure, cholesterol, and other medical topics. Training programs sprang up at Santa Fe Community College and the Community College of New Mexico in Albuquerque. Some were online, some in person. The UNM Office of Community Health developed a curriculum; so did Project ECHO. Some classes are paid for by the Health Resources and Services Administration (HRSA).

There have been problems with the NMDOH and the state Medicaid program, which has not yet applied for a waiver to allow Medicaid to pay CHWs directly. So far (in 2017) only 150 CHWs have become certified, mostly through the grandfathering process, with the NMDOH, projecting the total to rise to 450 in August 2017. Only one curriculum at the Central New Mexico Community College has been officially approved by the NMDOH and the state has no plan to introduce it more broadly. Regrettably, most CHWs are still learning from workplace programs, from one another, or from members of the larger team to which they belong at clinics or managed care organizations.

By some estimates, about 1,000 CHWs are currently on the job in NM, earning between $15–20 per hour. UNM pays $17 an hour. Nationally, there are over 120,000 at work, with a mean hourly wage of

$19.80 (compared to NM's average of $16.85).[25] In New Mexico, the average caseload is about thirty patients at any given time.

The salary is low compared to that of nurses and other health-care providers, but many of the largely female workforce lack college degrees. They welcome the opportunity to learn, particularly when there is a pathway to higher degrees and later to an increased wage (some clinics now pay $1 more per hour for certified CHWs).

Creating a Pipeline

Venice Ceballos, who's been a CHW for sixteen years, is trying to create a pipeline to affiliated careers for CHWs and community health representatives (CHRs). As the manager of CHW/CHR programs at Project ECHO, she's trained about seven hundred CHWs in everything from obesity to addiction. She sees a great future for CHWs. Although there is no direct pipeline to nursing, phlebotomy, respiratory, or other therapy programs which are now turning out graduates into a receptive job market, one could be developed. And there is a clear connection of the skills learned as a CHW to the fields of social work, public health, and community health education. It's the proper mix of hard (medical) and soft skills like motivational interviewing that are the key.

Ceballos is disappointed that, despite verbal support, state and federal Medicaid programs do not yet reimburse CHW for their services, which she says are of great value to the whole system. But Ceballos is working on that.

"I know the secret of reducing health care costs, and I will share it."

That was the opening line in the spring of 2016 of Venice Ceballos' TED-type talk about community health workers, which was filled with tales of CHWs solving patient problems and preventing emergency room admissions.

Ceballos, the daughter of Mexican immigrants, is fervent in her belief in CHWs. Her eyes twinkle and her ready smile softens as she tackles the subject. Here she is talking to another crowd in the wake of the 2016 presidential election. "As CHWs we see no color, we help individuals whether they were born in this country or not, whether they are LGBT or not...Fear cannot overcome us now...we will continue to promote love, hope, grace, and compassion and to remind ourselves that others depend on us."

Ceballos is not alone in her faith.

Molina Healthcare, a managed care organization that serves Medicaid patients in New Mexico and ten other states, has used CHWs since 2005 to track its high-cost patients. From 2007–2009 it joined with

Dr. Art Kaufman to study whether CHWs saved money on patients who had complex, overlapping diseases. They found that when CHWs were added to the mix, claims, emergency room visits, and prescription costs dropped by about $2 million over a twenty-five-month period.[26] After the study's results were published, Molina expanded its use of CHWs to more counties in New Mexico and engaged UNM to train Molina staff in other states.

"We've become a national leader in the growth and employment of CHWs," says Dr. Art Kaufman. Kaufman and his group are currently trying to expand the use of CHWs even further, beyond high utilizers to patients with chronic diseases, or on the cusp of becoming complex patients. Medicaid cuts have been a problem, but overall Kaufman is optimistic.

"CHW training and employment today is a broad collaboration of many stakeholders, overcoming their silos to enhance and employ this growing workforce," he says.

In a Nutshell

Problems

- High incidence of chronic diseases
- Shortage of doctors and nurses in rural areas
- Lack of support for patients who don't understand doctor's orders
- Need for follow-up and help in addressing housing, safety, and other issues that preclude healing
- Inappropriate use of emergency rooms

Big Idea

- Use non-medical professionals to reduce health-care costs and serve patients more personally

Partners

Primary-care clinics, HMOs, New Mexico Department of Health, community colleges, New Mexico Association of Community Health Workers, Pathways network, tribal clinics, Project ECHO.

What You Can Do

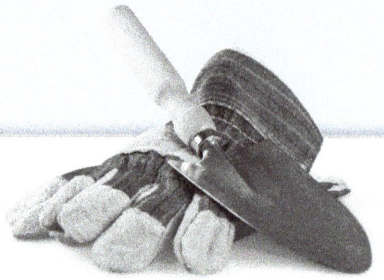

- Support adequate reimbursement for community health workers and community health representatives by Medicaid, Medicare, HMOs, and other insurance companies. Tell your elected representative that these providers save money and provide more personal care. Write to the New Mexico Department of Health.

- Ask your doctor about patient support services like visits from a community health worker, who could help after hospital discharge.

- If this seems like a caring career you would be interested in, check out training programs in your area. In New Mexico, programs are available at the Community College of Central New Mexico (Albuquerque), Santa Fe Community College (Santa Fe) and Project ECHO.

Resources

New Mexico Community Health Workers Association
1623 San Pedro NE
Albuquerque, NM 87112
505-255-1227 • B. J. Ciesielski, director
www.nmchwa.org/

TED-type Talk
Venice Ceballos, community health worker programs manager at Project ECHO: https://www.youtube.com/watch?v=ACfsjyR3Hxc&list=PLoL7mi3iOLMLO3BC_2M-ZkDgDYhLOW0Pn&index=

New Mexico Dept. of Health
Office of Community Health Workers
1190 South St. Francis Dr.
Santa Fe, NM 87505 • 505-827-2613
https://nmhealth.org/about/phd/hsb/ochw/

Central New Mexico Community College (CNM)
Community Health Worker
Certificate Program
900 University Blvd. SE
Albuquerque, NM 87106
505-224-3000
https://www.cnm.edu/programs-of-study/all-programs-a-z/community-health-worker

Project ECHO
Community Health Worker Program
1650 University Blvd. NE
Albuquerque, NM 87102
505-750-3246
http://echo.unm.edu/initiatives/community-health-workers/

Pathways
1650 University Ave. Suite 3300
Albuquerque, NM 87131-0001
505-272-0823
http://hsc.unm.edu/community/pathways/

SUN PATH
Healthcare Pathways
Santa Fe Community College
6401 Richards Ave.
Santa Fe, NM 87508
505-428-1000
https://www.sfcc.edu/programs/sun-i-best/

CHAPTER 9

Community Paramedics in Santa Fe Look Beyond 911 Calls

"If we're successful it's because we can bring behavioral and physical health providers together in a true interdisciplinary approach,"

— Andres Mercado, director, Santa Fe Mobile Integrated Health Program

Bringing resources in any community together to help patients with mental and physical problems is a tall order. It's beyond the purview of most doctors, nurses, and public safety personnel. Often families themselves cannot do it. But community health workers and a new kind of emergency medical technician (EMT) are picking up the slack. They are coordinating with hospitals, homeless shelters, food banks, and churches. In the process, they are redefining traditional roles, opening new career paths, and blurring traditional boundaries. And they are helping communities themselves come together to focus on the underlying needs of hard-to-serve, costly patients.

Andres Mercado had been a firefighter in Santa Fe for eighteen years, and he'd grown more frustrated every year. But last year, after his relentless advocacy, he finally found some relief when the Santa Fe Fire Department kicked off the state's first mobile integrated health team, a program that uses specially trained paramedics, along with a physician, a social worker, and a pharmacist to intervene and address the health problems of frequent 911 callers.

Mercado, a thirty-eight-year-old Santa Fe High School dropout and restless bundle of energy, was born in Puerto Rico and moved to Santa

Fe in his teens. He began volunteering with the Santa Fe County Fire Department when he was eighteen and was hired in 1999. He fit the profile for a firefighter—rugged, a fitness buff, an adventure seeker. He completed his higher education gradually. First the fire academy where, like all other firefighters, he was certified as an emergency medical technician (EMT), then Santa Fe Community College, a GED, University of New Mexico part time…and then, there was something else. After Bryan Conkling, a friend and mentor, hired him to work on a medical rescue helicopter, he did some soul searching. Still working for the fire department, he began studying the classics at St. John's College, finally earning a master's degree and meeting his wife.

"It made me realize that I can think freely, and challenge the status quo," Mercado said one afternoon over a cup of his favorite beverage, warm chocolate elixir.

Around that time he read an article in *The New Yorker* about Dr. Jeffrey Brenner and his "hot spotting" project in Camden, New Jersey. The article by Atul Gawande, now a classic among health-policy nerds, describes a project where crime statistics were used to pinpoint the frequent utilizers of Camden's medical facilities. Brenner and others then visited the complex patients, helping them untangle social as well as chronic medical problems. Hospital costs and admissions for the group came down drastically.

For Mercado, things began to come clear: "I had a super comfortable job, with a forty-eight-hour shift that left me lots of free time…but I was a cog in a machine. On the one hand, I was helping people but really I was complicit in a broken system."

Mercado was learning what other fire department EMTs around the country were beginning to realize. These days, there are fewer and fewer calls to local departments for structural fires. Most are 911 calls for medical emergencies, which department EMTs respond to with lights flashing, ambulances and fire engines tearing across town. Many of these are not true emergencies that warrant transport to emergency rooms, where costs range from an average of $2,000–$4,000 per visit. Yet EMTs are required to transport most of the callers.

Frank Soto, emergency medical services division commander for the Albuquerque Fire Department, says that in 2013 less than one percent of calls to his department were calls to extinguish structural fires. The rest were for emergency medical services. Of those less than ten percent were true emergencies.

In Santa Fe, Mercado says that out of approximately thirteen thousand calls each year, more than ten thousand are related to health issues. Many of them are repeat calls from people who face addiction, behavioral disorders, or other chronic diseases. Sometimes they are seniors who have fallen and need to be picked up. Or sometimes they are just lonely. The callers are often well known to the EMTs from previous contacts. They tie up expensive department resources and imperil the department's ability to respond to true emergencies, traffic accidents and urgent fires. More importantly, he says, each of these calls is a missed opportunity for navigation to needed resources.

In 2014, 243 people in Santa Fe used the 911 system at least four times. One man called the service seventy-two times, averaging an ambulance ride every five days.

"Seeing how the system fails is a motivator," Mercado said.

Another motivator, Mercado says, was Brian Conkling, whose push for a community paramedicine program in New Mexico was cut short by his untimely death in a hiking accident in the Sandias.

When Santa Fe Fire Chief Erik Litzenberg showed his staff a video calling for change and asked for new ideas, Mercado was ready. He had been studying what fire departments in nearby Colorado were doing, and he had a tentative plan.

What followed was a year of persistent phone calls, e-mails, memos, proposed protocols, and meetings with city and county officials, hospital administrators, police, behavioral health providers, nurses, EMTs, HMOs, doctors, and anyone else who would entertain his idea.

What emerged in 2016 was the Mobile Integrated Health Office (MIHO) program, whose flagship program, CONNECT, focuses on frequent utilizers of 911 and the emergency room at the local hospital, CHRISTUS St. Vincent. It is a team-based approach coordinated with medical and social services in Santa Fe.

The team's EMTs focus on twenty high utilizers at a time, cruising the streets, visiting shelters and jails, locating their clients, then doing medication reviews,

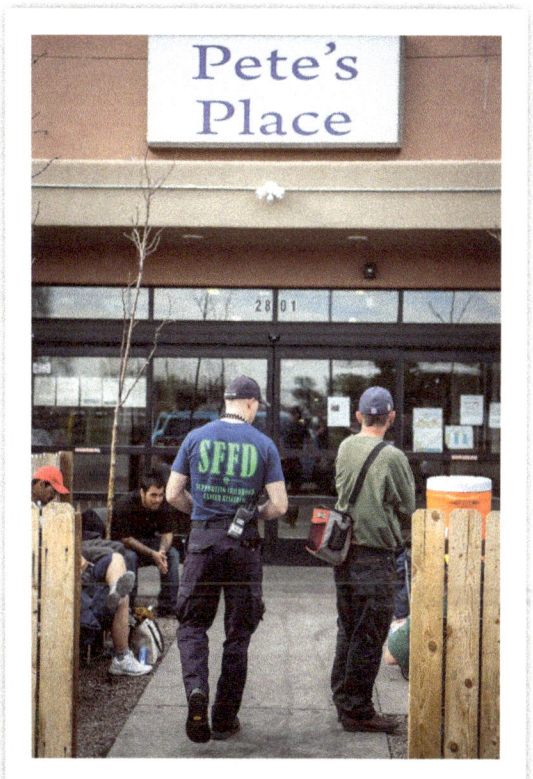

Paramedics in the Santa Fe Fire Department's Mobile Integrated Health Office, go to soup kitchens and homeless shelters to help a group of frequent 911 callers meet their health needs outside of the hospital emergency room.

Photo courtesy of Dham Khalsa Photography

safety assessments, and more. Most of the clients are homeless, facing addictions, or have behavioral disorders such as anxiety, depression, and schizophrenia. Many have experienced traumatic brain injuries They are a group seen by some as throwaways, people beyond help, but data shows that they do well with the right approach, says Kristin Carmichael, director of community health at CHRISTUS St. Vincent. Carmichael helped train the EMTs.

The team is composed of three EMTs, a coordinator, a part-time pharmacist, a physician, and a social worker. EMTs visit their charges once a week, establishing a relationship, letting the recipients drive the conversation, giving them choices, and helping them find long-range solutions outside of the emergency room.

"At first we couldn't locate them, but now they are calling us," said Mercado.

The program is currently funded by the city of Santa Fe, with smaller grants from the county, the hospital, and local clinics. It has been embraced by the city's mayor, Javier Gonzales, who hopes that the innovative project will become part of his legacy.

In January 2016, he spoke at the completion of the team's training and graduation ceremony. He commended the group for an "unprecedented level of compassion."

Gonzales said the Fire Department was the perfect fit for this because it is trusted by the community and had the required experience and infrastructure to provide mobile services. "Now, we can focus on prevention and navigation to avoid dangerous and costly emergencies," he said, adding that the program had a strong focus on data and outcomes and "the ability to clearly demonstrate public and financial values."

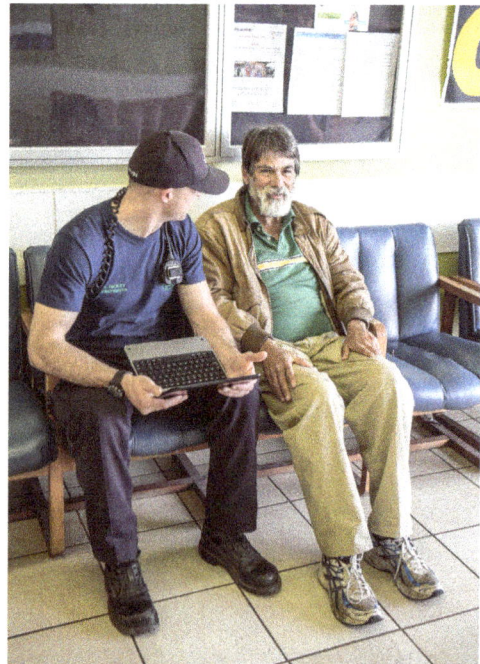

Santa Fe Fire Department Paramedic Erik Hickey (l) helps a client deal with the endless bureaucratic hoops that homeless and indigent patients must deal with.

Dham Khalsa Photography

The Trajectory Is Clear

Also at the graduation was Dr. Joel Rosen, a hospitalist at CHRISTUS St. Vincent. Rosen is a big supporter of using EMTs in the community. He calls EMTs "his eyes and ears," with far more access than he has. Rosen told a story about one of his patients, a fiercely independent eighty-five-year-old woman who was recently discharged from the hospital on oxygen. He was worried about her, but the earliest he would see her again was in four weeks. She was not doing well and was at risk of readmission, something hospitals are penalized for under new Medicare rules.

EMTs discovered that the petite woman could not leave the house because her oxygen tank was too heavy for her to move. They got her a smaller tank, and within forty-eight hours everything began to improve.

"The trajectory is clear," says Rosen. "The future is keeping people out of the hospital." It's a tough task with an older population, especially when patients are poor, homeless, or without transportation. Rosen would like to expand the Santa Fe EMT program to include home visits to a larger group of patients.

Already medically trained, EMTs are a good group to do it, in collaboration with behavioral health specialists, primary care doctors, nurses, home health agencies, and other partners. The key is collaboration.

Mercado spends most of his time recruiting partners—hospitals, HMOs, clinics, Medicaid officials—all of which will save money due to his group's prevention efforts. Convincing them to invest is not an easy sell since the institutions are always in tight financial straits and are reluctant to leave their silos to focus on a community problem. But in recent years the problem of drug abuse and the mounting number of overdose deaths have been hard to ignore. Santa Fe County now contracts with a mobile crisis response team composed of behavior health specialists. EMTs are using the anti-opioid drug naloxone (also known as Narcan) and training families and other first responders in how to administer it. The outreach visits act as springboards for conversations about how to prevent an overdose in the first place, as well as available treatment options.

Some of the HMOs have begun to contract with EMTs directly to manage complex cases. In Albuquerque, two HMOs, Blue Cross-Blue Shield, and the state's only health insurance co-op, New Mexico Health Connections, are piloting the use of EMTs from the Albuquerque Ambulance Service to do home visits to repeat callers and fragile patients discharged from the hospital. The ambulance company, which is owned by Presbyterian Healthcare Services, also has a contract with Presbyterian Hospital to visit frequent emergency room users and administer flu shots. It also contracts with Presbyterian Healthcare at Home (hospice care) to do assessments, lab draws, EKGs, breathing treatments, and immunizations.

Kerry Clear, Blue Cross-Blue Shield manager of community services, told *Governing Magazine* that one small patient cohort visited by the Albuquerque EMTs had cut its ambulance and emergency room use by 60 percent, and one super utilizer hadn't been to the emergency room in the eleven months he's been enrolled in the program.[27] Blue Cross is now looking to expand the program to other counties.

The savings are in line with the hundreds of programs that have sprung up around the country in the past several years. The National Association of Emergency Medical Technicians surveyed programs in both fire departments and private ambulance companies and found that 81 percent of those in operation for two years or longer reported success in reducing costs, 911 use, and emergency room visits.[28]

Nationally, hundreds of pilot programs—in Mesa, AZ, Prosser, WA, San Diego, CA, Fort Worth, TX, Reno, NV—are breaking new ground and beginning to fulfill what professional EMTs see as the future of the field. Closer to New Mexico, Colorado is setting the pace with programs in remote Eagle and San Juan counties, which are saving money on air transports and connecting scarce medical providers in rural areas. Activities in Western Eagle County near Aspen are based on a countywide report, "Healthy Eagle County." There the program draws on many community partners, including the county public health department and local hospitals. The group is looking to aggressively expand throughout Colorado, working with Randy Kuykendall, a former New Mexican now in the Colorado Department of Public Health and Environment's Emergency Medical and Trauma Services (EMTS) division. Colorado Springs has had a program in its fire department since 2012.

Back in New Mexico, Mercado is convening fire department personnel from around the state, bringing in experts from Colorado, and trying to spread the model program—with some success. The Las Cruces Fire Department now has one full-time employee dedicated to mobile integrated health, and Farmington is looking to begin a program for frequent callers.

The repurposing of EMTs, already trained as first responders, to prevent chronic disease and keep people out of the hospital was in line with the goals of the Affordable Care Act. Programs in Reno, Mesa, and Prosser got large grants from the Centers for Medicare and Medicaid Services (CMS). But the grants have largely dried up and programs have struggled to find new funding from states, localities, HMOs, and hospitals.

Mercado is undeterred. Sustainability is a problem, as always. But he is capturing cross-sector data to quantify the program's impact on the municipal budget, particularly the costs to the fire and police departments as well as incarceration costs. Many programs have focused on reimbursement from medical insurance companies only. Mercado hopes to demonstrate the economic impact to the municipality and share the stories behind this type of innovative service to capture the public value of such programs.

And time is on his side. The baby boom is coming. Federal and state programs will be looking for cost-efficient mechanisms to address complex, chronic diseases like diabetes and chronic heart failure and to keep frequent flyers out of the emergency room.

In 2016 Senator Al Franken, a champion of rural health care in Minnesota, introduced the Rural Health Care Quality Improvement Act to reform payments from Medicare and Medicaid for emerging practices—like community EMS—that improve health care quality in areas where there are shortages of doctors and nurses.

Configuration of the current health care delivery system is not set in stone. New teams, with different partners all acting at the top of their capabilities, are forming. New career paths are opening, and job descriptions are being rewritten to include previously unheard-of occupations like "community health worker" and "community paramedic." With the help of Andres Mercado, the firefighter with a degree in classics, Santa Fe is leading the way, arriving at a solution that meets multiple needs. Hopefully other New Mexico local governments and organizations, both public and private, will follow.

In a Nutshell

Problems

- Overuse of hospital emergency rooms by those with chronic conditions, behavioral-health issues, and social problems

- A broken EMT system that rewards transport to emergency rooms, uses fire department resources inefficiently, and drives up costs for the entire system

Big Ideas

- The Santa Fe Mobile Integrated Health Office, a team that includes EMTs, a part-time doctor, a pharmacist, and a social worker

- Repurposing trained EMTs to proactively address 911 callers' needs rather than simply taking them to the emergency room

Partners

City of Santa Fe, local homeless and other safety-net providers, CHRISTUS St. Vincent Healthcare, HMOs, local clinics, prisons, foundations, Santa Fe County, behavioral-health organizations.

What You Can Do

- Write, visit, call, e-mail, and text your local county commissioner and city councilor about the value of community paramedicine—the savings it represents and the better services it delivers to homeless, senior, and mentally ill people. Ask them to make it a permanent part of your fire department's mission and then to fund it adequately.

- Seek out foundations and charities you are involved with and ask them to contribute to their local fire department's community EMT efforts.

- Encourage the local media to cover success stories and take human interest photos featuring EMTs and their clients. Circulate the stories on Facebook and send them to elected officials.

- Thank a firefighter today.

- Sound like something you would like to do? Become a paramedic or a volunteer firefighter. There are EMT classes at community colleges everywhere and you can then take the next step into community paramedicine.

- If you are a nurse, or work at a senior citizens' facility, find ways to partner with community paramedics.

Resources

Santa Fe Fire Department
PO Box 909 • 200 Murales Rd.
Santa Fe, NM 87504
505-955-3110
http://www.santafenm.gov/fire_department

Mayor Javier Gonzales
News Conference on MIHO
https://www.youtube.com/
watch?v=PAFZtmdK2OQ&list=UUTgU_
rclEQSW7XN-sgaCUBA

Emergency Medical Services
Agenda for the Future
National Highway Traffic Safety
Administration
https://www.ems.gov/pdf/2010/
EMSAgendaWeb_7-06-10.pdf

2014 Survey of Community EMS Programs
by the National Association of EMTs
https://www.naemt.org/docs/default-source/
MIH-CP/naemt-mih-cp-report.pdf?sfvrsn=2

Albuquerque Ambulance Service
Presbyterian Health Care Services
4500 Montbel Pl. NE
Albuquerque, NM 87107
505-761-8200 or 505-449-5700
https://www.phs.org/doctors-services/
services-centers/supporting-services/
albuquerque-ambulance/Pages/911-
emergency-services.aspx#tabs

CHRISTUS St. Vincent Regional
Medical Center—Community Health
The HUGS Program
455 St. Michaels Dr. • Santa Fe, NM 87505
505-913-4917 • http://www.stvin.org/

St. Vincent Hospital Foundation
455 St. Michaels Drive
Santa Fe, NM 87505
505-913-5209
http://www.stvin.org/about-the-foundation

CHAPTER 10

Growing Your Own in Southwestern New Mexico:
Mandolin Player Has Cultivated Crop of Doctors, Health Professionals

Health-care reformers don't always need to create new professions like community emergency medical technicians (EMTs) or community health workers (CHWs) in order to improve the delivery of medical services. Sometimes they just need to reassemble the pieces more appropriately to fill in the gaps and ensure that supply meets demand. But it is easier said than done. Just ask Charlie Alfero in southwestern New Mexico.

Charlie Alfero has been playing the mandolin and guitar at Diane's Restaurant in Silver City with old hippies for 20 years. But that's not all he's been doing. In 1995, he started a community health clinic in the boot heel, one of New Mexico's remotest areas, which had not had a hospital—or a doctor—for years. He developed an innovative one-stop shop, a *health commons* to serve local residents who had to drive long distances for care. Then he pioneered the use of promotoras (community health workers) and developed Hidalgo Medical Services (HMS) into what was later called a *medical home* by the Affordable Care Act, where patient needs came first and prevention was part of the package.

But Alfero says he was never cut out to be a CEO, and a few years ago he moved on from HMS, the primary-care clinic he started, to work on his first love: health-care policy. Now the guy has more Power-

Charlie Alfero, now director of the Southwest Center for Health Innovation, has been playing the guitar and mandolin around Silver City, N.M. for years. He's also been revolutionizing rural health care, starting with Hidalgo Medical Services, and then a years-long drive to attract medical providers to the isolated area.

Points and policy papers than banjos and mandolins. And they're all about increasing the supply of health professionals in rural areas.

It's a matter of equity, Alfero says.

Hidalgo, Grant, and Luna counties—like other rural parts of New Mexico—have a chronic shortage of health-care professionals, especially primary-care providers—doctors, dentists, nurse practitioners, physician assistants, and specialists of all kinds. Making matters worse is the fact that many of their family physicians are nearing retirement age. And that has big consequences for the people who live there, and for rural residents all over the state.

With longer distances to travel for care, injuries and strokes result in death more often than in urban areas. The shortage of primary-care services is linked to higher rates of chronic diseases like diabetes and heart failure, and there is a lower life expectancy.[29]

To address the shortages in rural areas, the state has tried to lure doctors from out of the state, or from the University of New Mexico (UNM) School of Medicine in Albuquerque with loan forgiveness and tax breaks. The federal government has programs too. But for the most part it hasn't worked.

The reason has to do with a quirk of medical education that skews students to urban areas, and into specialties rather than primary care.

"Houston We Have a Problem"

To become a doctor means following a long, arduous pathway that begins with adequate math and science education at the primary and secondary level, a solid pre-med curriculum in college, then four years of medical school, followed by internship and residency, both designed as hands-on training, with mentors and preceptors. For rural students, medical schools are far from home. Residencies are based in hospitals and academic medical centers, equipped with the latest technologies. There are few opportunities for rural residencies, and the problem is that where budding doctors serve their residencies often determines where they will practice. That gives the edge to cities and larger communities.

"Houston we have a problem," says Alfero. And the problem is not just in the poor distribution of primary care and other medical specialties. "It translates into a physician workforce that is not focused on prevention or health, but on extending life through advanced technical interventions," he says. "The results are high costs and poor quality of life."

There are lost opportunities for economic development as well, since each physician practicing in a rural community generates approximately $1 million for the community, hiring on average eighteen people directly or indirectly. And the presence of a doctor helps attract retirees and businesses as well.[30]

To change the equation, Alfero partnered with UNM Health Sciences Center using a new program called the Health Extension Rural Offices (HEROs). It used the agricultural extension service model to link the urban medical center's resources to rural and underserved communities like Lordsburg and Silver City, where HMS also had offices. The goal of the program, which exists in other rural states, is to end health inequities by 2025. Alfero offered free housing in Silver City to family medicine, pediatric, psychiatric, and dentistry residents. He also worked with UNM to expand the number of rural residencies through the Affordable Care Act. Earlier, Medicare, which funds medical residencies, had reduced the number of slots funded nationwide.

In 2011 Alfero started a non-profit, the New Mexico Primary Care Training Consortium, aimed at increasing the number of family residency programs in all rural areas, not just in southwestern New Mexico. The year before he had developed the one-plus-two family-practice residency format, in which residents serve one year as an intern in a small city like Las Cruces or Santa Fe and then two years at a rural clinic. Soon thereafter, HMS became the first non-hospital teaching community health center in the state, and now the small rural clinic is overjoyed by the number of residency applicants each year.

"We had six hundred applicants for two positions for 2016," he says. "It's really unbelievable."

"We're creating a more holistic environment here that is healthier for the provider…there are a lot of people who don't want to be caught in a production mill."

The ultimate goal is to develop a network of training programs in decentralized locations all with family practice residencies spreading out like spokes from hospital hubs in Las Cruces, Farmington, and other small cities.

A Pipeline Runs Through Here

Another of Alfero's non-profits, Forward New Mexico, promotes health careers to middle, high school, and college students with summer academies at Western New Mexico University in Silver City. At the academies, the students hear from various professionals from Gila Regional Hospital in Silver City and HMS and get tutoring in science and math, including specific help to prepare for different national exams like the all-important MCAT (Medical College Admission Test). They interact with Arizona health providers as well.

For younger students, Forward New Mexico's Pathways to Health Careers sponsors "Dream Maker" clubs in two middle schools in Silver City and one in Deming. Every year there's a trip to Albuquerque to visit the dental hygiene program and the nursing and medical schools, with students usually sleeping on the floor of the New Mexico Natural History Museum. And there are hands-on activities to learn about suturing or even how to dissect a piglet.

The programs are planting the seeds early with the hope they will bear fruit later, in the form of rural providers. Alfero estimates the programs have reached 15 percent of youth in southwestern New Mexico, approximately nine thousand students.

HMS also hosts rural rotations for scores of medical students from UNM and elsewhere each year, introducing them to practice in a rural area.

Peter Holguin was one of the students, serving a six-week rotation at HMS in 2015. Unlike some of the other students he knew the area well. He was a graduate of Silver High School, but now he was seeing his old home in a new light.

"I'm learning a lot about the challenges New Mexicans have in getting health care, and the importance of rural medicine…not everyone lives in a big city," he said, wrapping up his experience for an HMS video on the program.

Holguin said that he loved how supportive everyone had been, and how people rallied around a new physician in training. The experience, he said, swayed him to want to serve in rural New Mexico, where he would like to take on the challenge of working without the plentiful resources available in other areas.

For Alfero and Alexandra Maus, Forward New Mexico's workforce program specialist, Holguin's reaction is not unexpected. "By spending time in our community, the students are more likely to return to practice here," says Maus. "And if they are *from* the community, the odds of them coming back are greatly increased," Alfero adds.

This homegrown likelihood is the premise of an innovative New Mexico program started in 2006, the UNM combined BA/MD program. Designed to keep medical students in New Mexico, each year the program nurtures a cohort of New Mexico high school graduates through their BA degree and on to UNM medical school, where a seat is reserved for them. Usually undergraduate tuition is paid for by the lottery scholarship, although medical school tuition is not.

HMS follows local participants in the program, providing moral support along the way and opportunities to train in southwestern New Mexico.

Alfero has also cultivated a relationship with an Arizona dental school, located in Phoenix, which recently set aside a slot for a qualified New Mexico student. His other non-profits, the Southwest Center for Health Innovation and the National Center for Frontier Communities, are also hard at work.

Altogether, it has paid off. Alfero estimates that the activities in the past few years have resulted in about fifty more health professionals—including nurse practitioners, nurse midwives, and physician assistants—in local facilities that had none before.

Alfero has a shelf of awards recognizing his efforts, most notably the Louis Gorin Award from the National Rural Health Association in 2013. He is the first New Mexican to receive one.

"The trick is taking an idea, proving it works and following it until it becomes a best practice," says Alfero, now toiling in the rural healthcare fields for thirty-five years. But it has to be a good policy to start with, based on outcomes and results, he says. "Otherwise don't do it."

Alfero's charts, PowerPoints and processes often move in concentric circles—first setting internal priorities, developing consensus within the organization and community, and then getting the necessary resources.

"You can't wait for somebody else to do it. You've got to create the program, what's best for you," he says. And to sustain and grow it, you have to be a policy advocate.

"It's only sustainable if it's in state law or federal policy," Alfero says, "If it's in the financing system, in the payment contracts, or if it's revenue—not expense based.

"And you can't do that unless it's good policy."

In a Nutshell

Problem

- Lack of rural healthcare providers—doctors, nurses, dentists, nurse practitioners, physician's assistants

Big Ideas

- A new kind of medical residency program that encourages doctors and dentists to locate in rural areas (New Mexico Primary Care Training Consortium)
- Pipeline programs in elementary, high schools to interest kids in medical careers
- A BA/MD program that takes students from rural New Mexico communities, guides them as a cohort through an undergraduate pre-medical program at the University of New Mexico, and then guarantees them a place at University of New Mexico School of Medicine

What You Can Do

- If you are a teacher or a parent whose child/student is interested in medicine, nursing, or affiliated fields, guide them to appropriate programs and expose them to successful professionals in those fields.
- If you are a policymaker, fund programs that make it easier to pay off student debt and locate in a rural area.

- If you have math or science skills, help a student prepare for the MCAT or other exams.
- Celebrate graduations and other successes of medical students at all levels.

Resources

Southwest Center for Health Innovation
301 College Ave. Suite 16
Silver City, NM 88061
575-534-0101
http://swchi.org

Forward New Mexico
http://swchi.org/forward-nm

New Mexico Primary Care Training Consortium
http://swchi.org/nmpctc/

National Center for Frontier Communities
http://swchi.org/ncfc

Health Extension Rural Offices (HEROs)
University of New Mexico
Albuquerque, NM 87131
505-277-0111
http://hsc.unm.edu/community/hero/
Health Extension Toolkit available at:
http://healthextensiontoolkit.org

Combined BA/MD Degree Program
UNM School of Medicine
2400 Tucker NE
MSC09 5065
1 University of New Mexico
Albuquerque, NM 87131
505-925-4500
http://bamdas.unm.edu

New Mexico Health Resources
300 San Mateo NE Suite 905
Albuquerque, NM 87110
505-260-0993
www.nmhr.org

PART FOUR
Connecting New Mexico's Youth With Our Prime Asset: The Great Outdoors

What if New Mexico, with its educational system now rated at 49th in the nation and its high rate of dropouts and idle young people, tried something different? What if we re-framed education and job training to put kids outdoors, spending less time in traditional classrooms and doing real work that is valued by natural resource agencies and policymakers?

Three innovative programs that do just that have found that the result is more young people with skills in science, critical thinking, initiative, and character. Even more important, the result is a new generation with a personal connection to watersheds, rivers, forests, and mountains.

For twenty years, crews from the Rocky Mountain Youth Corps and other conservation groups have built trails and fences throughout the state, learning practical skills and building healthy relationships—often in the face of personal trauma. Since the mid-1990s, students from the Wild Friends program have been showing up at every legislative session, reminding policymakers of the importance of wildlife and learning about democracy—with all its warts. And since 1997, the Bosque Ecosystem Monitoring Program (BEMP) has been growing young scientists one litterfall and pitfall trap at a time.

In the future, the stewards and environmental champions forged by programs like these will show us another way forward—one that uses our public lands wisely, with the respect for our natural heritage and the assets that come with it in the form of rivers, forests, and wildlife. It gives me hope that a more-balanced development based on New Mexico's breathtaking scenery is possible.

CHAPTER 11

Wild Friends:
Unique Civics Program Helps Students
Find Their Voice While Standing up for Wildlife

Putting students in contact with the natural word, doing real work like collecting data on the bosque for BEMP, or building trails for the Rocky Mountain Youth Corps are two good ways to stimulate learning and build skills. But not all alternative programs are outdoors. The Wild Friends program connects students to another real world indoors: the world of policy making at the New Mexico Legislature. The genius of this decades-old program is its combination of civic engagement and environmental education. In an era when civics is absent from the curriculum and traditional classroom instruction is not always delivering good results, it is a ray of hope. Mentors, students, teachers, and legislators are—collectively—creating the platform for a new generation of leaders who stand up for what they have learned. That's good news for New Mexico.

Esteban Casas was nervous. The eighth grader from the South Valley Academy was the lead witness for Senate Joint Memorial 4 (SJM 4), a measure to create awareness of the importance of the now-declining population of bees and other pollinators. The memorial (a type of bill which contains recommendations, not funding) would start a labeling program for plants at local nurseries and create a pollinator garden at the state capitol. State senator Mimi Stewart, the sponsor of the memorial, was now approaching the witness stand and motioning for the student experts, all clad in turquoise T-shirts, to come forward and stand behind her.

Casas had been up since 5:30 that morning to make the trip to Santa Fe from Albuquerque's South Valley with nine other middle school students and his teacher, Jennifer Chavez-Miller. Along the way he had practiced his remarks and role-played responses to questions he might be asked. Earlier, his class had visited the Valle de Oro National Wildlife Refuge and heard experts talk about pollinators. He had memorized factoids and knew, for example, that sunflowers, asters, butterfly bushes, cosmos, lavender, and willows are pollinator-friendly plants. Along with thirty other students in the program, he had traveled to the capitol the previous day to get the lay of the land.

"I'd like to introduce some of my friends," said state senator Stewart, smiling at the members of the New Mexico Senate Conservation Committee. "They're the Wild Friends and I will let them speak about Senate Joint Memorial 4 for themselves."

Many of the committee members were familiar with Wild Friends, a twenty-five-year-old civics education program that brings hundreds of students to New Mexico's capitol each year to lobby for legislation about wildlife issues that they create themselves.

Some of the senators chuckled, and a flicker of recognition passed through the sleepy group assembled behind the curved dais at the front of the committee room. The chairman of the committee, Senator Joe Cervantes, nodded. Esteban knew that was his cue to kick off the discussion with an explanation of what the bill would do.

Esteban said he had been thrown off by the sergeant-at-arms who, moments before the committee convened, had announced loudly that no public comment would be allowed. She was mistaken, but the students, most of who had never been outside of their neighborhood in the South Valley, didn't know that.

Wild Friends (l to r) Alexia Mayarez, Ariana Gutierrez, Mateo Valencia and Stephanie Orozco testify before the New Mexico Senate Conservation Committee in January, 2017. Sen. Mimi Stewart, seated, was the sponsor of their wildlife bill to protect pollinators.

"I was nervous, but when they smiled and made a few jokes, I realized that this was easy," Esteban said later.

After the students from the Wild Friends made their case, the committee grilled them on the number of acres in agricultural production in New Mexico, how much the program would cost, and whether the state's land grant college in Las Cruces (New Mexico State University) would be involved (it would be). Their questions answered, the senators passed the memorial unanimously.

Esteban was elated. So were the other students, who gathered afterward in the hallway to talk about what just happened with state senator Stewart, a supporter and frequent sponsor of Wild Friends' bills. "I'd like to go back," he said, "to see what happened to some of the other bills. I noticed there was one about bear traps."

Esteban's newfound interest in the legislative process—and his confidence that he could make a difference—is just what the founders of the Wild Friends hoped for in 1991 when they started the unique non-profit, which combines civics education with wildlife science. Initially spearheaded by Ruth Musgrave, a New Mexico natural resource attorney, the small group started by brainstorming about a hands-on civics program that could engage students in something they really cared about. Musgrave, Carolyn Byers, Camy Condon, and Paul Nathanson plotted out of the Institute of Public Law, a part of the University of New Mexico (UNM) School of Law, which was shortly expanded to incorporate a Center for Wildlife Law.

"Carolyn Byers and I just started writing grant proposals," Musgrave said. "I took notes. I contacted everyone—John Denver and Maurice Sendak, who wrote *Where the Wild Things Are*." Al Utton, then a law professor, helped and, finally, Musgrave got a grant from the W. K. Kellogg Foundation.

It wasn't hard to make the pitch, which is even more compelling in 2017 than it was in 1991. It was this: representative democracy depends on educated citizens, yet civics education in the classroom has taken a big hit. High school graduates are more likely to be able to name the Three Stooges, rather than the three branches of government. Eighty-five percent did not know the meaning of "the rule of law," and only 5 percent of high school seniors are able to identify and explain checks on presidential power.[31] The upshot then—and now—is that citizens, not understanding how state, local, or federal government operates, often distrust politics at all levels. Voter participation suffers, and greater division results.

Legislators in New Mexico got it. By 1995, the legislature itself was making regular appropriations to the program, thanks to state senator Tom Rutherford, from Albuquerque, who then chaired the senate conservation committee. It didn't hurt that Dave Warren, his chief analyst, was Ruth Musgrave's partner. Other partners stepped up too, including the Public Service Company of New Mexico, NM Educators Federal Credit Union (now Nusenda Credit Union), Talking Talons Youth Leadership, and others.

More Than a Field Trip

Every year about four hundred students from grades four to twelve and their teachers participate in the program, which starts at the beginning of the school year. Initially targeted to primarily low-income schools, the program has been in scores of private, charter, and public schools from Jemez Pueblo to Silver City. The process begins when the students vote on which topic and bill to work on throughout the year. Wild Friends staff guides them using a few criteria, learned from hard knocks in previous sessions. The topic must be easy for legislators as well as students to understand, have a practical application, and draw on common ground between diverse interests. Ultimately it's the kids who decide. Pollinators have been a popular topic, but prairie dogs, butterflies, whooping cranes, safe wildlife corridors, and the prevention of poaching have been topics as well. The selection process itself is a lesson in democracy.

The students then research the topics as part of their science and civics curricula, using a study guide from Wild Friends and classroom visits from UNM law students, experts on the topic, and volunteer mentors, who are often retired. Then, using a form supplied by Wild Friends, they formulate a proposal for a new law or policy, which can either be a bill or a memorial. To figure out which—and what has the greatest chance of passage—they must understand the legislative process, requiring another whole series of lessons. Finally, the students send their well-honed draft to the legislative sponsor, who has the Legislative Council Service format it into the proper language for introduction.

Then the real work begins: getting it passed. Talking points and fact sheets are drafted. Target legislators are identified. Letters are written. Visits and testimony are planned. The imagination of the kids spans far beyond that of the typical lobbyist. Various school groups have brought hawks, fawns, and other critters to the Roundhouse, where they made appearances on the floor of the senate or in the rotunda—all to emphasize the importance of wildlife and the passage of that year's measure. Art is always included.

The Wild Friends Dance Troupe led by Lorin Erramouspe Abbey, has portrayed butterflies and whooping cranes, and another enthusiastic group of students once did a rap dance on the huge travertine marble table in the governor's office. Other groups have visited New Mexico Supreme Court justices, the secretary of state, and the land commis-

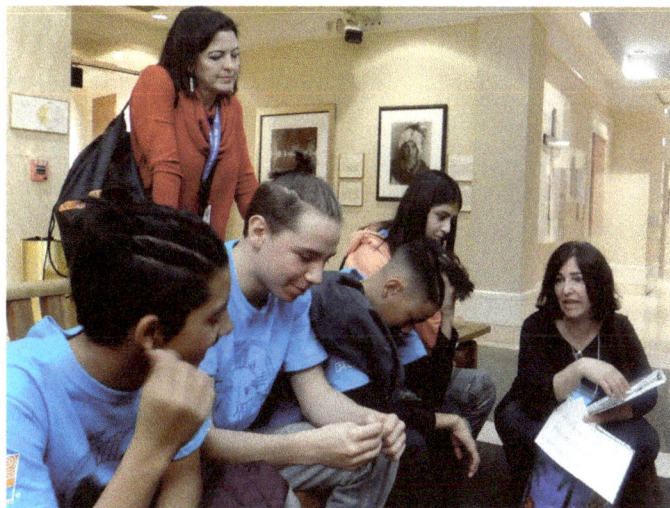

Wild Friends Director Sue George, kneeling, confers with students in the halls of the New Mexico legislature after their testimony before a senate committee. Their bill, Senate Joint Memorial 4, passed the legislature, after scores of students in the program came to Santa Fe to lobby for it.

sioner, as the Wild Friends have learned these officials are involved in laws as well.

But the heart of the program happens in the offices of state senators and state representatives and in the rounded halls of the legislature where students lobby their representatives and tell them about their bill. With a few notable exceptions, most are receptive to the young advocates, who are trained to make eye contact, shake hands firmly, and confine their remarks to a fact-based elevator speech.

Stephanie Sanchez started with Wild Friends in sixth grade at Polk Middle School. Now an adjunct professor of cultural anthropology at UNM, she continues to volunteer. She remembers walking down the hallway, pulling legislators aside, challenging them on the bill she was promoting and telling them "Hey, you represent me. I'm your constituent."

"It was really empowering, having access to decision makers like that," she said. One year, she was lobbying for a bill that would increase penalties for poaching, or hunting wildlife without a license. She got a lot of pushback from legislators who thought she was a naïve environmentalist, but she countered with her own experience: hunters in her family and the idea that it's often hunters who respect wildlife the most.

"Kids tend to lose their voice somewhere along the way in public schools, to not take up much space. You're not taught how to be a leader," she said. "But in Wild Friends you learn how to counter opposition and challenge people." Sanchez remembered the day when she spoke on the senate floor. "I remember choosing the outfit I would wear."

"This was more than a field trip," she said.

Hard Knocks and Common Ground

Since 1991 approximately fifteen thousand participating students have lobbied for twenty-six different bills and memorials on everything from wildlife-vehicle collisions to recycling at the state capitol. About 70 percent of the measures have passed—compared to the usual passage rate of about 20 percent. But the successes did not come easy, particularly in the early years. Wild Friends' first legislative outing was a disaster. Pushing a memorial to protect endangered species, the group was called out by rural legislators, who lectured them on the loss of their farms and ranches. It was a traumatic experience, recalled Musgrave. For several years, a few irritated legislators would purposely upset the kids by talking about shooting bald eagles, wolves, and coyotes.

"We were very naïve at first," said Ruth Musgrave. "We thought that an endangered species memorial would be a 'feel good' thing. But if you don't go for common ground you will get killed no matter how many cute kids you have."

"They found out that protecting wildlife and habitat was not a simple matter," said Jack Pickering, a volunteer who mentored the group well into his nineties. Pickering, who died a few years ago, was steadfast in guiding the students through competing interests, which they faced on numerous issues.

A few years after their initial defeat, the group redeemed itself with a Common Ground Memorial that affirmed common values across competing groups in the wildlife area. It has formed the basis of future legislation in the field.

State senator Stewart says the students gradually learned about some of the legislature's sacred cows and how not to "upset the applecart." But it still happens. Last year one representative gave the kids a scolding and threatened to kill their initiative. But Stewart reformulated the measure (also about pollinators), and the state senate passed it.

"They understand that if they do their work, become experts, testify before committees and answer questions they will be successful." Stewart says. "And that turns them into powerful citizens."

Jennifer Chavez-Miller, Esteban Casas' middle school teacher at South Valley Academy, says the whole program is "brilliant." "To have the kids do authentic advocacy and bill drafting—it's important work at the middle school level, and to be part of the civics process is life-changing."

In spite of its success, the award-winning program has been cut back in the past several years, as legislative budgets shrink and schools cut field trips and extracurricular activities, focusing instead on "teaching to the test." Sue George, now the director of Wild Friends, says the program draws on volunteers, law-school interns, and other partners. Parents and teachers often drive the kids to Santa Fe. Class visits to schools outside of Albuquerque-Santa Fe area are limited, and the group now works with more charter schools, which are more flexible.

Teachers, students, and supporters of the homegrown program, still housed at the UNM School of Law's Institute of Public Law, are determined it will survive. "A fifth grader told me after her field trip this year that she wants to be a legislator someday. That's what makes this all worthwhile," says Sue George.

 Meanwhile, one former Wild Friend, Gabrielle Swass, is studying biochemistry at UNM and thinking about medical school. She still remembers testifying in 2009 about how the state should map paths and construct wildlife corridors for the safe passage of animals across freeways. A few years later she was part of a group that threw the switch for lighting that marked a wildlife corridor in Tijeras canyon.

"We heard a bunny scamper by," she said, "and I knew it was possible to make changes in the world.

In a Nutshell

Problems

- Lack of civic education, knowledge of the democratic process
- Cynicism about decision-making and public institutions
- Threatened wildlife

Big Idea

- Wild Friends, a program combining student love of wildlife with education about state government. Each year, participating classes write wildlife legislation and personally lobby it through the New Mexico legislature.

Partners

Public and charter schools throughout the state, teachers, volunteer mentors, University of New Mexico School of Law's Institute of Public Law, legislators, New Mexico land commissioner, New Mexico State University, the New Mexico secretary of state, environmental organizations, dancers, artists, students, governors, judges, students, parents, Wildlife Rescue, Hawks Aloft, PNM, Nusenda Credit Union, beekeepers, landscapers, many others depending on the subject of the bills drafted.

What You Can Do

- Write, call, email, text your legislator and ask him or her to keep funding Wild Friends.

- Volunteer, go with the group to Santa Fe or assist classroom teachers by bringing your expertise (or your wildlife) into their classrooms. Help with field trips.

- Donate to the UNM School of Law: Wild Friends Program https://www.unmfund.org/fund/school-of-law-wild-friends-program/?_ga=2.88027928.1450576451.1499636353-934994994.1475106976

- If you are a parent, teacher, or friend of a child, take him or her outside to observe wildlife firsthand.

Resources

The Wild Friends Program
Institute of Public Law • UNM School of Law • MSC11 6060
1 University of New Mexico • Albuquerque, NM 87131
505-277-5089 • http://wildfriends.unm.edu

How the Legislature Works
http://nmlegis.gov/lcs/lcsdocs/NMHandbook01-05.pdf

Wild Friends Manual for kids teachers, volunteers and others, along with a guide to wildlife education activities and resource materials, can be found at the Wild Friends website (http://wildfriends.unm.edu) under Resources

CHAPTER 12

Cliff Crawford's Cottonwood Seedlings:
The Bosque Ecosystem Monitoring Program (BEMP)

"BEMP is setting the bar in how we bring together science, stewardship and education."

—Dr. Jennifer Rudgers, associate professor,
Department of Biology, University of New Mexico

D r. Cliff Crawford had cornered me. I had just asked a simple question about the bosque, the riparian forest of cottonwoods lining the Rio Grande in central New Mexico. "Is it true that the cottonwoods are dying, and unless we do something, they will all be gone in forty years or so?"

In 1996, in preparation for my first year in the New Mexico Legislature, I had just read the "Middle Rio Grande Ecosystem: Bosque Biological Management Plan" penned by Crawford and an interagency team in the mid-Rio Grande Valley. I needed to know, since the river ran through my district and the construction of a bridge through the bosque had sparked a constituent uprising.

Crawford knew the answer—and then some. And then more, and more about the problem and what could be done to preserve one of New Mexico's natural treasures. After hours of explanation, I learned that, with the construction of dams and levies, the river had been straightened and the flow constricted to reduce overbank flooding, which had fed the cottonwoods for years. That change, along with the growth of non-native species, the recurring southwestern drought and the fires it brought, put the forest at risk.

Crawford had the data, but he let me draw my own conclusions. As a University of New Mexico (UNM) professor, he had been studying

Cliff Crawford, founder of the Bosque Ecosystem Monitoring Project (BEMP), at work in the bosque.

Photo by Dan Shaw

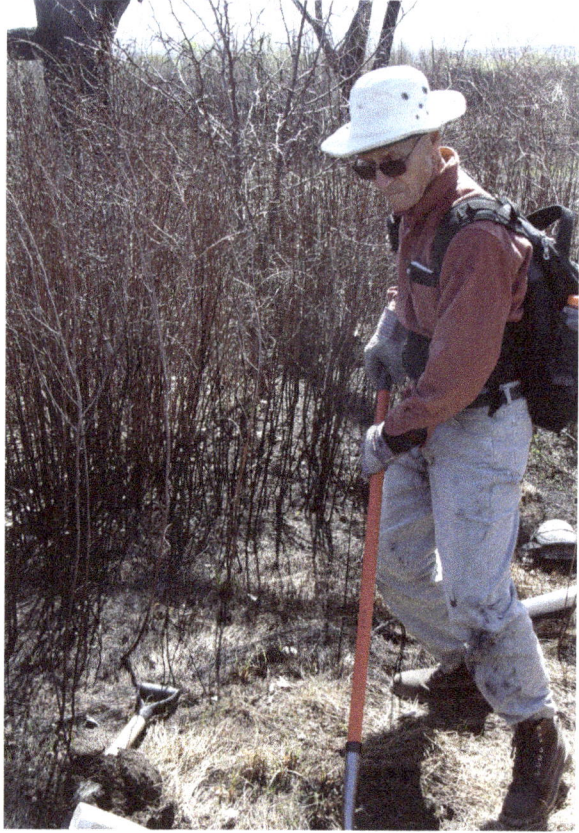

the problem since he started offering classes in bosque biology in the 1980s. But he didn't initially press the need for long-term management. He was forceful, yet humble and kind. I realized later that he was treating me not like a state legislator, but like one of his students.

"That was Cliff," says Dan Shaw, now codirector of the Bosque Ecosystem Monitoring Program (BEMP). Shaw said Crawford had a sense of wonder and excitement about learning that carried over into everything he did, regardless of whether he was talking to a second grader or another sophisticated scientist who knew the Latin names of all the species present in the bosque.

"Kindness oozed out of Cliff Crawford like sweat oozes out of most of us," said environmentalist and author Bill DuBuys, who worked with Crawford and the former United States Senator Pete Domenici to ultimately direct millions of federal dollars into bosque preservation based on recommendations in the 1993 management plan. "But he was a scientist through-and-through, passionately committed to the places he studied."

After even more hours of talking to Crawford, I knew that, for the bosque, it was only a matter of time.

But Crawford had an idea. Long-term management of the bosque and the river depended on data provided through accurate biological monitoring accessible to land managers in the area. Working with graduate students like Mary Stuever, Lisa Ellis, and other environmental educators, he provided evidence that middle school students could reliably collect ecological monitoring data. Crawford's plan would not only supply land mangers with needed data, but also provide hands-on educational opportunities for students from kindergarten to high school. It might even motivate students to become stewards of the bosque.

Crawford died in 2010, but not before his grand idea had grown from a small project funded by the National Science Foundation with four monitoring sites to an organization that engages ten thousand students a year from between thirty and forty public, private, and tribal schools up and down the Rio Grande. The program began as a partnership between UNM's biology department and the Bosque School, a private school on the banks of the Rio Grande in Albuquerque, when four sixth-grade classes set up the first monitoring site near the Alameda Bridge in Albuquerque. It engaged UNM graduate students and senior interns to mentor younger students as they collected field data according to scientifically rigorous protocols adapted to particular age groups. Data collected by the students and citizen volunteers went back to UNM to become technical reports about the health of the bosque.

The information on how flood, fire, climate, and human changes affect the ecosystem is important to state and federal agencies charged with managing the bosque. Before long the agencies began paying for it—through contracts that replaced, to some extent, the educational grants that formed the basis of BEMP's budget in the early days. Now, the twenty-year-old program operates at thirty-two sites from Ohkay Owingeh Pueblo in the north to Mesilla Park in the south with an annual budget of $750,000, two codirectors, fourteen staff members, and hundreds of teachers and volunteers.

"We are the sons and daughters of Cliff Crawford," says Shaw.

Green Trails for the Next Generation

Most of Mary Erwin's students at Wilson Middle School in the low-income "war-zone" area of Albuquerque have never been to the bosque, and they view the nearby Sandia Mountains as an exotic foreign country. But when they get down to their BEMP site in the bosque for their monthly monitoring trip, near the Rio Grande Nature Center, it's a grand adventure.

Their first job is to collect plant material (buds, seeds, flowers, twigs, stems, bark, and leaves) that has fallen into litter tubs that they set up on earlier visits. Then they read precipitation gauges at two locations,

BEMP participants (l to r) Hart Walker, Grace Klein-Robbenhaar, Jude Gutierrez, Abigail Nairn, Steve Davenport and Jazmin Soza, collecting data in the Rio Grande

Photo by Dan Shaw

meticulously recording the data in notebooks. After they collect the data they might hike around, make notes in their journals, or just sit on the riverbank watching the water flow and listening to the birds. Interns from UNM's biology department are often there to help mentor the younger children, and when students return to their classroom guest educators from the program visit to show how their data is used to track vegetation and biological diversity over time—all keys to understanding a complex ecosystem.

"When they see there is meaning to the work that they do, they will rise to any challenge," Dan Shaw says.

Some classes track arthropod activities with small pitfall traps used to capture bugs or monitor groundwater levels with low-tech, low-cost field equipment. Others have wrapped the bases of young cottonwood trees with chicken wire to prevent beavers from eating them. Some high school students are involved with fish or water-quality research, which they present at BEMP's annual symposia. There is something real for every level.[32] Collection of the information is not just an academic exercise. It's used by agencies like the Army Corps of Engineers and the Interstate Stream Commission to make multimillion-dollar decisions about restoration, a tribute to BEMP's reputation for scientific rigor and professionalism, something that Cliff Crawford designed into the program.

"Nobody else is doing what we do nationwide," says Shaw. "Data is being collected by 5th and 6th graders and it is informing multi-million dollar decisions."

But it's not just about data collection. It's the opportunity for kids to get outdoors, far from video games, mobile phones, and indoor malls where they usually play—at the risk of what author Richard Louv calls "a nature-deficit disorder."[33] And when they actually have something constructive to do in nature, it's what Crawford called "a grand adventure."

Through the years, middle school teacher Mary Erwin says her students have observed countless birds—great-horned owls, bald eagles, sandhill cranes, woodpeckers, pheasants, and more. They have seen coyotes and, their favorite—porcupines.

One of her students, a tough kid with oversized pants that fell far below his waist, had trouble simultaneously juggling his binoculars, running after birds, and holding up his pants. On the bus ride home, she learned about his home life and realized that being in the bosque allowed him to be the child he couldn't be anywhere else.

"Everything can't be learned in a classroom," Erwin says. "There's something to learning science by picking up sticks, poking at leaves and looking under logs that's essential to their humanness."

The BEMP program also incorporates hundreds of volunteers, parents, and members of wildlife organizations. Any given field trip might include the owners of the land on which the BEMP site is located—often government agencies like the Middle Rio Grande Conservancy District or the Rio Grande State Park. And activities do not end with the school year. There are summer camps and special projects, too.

It's "citizen science" at its best, engaging ordinary folks to collect information and then using it to increase a broad-based body of scientific research. "As we move into our 20th year, we tease out the impacts of drought and climate change from our data," Kim Eichhorst, BEMP codirector, told *Bio Science Magazine*. "If it were not for

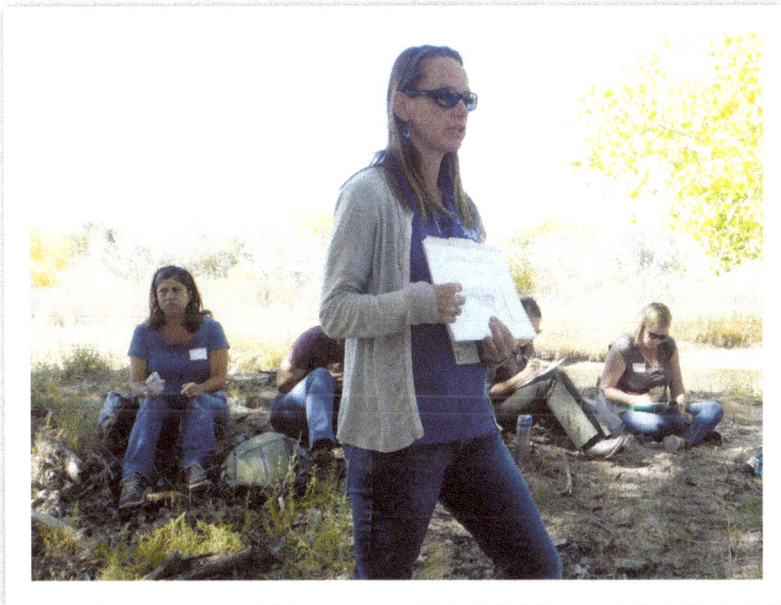

Kim Eichhorst, BEMP codirector, explains river flows during a 2016 fall field tour of BEMP's monitoring site at Sandia Pueblo.

citizen science we could not monitor 32 sites year round."[34] Eichhorst, a graduate student of Cliff Crawford's, was recruited by Crawford to succeed him as a director of BEMP when he retired from the UNM faculty to become a full-time BEMP volunteer. By that time she was a PhD. She has brought a scientist's sense of precision to the project, not to mention the graphs and charts with which she is always armed.

Growing the Next Generation of Scientists One Litterfall Tub, One Pitfall Trap at a Time

Rowan Converse was once a BEMP student scrambling around her class's monitoring area, taking measurements, reading graphs, and talking to older students from UNM. Now a Wesleyan College graduate, she's a full-fledged wildlife biologist—and she credits BEMP with giving her the confidence and the contacts. "I wouldn't even be in the sciences if not for BEMP," she says. Converse is not alone. Many BEMP students go on to study environmental science, biology, or wildlife ecology and conservation in college, later returning as BEMP interns or program employees. Then, many go on to become park rangers or natural resource managers.

To test this hypothesis, Converse took a survey of sixty former students and interns in 2014–2015. Although the sample was small, she found that 70 percent of those BEMP students majored either in natural resources, biology, or other STEM (science, technology, engineering, or mathematics) fields. And 67 percent said that BEMP was a motivator in pushing them in that direction. Even more important, 67 percent said that BEMP helped clarify their career goals.[35]

During the course of their experience with BEMP, students come in contact with a variety of natural resource professionals, from park rangers to hydrologists. They make presentations to them, get feedback, and begin to develop the skills that the professionals use on a day-to-day basis.

"Everything about BEMP has been a collaboration, from the very start," says Dan Shaw. The list of BEMP partners and participants is huge, incorporating groups from the United States Army Corps of Engineers and the United States Fish and Wildlife Service to local conservation districts, water and electric utilities, and even Intel and Los Alamos National Lab.

The partners—and the networks created by the project—have paid off for the students. "BEMP is fostering the next generation of natural resource managers," says Converse. "It's growing park rangers and biologists one litterfall tub, one pitfall trap at a time," adds Shaw.

At the same time, the monitoring data produced by the program has been vital to agencies managing the river and its riparian forest for regeneration, recreation, and fire prevention. BEMP monitoring sites are located in areas where restoration projects have occurred, making them useful in evaluating the outcomes of various projects.

As a result of BEMP data, the Middle Rio Grande Conservancy District has targeted certain areas for invasive species removal and adopted new guidelines for woodchip depth at sites where mulching is used to clear the invasive species. Forest officials have used precipitation data to close—or open—areas during fire season. And BEMP data has been used to approach questions like, is there any water savings from exotic plant removal? Or what is the best method of clearing debris and replanting after a fire?

Although they're quite technical, the answers to these and other questions are important in a state where rivers are running low, drought contributes to fire, and native species are threatened. But there's something else that is just as important, and it's the lasting contribution of the BEMP program: the relationships created between the thousands of students who participate and the natural places they inhabit. That is founder Cliff Crawford's greatest legacy—generations of bosque stewards and citizen scientists of all ages and backgrounds up and down the Rio Grande.

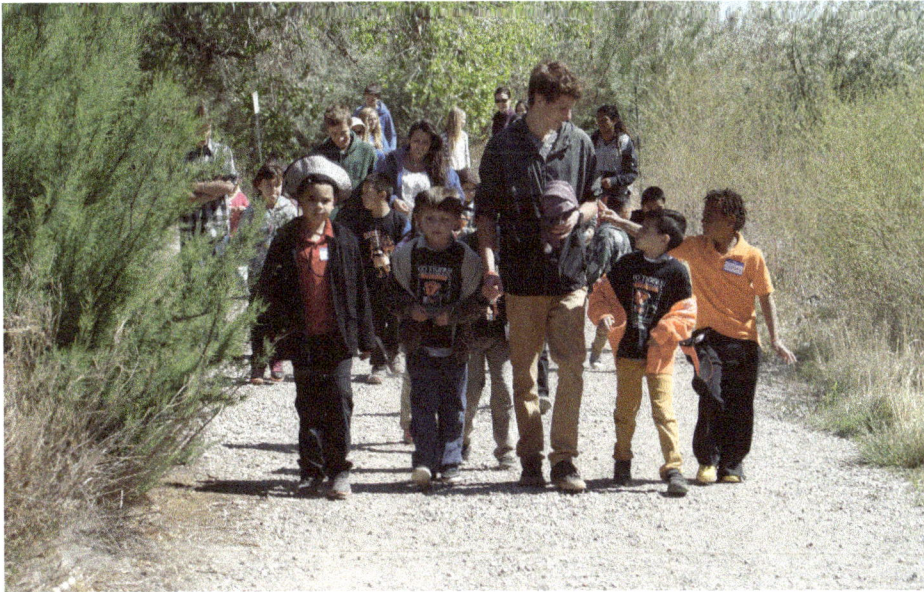

An older BEMP student leads a younger group along a bosque trail. The project is growing park rangers, biologists and stewards of the bosque.

Photo by Dan Shaw

In a Nutshell

Problems

- Decline and vulnerability of the bosque, the Rio Grande's riparian forest, as a result of fire and drought
- A nature-deficit disorder in many children with little contact with the natural world and few experiences outdoors

Big Idea

- Using students as scientists to collect data for natural resources agencies

Partners

University of New Mexico Department of Biology, Bosque School, environmental educators, public and charter schools up and down the Rio Grande valley, the United States Army Corps of Engineers, the Middle Rio Grande Conservancy District, the Bureau of Reclamation, the Valle de Oro National Wildlife Preserve, the Rio Grande Nature Center, United States Fish and Wildlife Service, Albuquerque Open Space Division, local conservation districts, water and electric utilities, Los Alamos National Labs, Intel, Rio Grande pueblos, New Mexico State Parks, Office of the New Mexico State Engineer, New Mexico Water Resources Department.

What You Can Do

- If you are a teacher, see if your classroom can join the BEMP program. Use the program's books, maps and other materials in your classroom. Use the Bosque Education Guide available on line at http://www.nmnaturalhistory.org/educational-resources/sections/bosque-education-guide or from the New Mexico Natural History Museum or the Rio Grande Nature Center. The Nature Center holds periodic workshops on how this interdisciplinary curriculum can be used in your classroom.

- If you are a land manager, contact the BEMP project to review its reports, commission data collection, or host a site on your land.

- Volunteer for the BEMP program, help with transportation, or go on field trips with students to the bosque.

- For a greater understanding of the one of New Mexico's prime outdoor resources, read the "Middle Rio Grande Ecosystem: Bosque Biological Management Plan" http://westernwaters.org/record/view/113165.

- Join one of the many civic and environmental groups protecting the bosque—Friends of the Rio Grande Nature Center, the Rio Grande Chapter of the Sierra Club, Friends of the Bosque del Apache Wildlife Preserve, the Bosque Action Team, Wildlife Rescue, the Aldo Leopold Foundation, or Hawks Aloft, among others.

- Go for a bird walk in the bosque. Join the Audubon Society's annual Christmas Bird Count.

Resources

The Bosque Ecosystem Monitoring Program
4000 Bosque School Rd NW
Albuquerque, NM 87120
505-898-6388
http://bemp.org/

UNM Department of Biology
MSC03 2020
1 University of New Mexico
Albuquerque, NM 87131
505-277-0758

Mid Rio Grande Stormwater Quality Team
http://www.keeptheriogrand.org/bosque-eco-system-monitoring-project/

Rio Grande Phenology Trail http://bemp.org/rgpt/

The Long Term Ecological Research (LTER) Network
at www.lternet.edu has special projects related to climate
change for young people.

For a **directory of citizen science projects** go to: www.citizensci.com.

The **Audubon Society**'s Christmas Bird Count program is one of the oldest
examples of citizen science: www.audubon.orgbirds/citizen/index.html.

Middle Rio Grande Ecosystem: Bosque Biological Management Plan
http://westernwaters.org/record/view/113165

Datasets from BEMP monitoring projects available at
http://bemp.org/data-sets/

BEMP reports are at http://bemp.org/reports/

Converse, Rowan, Dan Shaw, Kim Eichhorst, and May Leinhart. "Bringing
Citizen Monitoring into Land Management: a Case Study of the Bosque
Ecosystem Monitoring Program," *Journal of Science Communication 15*
(2016).

Porky's Quest: An Adventure in the Rio Grande Bosque, a children's book
by Lauren Bennett, and *Eco-tracking on the Trail of Habitat Change,* by
Dan Shaw, are two of the many books and educational resources available
from BEMP at http://bemp.org/education-resources/.

The Bosque Education Guide provides an interdisciplinary curriculum
adaptable to classrooms or groups. It is available on line at http://www.nm-
naturalhistory.org/educational-resources/sections/bosque-education-guide
or from the NM Natural History Museum or the Rio Grande Nature Center, which periodically holds workshops on how to use it.

Richard Louv, *Last Child in the Woods,* Algonquin Books 2005
http://richardlouv.com/books/last-child/

CHAPTER 13

Rocky Mountain Youth Corps, Youth Conservation Programs Inspire Motley Crews to Give Back and Build the Foundation for Healthy Communities

"Hope comes in the form of taking action and doing the dirty work. This work in the wilderness has saved our lives, and we will bring back our skills to the city."

—Alyssa Armstrong, crew supervisor,
Rocky Mountain Youth Corps,
Valle de Oro National Wildlife Preserve

New Mexico has one of the highest high school dropout rates and levels of idle youth in the country. And as we'll see in Chapter 16, completing college is a heavy lift, especially for those from a low-income background. Disillusionment, drug abuse, and crime rates run high, and there is an exodus of teens and young adults seeking jobs in Colorado, some of them in the marijuana industry. But given the chance, many are willing to put their energy and enthusiasm into something positive. One common loyalty is to New Mexico's precious public places, and many are eager to preserve them. All over New Mexico, the Rocky Mountain Youth Corps (RMYC) and other programs are giving young people something to say yes to, something to build, and something to take pride in. In the process, communities benefit, young people get a taste of their own power and new paths to both personal and community development open wide.

A Rocky Mountain Youth
Corps member at work in
New Mexico

Photo courtesy of Rocky
Mountain Youth Corps

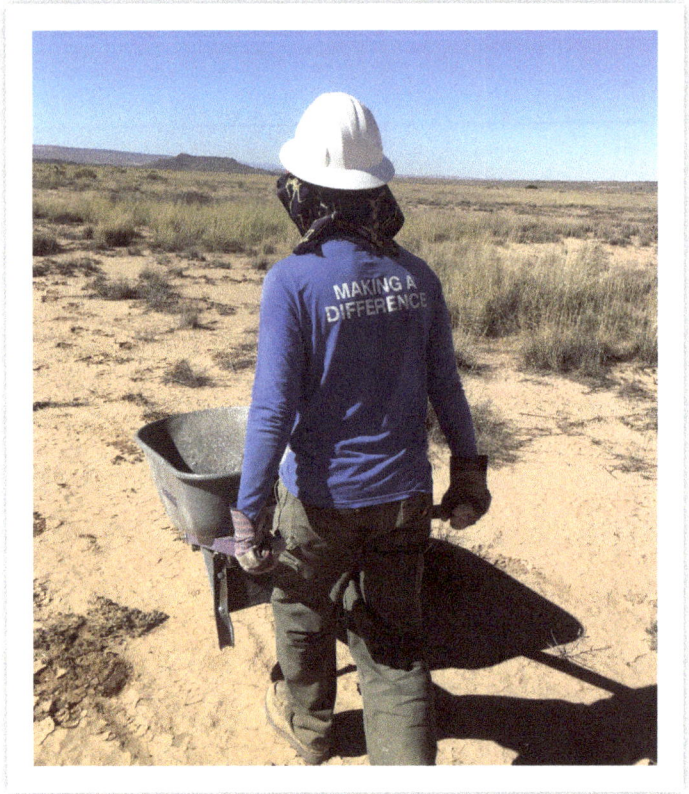

A Rocky Mountain Youth Corps member at work in New Mexico

Photo courtesy of Rocky Mountain Youth Corps

When you ask the members of the RMYC to share highlights of their experiences in the state's twenty-two-year-old program, no matter where they are from, they tell you that hard work and team spirit taught them they could do more than they ever thought they could.

"I'm stronger and smarter than I thought," said Augustine Quintana, from Santo Domingo Pueblo. Quintana had struggled after high school with temporary jobs that he didn't like, but now, with new skills under his belt and a newfound appreciation for nature ("It takes care of you and you take care of it," he says), he is off on his life's journey. This coming fire season, he has signed on with the United States Forest Service (USFS).

Quintana, twenty-two years old, is one of over two thousand teens and young adults to benefit from a number of youth conservation programs that in the past few decades have mobilized them to build trails, thin forests, and remove invasive species on New Mexico's plentiful federal, state, and local park lands. The programs are all descendants of the Civilian Conservation Corps (CCC), which put thousands of unemployed young men to work in the 1930s building dams, fighting fires, and conserving natural resources. Elephant Butte Reservoir, Bandelier National Monument, and many other familiar facilities in New Mexico were constructed by men camped out in the nearby woods. Some of them are now being restored by today's conservation crews.

Pick-and-Shovel Soldiers Abound in New Mexico's Vast Outdoors

Although the RMYC is the largest of the conservation corps operating in the state, there are others. Funding for many comes from the New Mexico Youth Conservation Corps (NM YCC), which was created in 1992 to spur youth development. Each year the NM YCC Commission selects and funds conservation programs from around the state, using funding from a small add-on to governmental gross receipts taxes on items like ticket sales. In 2017, the funding came to $3.8 million spread out to thirty-one different projects from Ruidoso to Aztec.

"Most of the programs are summer programs, and are very locally driven," said Wendy Kent, NM YCC executive director. "I'd like to believe that a lot of these young people stay in their communities, although there are many competing pressures." A key feature of the program is that participants who put in fifty-two weeks over a four-year period are eligible for a cash bonus ($500) or a tuition voucher ($1,500) good at New Mexico colleges and universities. In addition to the education, participants get training and many go into the USFS, positions in state or county parks, or sometimes local fire departments, where they fight wild land fires.

One of the youth conservation programs—the Forest Stewards Guild—is allied with the USFS. Since 1999 about seven hundred rural young people have been through the program, which employs teens between sixteen and nineteen years old. Based in Santa Fe, the crews work out of ranger stations, preparing fire lines, marking trees for other crews to thin (the minimum age for working with a chain saw is eighteen), stabilizing structures and building fences.

Eytan Krasilovsky, executive director, says the non-profit guild recruits through school guidance counselors, district foresters and workforce development centers. There's a "big mix," he says, and, depending on the relationship with the local foresters, there is a pathway to jobs in local forests. In Cuba, NM, for example, lots of kids have been placed in USFS jobs thanks to the efforts of Richard Montoya.

With a staff of four and an annual budget between $450,000 and $500,000 in both private and public funds, the Forest Stewards Guild offers college credits in forest management that are accepted at Santa Fe Community College. Some of its graduates have gone on to study forestry at Highlands University and natural resources management at New Mexico State University and Luna Community College. Krasilovsky estimates that, since its inception, the Guild has invested $3 million in rural New Mexico communities.

Another program, the Southwest Conservation Corps, is a regional program with offices in Durango and Salida, Colorado. Its New Mexico programs, based in the Acoma and Zuni pueblos, as well as Gallup, are centered on ancestral Native American lands, with one barrio program, La Plazita, in Albuquerque's South Valley. The program partners with the Bureau of Indian Affairs, public lands, parks, tribal colleges, and AmeriCorps VISTA. Crews integrate cultural practices into their work, which includes native agriculture and restoration of ruins, as well as the more typical trail and fence building.

Rocky Mountain Youth Corps members repairing a boardwalk at the Bosque del Apache National Wildlife Refuge in Socorro, N.M. Photo courtesy of the Rocky Mountain Youth Corps

Rocky Mountain Youth Corps: From the Start, a Model Based on Faith in Local Youth

It's not often that the White House dubs someone a "Champion of Change." But in 2011 that honor was bestowed on Carl Colonius, a founder of and the driving force behind Taos's RMYC. It was a tribute not only to the self-styled farm boy from northeastern Ohio, but to the innovative job training and rural economic development model he pioneered over twenty years ago. At 6'6" Colonius, an avid outdoorsman, is big. And so are his ideas.

In the late 1980s, Colonius was attending law school in California, and every morning he rode his bike past the office of the San Francisco Conservation Corps, near the Presidio. One day he saw the staff loading and unloading equipment and he stopped by. The director reeled off the mission of the program, founded in 1983 by now-Governor Jerry Brown and then-Mayor, now-Senator, Diane Feinstein. It was to put teens and young adults sixteen to twenty-five years old to work cleaning up Golden Gate Park as they got training and earned a GED through San Francisco Community College.

The concept sort of "hatched" in the early 1990s, Colonius says, in conversations about social change and northern New Mexico with the group's cofounders, Steve Patrick, Seth Miller, and Horacio Trujillo. The youth population of the scenic area, once dominated by agriculture, was particularly at risk, the group thought. With unemployment high and income low, frustration ran high and families often turned to drugs and alcohol. About 14 percent of teens from sixteen to nineteen years old were neither in school nor at work.

One of the ideas to address this problem was an outdoor gear shop staffed by local youth who would also provide tours based on local culture and historic attractions. "But then we discovered the youth corps model," Colonius said.

It would be several years before the first crews started clearing brush and building trails in the Taos area. Colonius had to try it out for himself, which he did by working on crews in California, returning to New Mexico in 1995. During the interim, the idea of community service to overcome poverty and build capacity had taken hold at the national level. In 1993, the Corporation for National and Community Service was founded during the first year of the Clinton administration. Two of its programs, AmeriCorps and Senior Corps, picked up where VISTA (established in1964) and the Peace Corps (established in 1961) left off.

Colonius and an advisory council composed of Ted Allen, Stephanie Daw, Michael Kramer, Dan Lobato, Seana Lowe, Seth Miller, Tony Povilitis, and others, set out to raise funds and search for partners. There was no shortage of problems to which local youth could provide solutions.

During the first summer in 1995, crewmembers from Questa and Taos renovated a park behind the Questa health center and built a basketball backstop. With a grant from the McCune Foundation and the NM YCC, they repaired and replaced playground equipment and constructed an irrigation system for an organic garden, with herbs, lettuce, and corn, which they hoped would be used in a restaurant patterned after Chez Panisse, Alice Waters' famous Berkeley mecca.

RMYC maintains it connection with Questa, population 1767, and in the summer of 2017 two conservation-based crews partnered with the village and the USFS there.

RMYC Motto: "Work Safe, Take Pride, Make a Difference"

Today, RMYC's members still wear the trademark blue T-shirts with one of the corps' three mottos, "Make a Difference," emblazoned on the back. And they still meet each morning in a "PT (physical training) circle" where they stretch, warm up, and connect with each other, sometimes in very silly ways. But oh how the non-profit group has grown. With both day and overnight crews working everywhere from the Gila Wilderness and Bosque del Apache to Bandelier National Monument and Ghost Ranch, they are building New Mexico's outdoor infrastructure.

Corps members begin each day's work with a morning huddle and stretch.

In 2016 alone, the crews constructed 161 miles of trails, thinned 147 acres on public and private land, built and repaired countless fences, erosion control structures, kiosks, and trailheads. They have removed invasive species, conducted tree surveys and mapping projects. Almost all of the work was done in partnership with various federal, state, and local agencies, which often paid for the services and served as mentors for corps members, teaching practical skills needed for land and natural resource management.

About 170–180 young adults participate each year, and the crews are diverse—educationally, ethnically, and geographically. Most participants are from New Mexico, with a high percentage of Hispanic and Native American youth, but there are some from out of state as well. In 2016, about 29 percent did not have a high school degree or a GED, but they work alongside college students (31 percent) and those with degrees (10 percent). The diversity, staffers say, is a key to the success of the program.

Corps members who serve on "spike crews" camp together for eight days, experiencing life without a water faucet or indoor toilet. They learn to rely on each other, to carry heavy loads, move rocks, and hike long distances. Day crews operate in the summer, traveling to work sites in vans. The work is just as hard.

In addition to conservation work, RMYC operates a diversity of projects, including an alternative school called the "Learning Lab" for middle and high school students and a program that aims at reducing substance abuse in the Taos community. As part of that program, the group sponsors "Booze-less Thursdays" in Taos.

In 2014, RMYC opened a headquarters in Albuquerque at the new Valle de Oro National Wildlife Refuge, where crews are working to build out the refuge in the South Valley to serve a larger urban population. Local programs have included reconstruction of a ramada (a shelter with a roof but no walls) at the Petroglyph National Monument and a youth ambassador program to engage younger children. In 2017 a disaster relief crew was deployed to Louisiana to continue the clean up from heavy flooding in the area. In the summer of 2017 another will work with deaf students from Albuquerque's Sign Language Academy.

The entire organization now has an annual budget of $2.4 million and a staff of fifteen full-time employees. Since its inception, approximately two thousand young adults have been crewmembers. Local partnerships abound, and funding comes not just from the state and federal government, but from foundations, individual contributions, and fees paid for services. But the mission is still the same, says Ben Thomas, the executive director of RMYC since 2014.

Corps members Ariel Kalson (l) and Augustine Quintana (r) build a fence at the Valle de Oro National Wildlife Refuge in Albuquerque's South Valley.

"We engage young adults in a team to meet community needs," he says, "and provide a stepping stone to new opportunities." Often this is the opportunity to pursue more education, sometimes it's a career in a natural resources field.

Thanks to the group's affiliation with AmeriCorps, members receive an educational award, along with their stipends of $760 for every two-week period. The award is proportional to the number of hours worked and may be used to pay off college expenses, including debt. It can range from $1,230 to $5,815. Corps members have seven years to use it, adding flexibility to the benefit.

The awards are a definite draw, but it takes a certain kind of person to want to do the outdoor work. Sometimes it's young adults tired of dead-end jobs or experiencing a crisis of confidence. Sometimes it's people who are in love with the forests, rivers, and deserts of New Mexico and want to protect them.

Ben Thomas came to New Mexico in 2004, fresh from the University of Montana, hoping for a career in the USFS. He replied to an advertisement for an AmeriCorps summer position in Taos, a bridge, he thought, to his final destination. Like other Corps members, he was inspired, and he stayed on, becoming the director in 2014, when Carl Colonius retired to start other adventures.

"The RMYC attracts risk takers and truth seekers to the wilderness," says Alyssa Armstrong, twenty-six years old, who has worked for a variety of youth corps programs for five years. An admitted romantic,

Armstrong says that the experience is often a rite of passage, then a homecoming, and a return to a family some have never known.

The hot, hard, dirty work forms bonds, and team members learn from one another. College graduates are shored up by high school dropouts when they can't make it up the hill or use a hammer properly. Crew-members who have never left the local area learn from non-New Mexicans who have taken classes in environmental science, or other fields.

I was lucky enough to meet some of these young men and women this year as they finished their service and reflected on what they had learned. One of these was Andrew Riggs, who had previously been incarcerated as a juvenile for two years.

"I didn't know whether I could ever escape the consequences of what I did, but I got the opportunity to serve and that has made me feel like a valued part of society," Riggs told a group of his corps comembers at an end-of-year ceremony. Riggs, who became an assistant crew leader, said he didn't think that he was capable of leading, or even reaching out for his dreams. Now he knows different.

Another corps member, Alex Eustace, twenty years old, from Zuni Pueblo, is eager to bring what he's learned back to his own community. He's been in three different conservation programs and will soon be working with the National Park Service at El Morro National Monument to stabilize ruins, something very meaningful to him, since it's his people, his history. "It really shows you what young people can do," he said, "and it sets you up for real life."

Stabilizing walls at historic sites is part of the job for members of various regional conservation corps in New Mexico.

Photo courtesy of the Rocky Mountain Youth Corps.

After her stint in the program had ended, Sara Rodriguez, who graduated from Truman State University in Missouri, could not throw away her crusty, stained work gloves. The gloves—and the gritty work they represented—meant a lot to her. "In school we learn that we are doomed, that the environment is being destroyed, but here we are partnering with people who are doing something about it. And they are all in." Rodriguez said her life goal is to make a difference …"even if it is the slightest, most miniscule difference when it comes to the environment."

...But Can the Beat Go On?

Each year the staffers at the RMYC churn out the statistics and evaluate the success or failure of that year's program, down to the quality of the surface materials on the trails and the number of corps members who are certified in CPR. Few members drop out of the program, and, upon completion, about 61 percent continue their education, with 21 percent getting a job. Many become certified in various skills learned in trainings held during their service. The educational award is key.

"In years to come, people will begin to see AmeriCorps' educational stipends and loan repayments (valued from $1,200–$5,200 depending on the hours served) as important for this generation as the GI bill was in another time of transition," says Carl Colonius.

But with President Trump threatening to cut funding for national programs like AmeriCorps, non-profits serving young people are under the gun. And natural resources are in need of protection from policy shifts toward resource extraction, not conservation.

"If AmeriCorps goes down, it will impact us, but not sink us," says Ben Thomas. Over the years, the organization has diversified its funding sources, and its natural resource partners now pay for services rendered. But for the young people, it will be a blow.

Fortunately, RMYC and other New Mexico conservation corps are not just about formal education and resume building, but about character and community, public service, and stewardship. The program's sons and daughters are all over the state, working in state parks, national monuments, fire departments, and Native American agencies. One of them is in even the United States Senate. Martin Heinrich is an AmeriCorps alumnus.

"Yeah, times are uncertain, but we're just going to keep showing up," said Brad Knipper, Conservation Program Coordinator in the middle Rio Grande region.

For New Mexico's youth and the state's natural heritage, that will make all the difference.

In a Nutshell

Problems

- A reserve army of unemployed youth who don't fit in traditional programs
- Public lands throughout New Mexico, which need maintenance—trail building, fence repair, shelter and dam construction, or forest thinning
- Heavy burden of college debt for young people

Big Idea

- Community service that puts young adults to work outdoors, builds infrastructure in parks, forests, and preserves; trains a new generation of resource managers and helps them pay down debt

Partners

Valle de Oro National Wildlife Preserve, United States Forest Service, New Mexico Energy and Natural Resources Department, Bandelier National Monument, Petroglyph National Monument, AmeriCorps, colleges and universities, United States Park Service, Rio Grande del Norte National Monument, PNM, City of Albuquerque, City of Taos, El Morro National Monument, Native American tribes and pueblos, retired foresters, and land managers.

What You Can Do

- Write, lobby, e-mail, and call your United States Representative and Senators to fund AmeriCorps and preserve public lands.
- Contribute to the Rocky Mountain Youth Corps, Forest Stewards Guild, La Plazita, or the Southwest Conservation Corps.
- If you are employed by a national park, monument, or land management agency, partner with one of these groups (Rocky Mountain Youth Corps, Forest Stewards Guild, La Plazita, or the Southwest Conservation Corps) and help corps members learn new skills like using equipment or building a stone wall.
- Offer to be a mentor and teach a class during one of the Rocky Mountain Youth Corps' sessions. Share your experience.

Resources

Rocky Mountain Youth Corps • Upper Rio Grande Office
Ben Thomas, Director • 1203 Kings Drive #3 • Taos, NM 87571
575-751-1420 • http://youthcorps.org/

Middle Rio Grande Office
7851 2nd St. SW • Albuquerque, NM 87105 • 505-263-7585
Jordan Stone, Program Manager • Brad Knipper, Program Coordinator

AmeriCorps
Corporation for National and Community Service
https://www.nationalservice.gov/impact-our-nation/state-profiles/NM

Conservation Legacy Programs

- The Southwest Conservation Corps
  701 Camino del Rio #101 • Durango, CO 81301
  970-259-8607 • Teresa DiTore • tditore@conservationlegacy.org
  http://sccorps.org/

- La Plazita Institute
  831 Isleta Blvd. SW • Albuquerque, NM 87105
  505-508-1802 • http://laplazitainstitute.org/

- Ancestral Lands Project
  http://sccorps.org/join/ancestral-lands/

  Navajo Projects
  207 E. Second St. • Gallup, NM 87301
  505-722-9755 • Lance Hubbard
  lance@conservationlegacy.org

  Pueblo of Acoma
  P.O. Box 208 • San Fidel, NM 87049
  505-408-4101 • Aaron Lowden
  aaron@conservationlegacy.org

  Pueblo of Zuni
  67 Rte 301 N. • P.O. Box 203 • Zuni, NM 87327
  505-870-0101 • Ryan Aguilar
  ryan@conservationlegacy.org

Forest Stewards Guild Southwest Region Program
2019 Galisteo St. Suite N7 • Santa Fe, NM 87505
505-983-8992 • http://www.forestguild.org/southwest
Eytan Krasilovsky • eytan@forestguild.org

New Mexico Youth Conservation Corps
811 St. Michaels Dr. Suite 104 • Santa Fe, NM 87505
505-690-1831 • http://www.emnrd.state.nm.us/YCC/
Wendy Kent, executive director • wendy.kent@state.nm.us
For a complete listing of 2017 grantees:
http://www.emnrd.state.nm.us/YCC/yccnews.html

PART FIVE
Growing the Middle Class — One Family at a Time

Poverty is a crushing issue in New Mexico, at the root of many of the state's problems. We are the second-poorest state in the nation, behind Mississippi, and our unemployment rate is among the highest in the country. Roughly 20 percent of the population lives at or below the poverty line, and the figure hasn't budged much for decades. Children, in particular, pay the price as many families are caught in a generational cycle of scarce income and low levels of education, resulting in dependence and insecurity.

Welfare reform, food stamps, free school lunches, and housing vouchers are just a few of the ways that the federal and state governments have tackled this problem. Economic development efforts are rarely targeted to low-income citizens who often have little formal education. Yet, in recent years applicants for food stamps and other benefits have been required to have a job, be looking for one, or be enrolled in some kind of training program. But where are those jobs? The retail sector? It is shrinking. Service industries? Not great income generators. The sad truth is that few permanent new jobs are trickling down to the folks that need them the most despite the state's efforts to recruit and subsidize high-tech companies and start-ups.

But sometimes it pays to start small.

In Albuquerque, two enterprising women, sick of traditional approaches to alleviating poverty, have started organizations to help families join the middle class. Ona Porter's Prosperity Works helps people build on their own assets and learn financial skills, freeing them from predatory lenders and bad credit. Susan Matteucci's little factory on 4th Street provides living wages, daycare, and family support for a group of Spanish-speaking women. They are gradually pulling themselves—and their children—up the economic ladder.

How do they do it? One organization provides the security of a steady wage. The other offers an incentive to save. Both supply mentors, support, and education—usually in Spanish, but always on a level to which participants can relate. And both draw on the innate strengths of women. A group process gets going. A team mentality takes over. Participants share practical solutions and begin to trust one another. Confidence levels rise and attitudes begin to shift.

These seemingly tiny steps add up to a big return: a sense of power and self-determination that is the key to economic advancement for an overlooked group. This is an important accomplishment, since real community development depends on advancing those at the bottom as well as those at the middle and the top.

CHAPTER 14

Prosperity Works' Approach to Poverty Addresses Root Causes

"This approach frees people from poverty because when people have even a small amount of reserves their world view changes quickly and permanently."

—Ona Porter, president and CEO, Prosperity Works

By 2004 Ona Porter was tired of fighting the war on poverty using the traditional tools—income supports, food stamps, and other welfare programs. She'd logged years in the business community working on family-friendly policies, served time as a children's advocate, and been recruited to become the executive director of the association of New Mexico's Community Action Programs (CAPs). Formed during the 1960s, New Mexico's six non-profit CAP agencies have been on the front lines in a state that perennially has one of the lowest per capita incomes in the nation. But with the wolf always at the door, the demand for providing safety net services like food, bus passes, emergency housing vouchers, and payments to prevent utility disconnections overwhelmed them. They had few resources left to focus on initiatives required to move people out of poverty.

They were not, Porter realized then, getting ahead of the curve. Marching to protest the United States' invasion of Iraq that year, Porter began to cry, thinking about the misuse of resources desperately needed here at home. It was then that she decided to take on poverty in a new way.

The daughter of blue-collar parents and a graduate of the Inter-American University in Puerto Rico, Porter thinks she was born with an extra gene—a social justice gene. "I don't want to address the symptoms but get to the root cause of things," she told me as she took a break between lobbying the legislature to reduce the rates of payday loans in February of 2017. "I'm too old and too fat to just take the rough edges off of poverty." (She is neither.)

Porter's "big idea," to help low-income New Mexicans is not completely original. But its implementation by Prosperity Works, an organization begun by Porter in 2006, has been unique and effective. Porter states the idea simply: "Income gets you by. Assets get you ahead."

But acquiring assets seems like an impossible dream for families just squeaking by, right?

Not for Porter and the proponents of individual development accounts (IDAs), special savings accounts that match the deposits of low and moderate-income savers, provided that they participate in financial education and use the savings for targeted purposes like postsecondary education, homeownership, or building a small business. These financial instruments have the potential to lift families out of poverty, step-by-step, and help them join the ranks of the middle class.

Porter says that the opposite of poverty is not wealth but opportunity and social justice. Low-income people already have many assets and skills, and, given the opportunity to thrive, they do amazing things. "These are whole and complete people with goals for themselves," she says. "Very low-income people know how to make their money go further...and look, if you can raise three kids on $12,000 a year, you have knowledge and skills to share."

The asset-building approach started to gain steam at the federal level in 1996 as part of President Bill Clinton's welfare reform program. Previously, assets owned by low-income people were counted against welfare benefits, thus penalizing savings. The Assets for Independence Program, sponsored by Representative John Kasich and other Republicans as part of the Contract with America, was established in 1998 to start the matching funds. Since then it has provided $214 million in federal funds to 880 sites around the country, including New Mexico.

In 2003, New Mexico established its own program, but failed to appropriate any funds. In 2006 the New Mexico Legislature, on an almost unanimous basis, funded the Family Opportunity Act, with $1.5 million for IDAs. Although the funding was not recurring, there was a consensus behind the new approach from both liberals who dreamed of reducing poverty and conservatives who saw building individual wealth as the key to economic opportunity.

A few community-based organizations had been offering IDAs, including the Women's Economic Self-Sufficiency Team (WESST) in Albuquerque, the Northwest Community Development Corporation in Farmington, and the Navajo Partnership for Housing. But there was little coordination and few standard practices.

Porter created Prosperity Works in 2006 to act as an intermediary organization to assist community-based non-profits and financial institutions around the state create programs to build the assets of working families. An aggressive—but family friendly—strategy was called for in a state where many citizens are unfamiliar with financial institutions.

According to the FDIC, in 2015 9 percent of New Mexican households were "unbanked," with no checking or savings account, and 27 percent were "underbanked."[36] Those who were underbanked possessed a checking or savings account, but also used payday lenders, check cashing services, refund-anticipation loans, pawnshop loans, and auto-title loans to make ends meet. These alternative financial services come with huge interest rates (some as high as 1,300 percent) and often create a death spiral of debt for people who are already economically distressed.

Prosperity Works now partners with twenty-three different community and tribal organizations around the state, providing training, technical assistance, capital, and oversight. Partners learn how to organize financial capability classes and work with cooperating financial institutions. The local partners, together called "the New Mexico Assets Consortium," provide "asset coaches" who help participants build family budgets, remove financial barriers, and reach their savings goals.

To those willing to set goals and learn how to manage their finances, Prosperity Works offers a four-to-one match on savings up to $1,000 to working individuals whose household income is not more than 200 percent above the poverty line, or about $32,000 for a family of two. Participants must not possess more than $10,000 in assets, excluding a house and a car.

A key part of the program is a required ten-week financial-capability course.

A Course Worth Its Weight in Gold

By day Barbara Lopez teaches third grade at Coronado Elementary School in Albuquerque's Barelas neighborhood. But on one night a week her classroom is transformed into a financial services lab for about fifteen adults, who arrive fresh from their jobs as babysitters, cleaning-service, restaurant, or construction workers. Some are college students, others have not finished high school. Still others graduated long ago. They are all there to learn how to manage their finances, become savvy consumers, reduce debts, and save more.

Lopez, who previously worked in financial services with Citigroup, has been teaching the classes (in both English and Spanish) for twelve years. She is employed by Encuentro, a local group that works with immigrants and partners with Prosperity Works. She gets to know everyone and can identify those who are ready to open an IDA account.

Class discussion often centers on medical and student loan debt, collection agencies and credit ratings. "Most of them haven't done a budget before," says Lopez. "They don't know the difference between wants and needs, and there has never been an emphasis on saving." One exercise is to write down everything they are spending money on to discover where the "leaks" are. This helps them see for themselves where they might be able to save.

Lopez says that sometimes she'll help them fix credit reports and make a plan to get out of debt. Encuentro will help them write letters and wend their way through various bureaucracies, as well.

"I can teach them to set priorities, but it's up to them to make changes," she says.

Even a small setback can really derail things. "But we talk about how other people have bounced back," Lopez says. Mutual support is key, and the mix of different types of experiences people bring to the financial training classes helps. One member of the class I attended, a Mexican immigrant, was a degreed psychologist. She was unable to get a job here because she didn't have a New Mexico credential. But she had skills that others did not—and was willing to share.

"About 15 percent of the seats in the classes are reserved for the community at large," Porter says. Generally these are middle-class people seeking financial education, and often they become advocates for the others in the class, or for policy changes to allow people to get ahead. For many of the community participants, this is their first encounter with the challenges that low-income people face on a daily basis. Pejorative views that they may hold as a result of the dominant culture narrative are replaced with understanding and compassion.

Just knowing someone who is middle class is important. "There's a direct relationship between your ability to escape poverty and the number of middle- and upper-class people you know," Porter says.

Step-by-Step to Success

Unlike most IDA recipients, Richard Noland was already a college graduate when Prosperity Works opened an account in his name. In 2010 Noland, a long time bicycle lover, was struggling with student debt and a small web-based bicycle rental business. He had started the business with the proceeds from an insurance settlement from a car accident and was operating out of a storage facility when someone recommended the program to him. He took the training, managed to save $1,000, and eventually withdrew $4,000 from the account. He used it to expand the number of bicycles for rent to seventy. In 2012

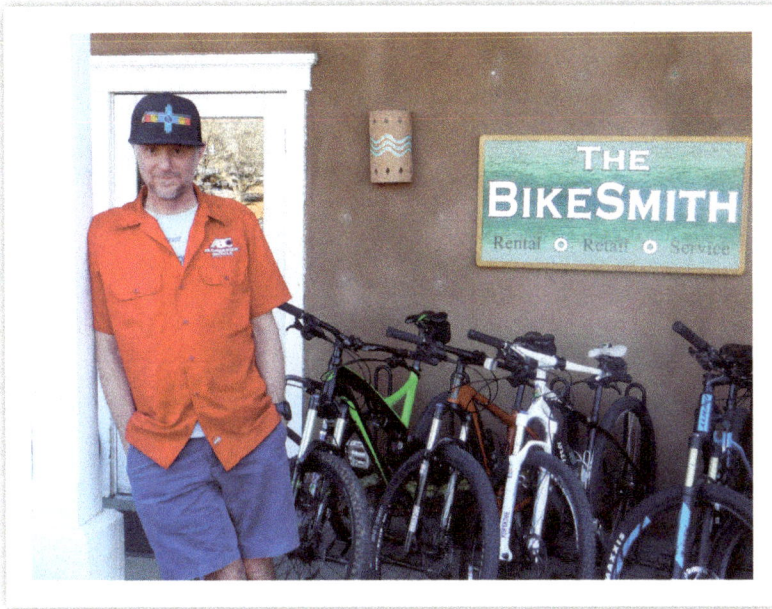

Richard Noland, owner of The BikeSmith in Albuquerque, used one of Prosperity Work's individual development accounts to build what is now one of the top five bike shops in the city.

he opened The BikeSmith, a shop off Rio Grande Boulevard near the bosque, perfect for bicycle rentals. He has expanded to sell and repair all kinds of bikes. He now employs six people and recently earned the title of one of the top-five bicycle shops in Albuquerque.

It wasn't just the money.

"The financial literacy course alone is worth its weight in gold," Noland said. It taught him how to put his finances in perspective and create a plan.

In southern New Mexico, with the help of the Community Action Agency of Southern New Mexico, eleven IDA savers who have gone through the Prosperity Works training have started or expanded day-care businesses. Most of the businesses are home-based operations. Dina Ramirez, owner of Arcoiris Day Care in Sunland Park, added a room to her house, which allowed her to increase her license from caring for six children to twelve. Martha Mireles, seventy-one years old, brought her home in Chaparral up to code, made improvements, and purchased insurance. Once an impulsive shopper, she has learned to save and operates Mireles Day Care, which cares for six children and provides income for Mireles and her husband.

Many of the women business owners did not finish high school; some did not own their own homes. All mention the financial education as the key to their success.

Noland and the women are only a few of the 1,495 people who have established IDAs totaling $8.3 million since the program's start. In the past ten years, the matched funds have fostered approximately seven hundred locally owned businesses and created 1,150 jobs. They have helped six hundred residents launch a college education, injecting $1.9 million into local educational institutions. And they have assisted four hundred families secure safe and affordable housing, accounting for $57 million in mortgages.

Clearly, the asset-building approach is not just a way out of poverty for some, but an economic development tool for the larger community. In Texas, where IDAs are also used, the Center for Public Policy Priorities found that for every $1 invested there is a return to the state economy of $5 in new businesses, increased earnings, new or rehabilitated homes, reduced welfare, and greater educational attainment.[37]

There's another benefit as well: resilience—a quality that both states and individuals need to weather economic ups and downs. A 2010 report showed that IDA homebuyers were two to three times less likely to lose their homes than other low-income people[38] and 59 percent were likely to stay employed.[39] "It's all about a change in mindset that is fueled by new skills and opportunity," Porter says.

Finding Partners, Building New Programs

To grow the program, Porter has worked hard to raise private funds and work with financial institutions, which stand to gain new customers, new deposits, and new relationships with their communities. "I don't understand why more advocates don't partner with the business community," Porter says. "Going to them with a hand out and not understanding that they have so much more to offer is a huge mistake. They have the capacity to move our agenda when we do not, and they know that they thrive when families and communities thrive." Rio Grande Credit Union, My Bank, and First American in Las Cruces have been valuable partners. Southwest Capital Bank in Albuquerque has been helpful in another Prosperity Works program for kids.

"Prosperity Kids" allows low-income families to save money for postsecondary education for their children by seeding small accounts in a child's name with $100, then matching family deposits made into each "Children's Savings Account" (CSA) up to $200 for ten years. In keeping with Prosperity Work's comprehensive approach, the program does not end there. A prerequisite for enrollment is a ten-week *Abriendo Puertas* (Opening Doors) class offered in collaboration with the Partnership for Community Action, where parents are taught to be advocates and teachers for their children. Five hundred thirteen children and their families from thirteen elementary schools in Albuquerque's South Valley participated in the pilot. Parents are also eligible for emergency accounts funded by Prosperity Works for up to $100 per year for five years if the parents can show that they are supporting healthy outcomes for their kids by doing things like volunteering in their classroom or creating a good place to study at home. The accounts come with a secured credit card, so families can build credit.

"We are not paying for college with these accounts but creating a future orientation and college identity," Porter explains. Studies back her up. Kids with a savings account in their own name are four to six times more likely to go to the university and complete their studies. Parents are more engaged. Children are ahead of their peers in social and emotional development when they enter preschool, and ahead in math and language when they enter third grade, according to Dr. Willie Elliot of the University of Kansas.[40]

The 513 enrollees in the pilot saved approximately $60,000 in fifteen months. Now Prosperity Works is working to ensure that every child born in New Mexico has an account opened at birth. This year (2017) the New Mexico House of Representatives passed a measure to identify a permanent source of revenue (like a fee to license financial products) that could be used to teach financial literacy and expand the Prosperity Kids program statewide.

Constant Advocacy the Price of Sustainability

Porter and other supporters of the "big idea" of assets as the key to opportunity and poverty reduction are in constant motion. In one legislative session alone, they were the lead lobbyists to reduce rates charged by payday lenders to 36 percent. They proposed a measure to eliminate the use of credit information in employment, and another to require the state to provide an alternative loan product to state employees. As Porter says, "people must be stable before they can grow. That means increasing income, decreasing costs or both. Our proposals are always aimed at eliminating barriers and creating avenues for financial inclusion and opportunity."

The advocacy will never end.

Public funding for individual development accounts is always at risk at both the state and federal levels even though the program packs such a big bang for such a small buck. And with a new administration in Washington, there's even more danger.

Yet the evidence keeps mounting that the mind shift that comes from having a few dollars in the bank packs a big wallop. It's a frustrating proposition for change-makers like Ona Porter. Focusing on root causes is never an easy fix. But Prosperity Works is in it for the long haul, ready to use many tools—advocacy, constant communication, community engagement, and even litigation to reach its goal: a New Mexico where everyone has the opportunity, knowledge, and relationships they need to achieve economic security and prosperity.

In a Nutshell

Problem

• Families can't save enough to invest in themselves by starting businesses, buying homes, going to school, or paying off debt. As a result they are trapped in poverty and dependence.

Big Ideas

• Providing assets and training to allow low-income families to get ahead and not just get by

• Individual Development Accounts, which match savings 4:1 for a home, business, or education after financial literacy classes are completed

• Children's Savings Accounts to create a college trajectory and begin to build intergenerational wealth

Partners

Twenty-three non-profit community and tribal organizations around the state which are members of the New Mexico Assets Coalition; local financial institutions including Rio Grande Credit Union, My Bank, First American in Las Cruces, and Southwest Capital Bank in Albuquerque; Encuentro, Partnership for Community Action, Prosperity Now, state and federal policymakers, Atlantic Philanthropies, W. K. Kellogg, Tides Foundation, New Mexico Community Foundation, Mott Foundation, McCune Charitable Foundation, Ford Foundation, CNM Foundation, Bank of America Charitable Foundation.

What You Can Do

- Contribute to Prosperity Works.

- Attend a financial literacy course as a community member.

- If you work at a financial institution, suggest partnering with Prosperity Works.

- Lobby the state legislature, write, call, or e-mail your legislator and ask for consumer protection against predatory lending, credit, and financial requirements that discriminate against low-income people. Ask them to support individual development accounts and financial literacy programs like those coordinated by Prosperity Works with recurring funding.

- Spread the word to people you know who might benefit from an Individual Development Account (IDA). Tell the media about the organization's success stories.

- Contact your United States Congresspeople and ask them to maintain and increase funding for the Assets for Independence Program.

- Join Prosperity Now, a national network, to advocate for programs like Prosperity Works that build assets, as well as for affordable housing, consumer protection, and a safety net that works.

Resources

Prosperity Works
909 Copper Ave NW
Albuquerque, NM 87102
505-217-2747
http://prosperityworks.net

NM Association of Community Partners
3220 Carlisle Blvd. NE
Albuquerque, NM 87110
505-321-4638
http://nmcap.wordpress.com

Partnership for Community Action
722 Isleta Blvd. SW
Albuquerque, NM 87105
505-247-9222
http://forcommunityaction.org

Encuentro
714 4th St. SW
Albuquerque, NM 87102
505-247-2920
http://www.encuentronm.org

Think New Mexico
1227 Paseo de Peralta
Santa Fe, NM 87501
505-992-1315
www.thinknewmexico.org

Prosperity Now
1200 G St. NW
Washington DC 20005
202-408-9788
https://prosperitynow.org/

Sherraden, Michael. *Assets and the Poor:
A New American Welfare Policy*. Armonk, NY: ME Sharpe, 1991.
Available through local bookstores and online at Amazon.

CHAPTER 15

Southwest Creations Collaborative Combines Business and Social Mission in a Small Albuquerque Factory

Even more than other projects profiled in this book, Southwest Creations Collaborative follows the model of a true social enterprise. A non-profit with a social mission (alleviating poverty and creating intergenerational wealth), it is also a business that sells products. Eighty-five percent of its revenue now comes from the sales of the goods it produces. The secret of its steady growth is the daycare and support services it provides for the women who work there and its adherence to the founder's big idea that, given an opportunity to earn steady income, women will invest in their children.

From a strictly business point of view, the mid-1990s wasn't a propitious time to start a textile operation, even a small one. Clothing manufacturers were fleeing the United States for cheap labor in the Philippines and Vietnam. Garment districts in New York and elsewhere were in decline. But that didn't stop Susan Matteucci, who had a broader vision.

Matteucci was fresh from Mayor Harold Washington's Chicago, where she had dreamed of joining the administration when the progressive mayor died in 1987. She decided to pursue a Master of City Planning degree and as part of her community development studies at MIT, she discovered the Grameen Bank. Its founder, Muhammad Yunus, pioneered the use of microloans to support poor women who wanted to start small businesses in Bangladesh. A Chicago organization, the Women's Self-Employment Project (WSEP), was then implementing the Grameen lending practices in Chicago's African American community. It was the first urban organization in the United States to do so. Matteucci wrote her master's thesis on the project and then went to work for WSEP establishing the Full Circle Fund, where she worked with small groups of women to develop business ideas.

Matteucci wasn't completely sold on the idea that individual entrepreneurship—based on one woman's own labor—was an effective way for low-income women with few skills and child-rearing duties to pull themselves out of poverty. But she kept exploring, meeting Pushpika Frietas, an Indian woman living in Evanston, IL, who had started a catalog, *Marketplace Handwork of India*. The catalog featured pillows, dresses, and other fabric items hand sewn by Indian women who were formed into different cooperatives. In the smaller groups, the women learned new skills like embroidery and the use of a sewing machine. Affiliated programs offered educational and enrichment opportunities designed to help the artisans overcome personal, cultural, and financial obstacles. The result was that the artisans became role models for their families and leaders in their communities, opening the prospect of change.

For Matteucci, the ideas were percolating. And then, with her husband, she came to New Mexico.

Determined to launch a project for low-income women here, Matteucci obtained a small grant from the Mott Foundation for a sewing project along the lines of Frietas'. Then she asked Sister Bernice Garcia and Father David Gallegos, of the San Jose Parish in Albuquerque, if they would help recruit women from their flock of Spanish-speaking immigrants. One Sunday after mass in 1994 they made an announcement inviting parishioners to a small handcrafting workshop to be held in the parish hall. Much to her surprise, seventy-five women showed up.

"We didn't have the money to pay them, and I didn't even speak Spanish," Matteucci recalled. "It was the worst organizing principle ever." Nevertheless, twenty-five women agreed to participate, and Southwest Creations Collaborative (SCC) was born.

Matteucci had to use her credit card to buy the sewing machines, since foundation funding was not available until May. But Matteucci worked her Chicago contacts, and the New Mexico Community Loan Fund offered credit. Levi Strauss, which then operated a jeans factory in Albuquerque, matched the Mott grant.

During the first two years, San Jose Church provided space in a large room for three days a week. A cutting table and sewing machines were set up, and the women began to gain skills, enjoy the work and each other's company.

Rosa Maria Villarreal (r), Southwest Creations Collaborative's (SCC) office manager, is a founder of the social enterprise. Her whole family, including her granddaughter Camilla (l), has benefitted from the educational services and day care it offers for 25 cents per hour.

Photo courtesy of SCC

One of the early participants was Rosa Villarreal, who had recently immigrated from Mexico. Unlike most other participants who didn't have much education or training, she had been an accountant but, with little English, was unable to find work. Another was Flora Lopez, who was reluctant to join the program at first but who soon realized she liked being out of the house. Both are still with the program today. Villarreal is the office manager and Lopez is the leadership development director. Matteucci considers them cofounders of the non-profit.

Jobs at SCC were initially part-time, paying $6.50 an hour, but, in an unusual twist for a start-up, on-site childcare was provided for twenty-five cents an hour. It was to become the key feature of SCC. The first customers for the group's sewn goods were found through the *Marketplace Catalog*. A few local businesses bought items to take to gift shows or sell retail.

Soon the new organization needed more space and the women needed full-time work. In 1996 SCC moved its operations to a Quonset hut on Woodward Ave. SE near the church. Childcare was provided in a mobile home on site, and the search for new contracts began in earnest. Yes, the operation was a poverty-alleviation project, supported by grants, but it was also a business that could no longer rely on catalog sales that were oriented toward India.

As Matteucci searched for a market niche, SCC took on a variety of jobs and employees gained experience in high-volume manufacturing—both of sewn soft goods and hand-assembled products that demanded precision and artistic attention to detail. By 2002 the group secured a long-term contract with Clariant, a desiccant manufacturer (those "do not eat" packets found in pill bottles and peanut packing materials), and in 2005 it moved into a 10,000-square-foot facility on

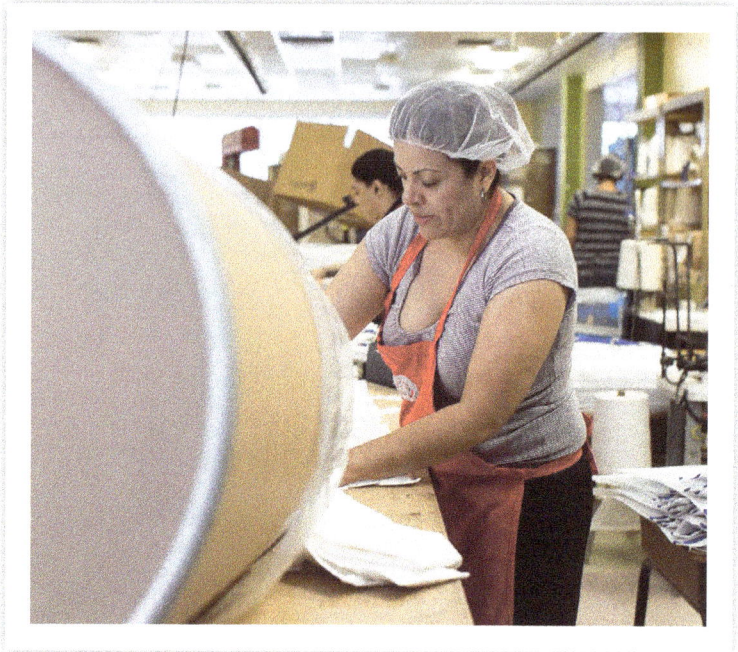

Southwest Creations Collaborative specializes in precision assembly, sewn soft goods and high-volume manufacturing. Eighty per cent of employees are Latina immigrants whose steady wages are invested in families and education. Here, Guadalupe Torres is at work.

Photo courtesy of SCC

4th Street in downtown Albuquerque. Ironically, the facility had been the location of an old women's prison.

But in spite of its security features, the new factory is anything but a prison. With steady, full-time wages of $12.00 an hour, childcare, and family programs, it has opened doors for its thirty-seven current employees—and their families. There is little to no employee turnover, and the women take obvious pride in their work, which is displayed in a small showroom and on racks on the factory floor, hung with tote bags, pillowcases, and children's clothing. Although tiny specks of fabric float above the airy, light production area, the floor is spotless. And all paths lead to the heart of the operation, the daycare center, located at the rear of the whirring factory.

The provision of childcare has been the key to the productivity of SCC employees, 80 percent of whom are Latina immigrants from Mexico. It has allowed them to focus on their job and increased loyalty to the group, which has been remarkably stable over the years. Both children and grandchildren of employees are now daycare alumni.

"The core of our business has always been that if you give a woman a chance to earn an income, she's going to invest it in her kids," Matteucci says. And if you build programs around that idea, families will begin to gain income and create intergenerational wealth.

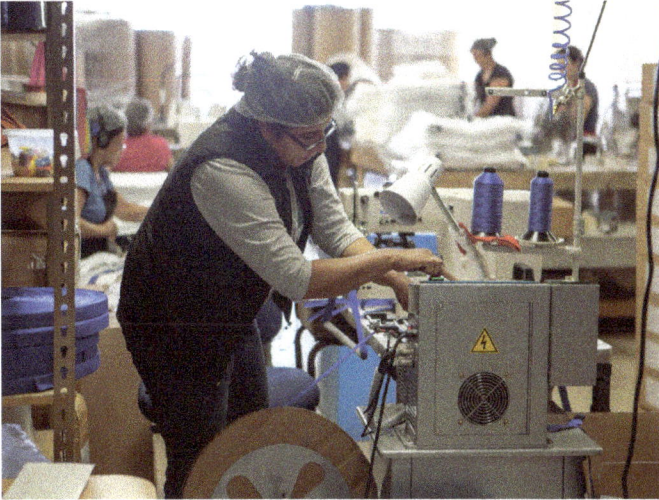

Maria Grajeda works on SCC's production floor.

Photo courtesy of SCC

Family Programs, Adult Education at the Heart of Southwest Creations

Flor Lopez heard about the meeting of women that Sister Bernice was organizing at San Jose Parish in 1994 from a friend. She was eager to earn extra income from sewing projects, but she didn't want to leave her two baby girls, then six and eighteen months, at home. But when she realized that daycare would be provided she was ready to put her embroidery skills to work—for money. Family is the most important thing for Lopez and many of the other immigrant women who attended that first meeting. It is still the most important thing for the women who work at Southwest Creations Collaborative.

Now the leadership development director, Flor Lopez is in constant contact with SCC's employees and their families, working to strengthen their achievements and community ties. "I'm kind of a mother for employees and their families," says Lopez. Through the company's *Buena Familias y Escuelas* (Good Families and Schools) Program, employees get paid leave to volunteer at their child's classroom once a month. Lopez teaches the parents how to interact productively with the schools and deal with report cards. Three times a year SCC hosts a dinner dialog with teachers, parents, and administrators at the factory. Parental involvement, which is often a problem for working parents, is built in at SCC.

Andrea Plaza of *Encuentro*, an immigrant-rights organization, was instrumental in starting the adult education programs and keeping it relevant to the target population.

As the children began to do better, parents begin to invest in their own education. SCC makes it easy with a $300 per semester stipend for college classes and free on-site adult education, including English as a second language, citizenship preparation, GED courses, and various certifications. The classes are also available to family members, but they are required for employees. Lopez has developed curricula and makes sure everyone is on track.

It isn't always easy. Lopez has been known to call in angry high school students at risk of dropping out. She strategizes with mothers, looks at their kid's grades, gives pep talks, or connects them with advisors at the Central New Mexico Community College.

Flor Lopez, SCC's leadership development director, counsels families, coordinates GED classes and citizenship training. The 360-degree support is the secret of SCC's success.

"I want them to know I care," Lopez says, "and I want them to appreciate their parent's work."

"What other employer asks you to bring in your child's report card?" asks Jessica Aranda, a former SCC program director. It might seem intrusive to some, but she says it works.

Ninety-eight percent of employees have gotten their GED. Many have passed their citizenship exam. And their children have done well. Ninety-eight percent have graduated high school and 86 percent have gone on to college.

Lopez's own daughters are cases in point. Both are graduates of the SCC daycare and beneficiaries of the family programs. One daughter has a master's degree in nuclear engineering from Texas A & M; another graduated from UNM and works at a law firm; the youngest is currently a student at UNM.

Hacia la Universidad: Driving Families Toward the University

In 2011 SCC spun off Flor Lopez's informal curriculum into a formal program designed to help more working families get their children ready for college, starting from an early age. Sasha Pellerin, director of the program, called *Hacia la Universidad* ("Toward the University" in Spanish), was the first in her family to go to college, and she is familiar with the barriers that Spanish-speaking immigrant families face.

"For those who lack information, and don't know what to expect, it can be overwhelming," she says. To help parents (who sometimes have not graduated high school themselves) navigate the path from preschool to college, the program offers workshops, tutoring, mentoring, college tours, and 360-degree support services. The interactive workshops are based on themes geared to the child's age and include topics like how to read a report card, plan a high school schedule with college in mind, and prepare and pay for the ACT exam.

"We meet families' needs wherever they are, from those with high school valedictorians to those with kids who haven't attended class in three months," Pellerin says. The common denominator is high expectations.

Financed by the W. K. Kellogg Foundation, United Way, the Frost Foundation, and revenue earned by SCC's social enterprise, *Hacia la Universidad* is part and parcel of SCC's efforts to alleviate poverty and build economic and educational opportunity across generations. Results from an initial four-year pilot program (2010–2016) with 310 families suggest it is on the right track. Ninety-two percent of the program's students graduated from high school (compared to 63 percent overall in Albuquerque public schools) and 81 percent attended college (compared to 69 percent of Albuquerque public high school graduates)[41]. Since the pilot, the program has expanded and now serves 600 families.

A Double Bottom Line

In spite of the economic recession, SCC has grown from a small collaborative with twenty-five workers operating out of a parish hall to a sustainable social enterprise. Annual revenues have grown from $30,000 to over $1.5 million. The payroll is $850,000. The workforce has been stable and become more and more able to handle assembly of everything from glass mosaic tiles to doggie collars. With some bumps along the road, the operation has found a niche in high-end home décor and other sewn products for clients like the West Elm catalog. It is currently working with partners to expand to a new social-enterprise campus.

Although it has become a relatively large business by New Mexico standards, SCC is still a non-profit with a social mission, and its list of funders has grown. But now 85 percent of its revenues come from contracts. That's a double bottom line that doesn't often exist in either the non-profit or for-profit communities.

Matteucci's model was based on her initial idea that stable, income-producing jobs for women—rather than loans and home-based businesses—are the best bet to alleviate poverty, one family at a time. It's a different route than that taken by Prosperity Works (see previous chapter), but in New Mexico there's plenty of poverty to go around.

Matteucci has been slow and steady, guiding the company through two moves and many contracts. She has never missed a payroll, even during some hard times, and she is the first to tell you it's a group effort, not hers alone.

Can the SCC model be replicated?

"Sure," says Matteucci. "A lot of businesses could run like this, with daycares, and support services for their employees." More important, she says, are the affiliated social programs to strengthen families and create a college-bound culture. Combined with steady income, those enable employees and their families to begin to build intergenerational wealth.

Over two decades SCC has helped 125 employees, created family assets, and opened doors for hundreds more through *Hacia la Universidad* and its family support initiatives. It is proof that a social enterprise can be sustainable and maintain its vision while providing jobs, training, and daycare, all while advancing social change.

In A Nutshell

Problem

The persistent poverty of low-income
Mexican immigrant women

Big Ideas

- Given an opportunity to earn steady income, women will
  invest in their children.

- The provision of steady employment paired with affordable
  daycare and counseling to support low-income working
  women and their children

Partners

Employees, customers, families, board members, San Jose Parish,
Encuentro, Hacia la Universidad, Mott Foundation, W. K.
Kellogg, Levi Strauss, and other donors.

What You Can Do

- Contribute to Southwest
  Creations Collaborative or
  Hacia la Universidad.

- Contact Southwest Creations Collaborative if your company or
  project needs precision assembly work, industrial sewing, tile or
  jewelry assembly, knitting, embroidery, or other work.

- If you have a child or know of someone who could benefit from
  Hacia la Universidad's mentoring and guidance, contact *Hacia la
  Universidad* for a schedule of trainings and workshops.

- Contact *Hacia la Universidad* to volunteer as a tutor, mentor, or
  driver for field trips to local colleges and universities.

Resources

Southwest Creations Collaborative
1308 4th St. NW
Albuquerque, NM 87102
505-247-8559
http://www.southwestcreations.com

Several websites related to social enterprise and social entrepreneurship:

- Ashoka Foundation, www.ashoka.org

- Skoll Foundation, www.skollfoundation.org

- Social Enterprise Institute, www.se-institute.org

- Social Venture Partners International, www.svpi.org

- Grameen Bank and Grameen Foundation, www. grameenfoundation.org

- Newman's Own, www.newmansown.org, and

- Newman's Own Foundation, www.newmansownfoundation.org

"Social Enterprise Typology," by Sutia Kim Alter, Virtue Ventures, LLC, 2007. Available at http://www.virtueventures.com/setypology/. This report was commissioned by the Inter-American Development Bank's Social Enterprise Program in 2003 and updated in November 2007. It provides an extensive description of the basic concept of social enterprise, types and models of these organizations, and strategies for successful operation. Several case studies are included in the report.

Yunus, Muhammad and Alan Jolis. *Banker for the Poor: The Story of the Grameen Bank,* Aurum Press Ltd, 2003

Women's Self-Employment Project
11 S. La Salle St. Chicago, IL 60603
312-606-8255

Hacia la Universidad
c/o Southwest Creations Collaborative
1308 4th St. NW
Albuquerque, NM 87102
505-227-9279
http://www.southwestcreations.com/hacia-la-universidad

PART SIX
Grassroots Efforts Get New Mexico Kids into College— Against the Odds

America's system for free public education is supposed to be a symbol of democracy, a great equalizer that opens the road to economic opportunity for everyone, based on achievement, not wealth or background. There are no more hackneyed phrases on the campaign trail or in daily editorials than "our young people are the hope for the future," or "education is the most important thing we can do." Everyone seems to agree—except when it comes to funding schools and colleges properly or coming to a consensus on how to raise achievement levels for all students.

In New Mexico, today's college experience is difficult for almost all families. Tuition is rising, help from the lottery scholarship is shrinking, and federal aid programs may face cutbacks. But it is particularly hard for low-income families. For them, the path to college is fraught with tough tasks and high hurdles. Many are unfamiliar with schools outside of New Mexico and cannot conceive of sending their children out-of-state for a long period of time. And when low-income students do get to college, the statistics for the proportion of low-income, first-generation students who actually complete it are astonishing— only 10 percent.

Most students from low-income backgrounds do not get the help they need at any level. The number of high school guidance counselors has been cut, and those left standing advise hundreds of students. College exam prep courses are expensive and advice from someone else in the family who went through the same process is scarce. By the time low-income students reach high school it may be too late anyway. College readiness begins as early as elementary and preschool. The previous section spotlighted a number of Albuquerque programs that are tackling this problem. Southwest Creations' *Hacia La Universidad* and Prosperity Works' *Abriendo Puertas* are preparing families early. But the people and the programs described in this section take it to another level, using personal guidance, community support and mentoring from committed, savvy adults.

CHAPTER 16

Closing the College Gap:
Getting Low-Income Kids Into College
One Student at a Time

"Teenagers are the single most influential group in a low-income community. If the teens are well engaged, it shifts the dynamic in that neighborhood. You are never going to see a lasting transformation in low-income communities until there is a critical mass of college-educated youth in those communities."

—J. B. Schramm, founder, College Summit

It was the mid-1980s and over 65 percent of the students at the high school where he taught were not graduating. Rio Grande High School, located in Albuquerque's South Valley, had always been a tough school. It's part of what drew Alan Marks to teach there. But it took a few years for Marks to realize how bad the situation was. Every year about eleven hundred freshmen would enter the school, he said, and three hundred would graduate. Of those three hundred, only thirty would go to a four-year college.

Parents were up in arms. The dropout rate was just one issue. They sued the school district for not allocating enough funds to the low-income Hispanic area, while richer, whiter areas in the Heights of Albuquerque got a disproportionate share of the funding. To remedy the situation, the school was reorganized into academies. The leadership was changed. More money came in. But by the 1990s, the dropout rate had only gotten worse.

By that time Marks was well on his way to changing the game for many of his Rio Grande students. His plan was rooted in a simple, but radical, belief. They were capable of being successful in college.

"I looked around at the kids who were going to school there and just said, 'this is unacceptable.'"

In 1982 the lawyer-turned-educator set out to do something about it. He organized his first summer field trip for a few high school sophomores to colleges on the West Coast. After some convincing, seven families allowed their kids to go with Marks, who took them to the Claremont Colleges outside of Los Angeles, nearby Occidental College, Stanford University, and Mills College, near San Francisco. For the students, most of whom had never left the state, it was a life-changing experience, and they all went on to Ivy League colleges. For Marks and other educators, it was part of the answer to a problem that extended far beyond Rio Grande High School.

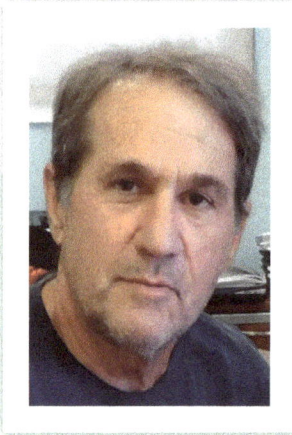

Alan Marks

Radical Teacher Opens Doors, Shifts the Paradigm

Stanford, Brown, MIT, Princeton, Harvard, Yale, Dartmouth, Pomona, Amherst, and Vassar. Alan Marks can tell you which student went where, when, why, and what he or she is doing now. Almost. Over the more than three decades that the good-natured Marks has taught and lived in the South Valley, he's mentored, nudged, advised, nagged, and otherwise helped over one hundred students get into top colleges with full scholarships. That's a lot to keep track of, even for Marks, who has taught almost every subject in the high school book.

But he knows, because many have become leaders in education, medicine, and the arts, and have returned to give back to their communities. That gives Marks, now focusing more on his orchard than his students, a sense of satisfaction.

Back in the 1980s, Marks acted on his own, first driving a van of Rio Grande High School sophomores to the West Coast in 1982, then flying other groups east to visit Ivy League schools there. The kids worked summer and after-school jobs to pay their way. Marks sometimes picked up the slack. He made the college contacts himself, convinced that the college admissions offices would be interested in the remarkable, plucky kids from New Mexico. He tried to connect his students with college students who were Hispanic. Along the way, he took them to Broadway shows, museums, and landmarks.

"I had never been on an airplane, never seen a big city before," Katarina Sandoval recalled. She stayed in the Brown University dorm with other students of color. "There were people who were going there who looked like me...I realized that there's this whole other world out there."

Sandoval was accepted at Brown and Princeton, but decided to go to Stanford. Later, she got a higher degree from Harvard, and in 2000 became the cofounder of South Valley Academy with Marks. She never forgot the sense of possibilities that her college field trip stirred up.

Santiago Macias and his older sister Santana also went on the college trips during the early 1990s. "It opened our eyes, exposed us to schools we never even thought of, and allowed us to dream," says Macias, who graduated from Occidental College and then the University of New Mexico School of Medicine. Macias is now a doctor in the South Valley. His sister is a doctor as well.

Arranging college field trips was only one of the things that Marks did for his students. He made sure that they were enrolled in the right math classes, could pay for the PSAT test, and didn't miss important deadlines. Soon his activities expanded beyond Rio Grande High School to Albuquerque High, Bernalillo High, Isleta Pueblo, and even further afield in New Mexico.

"He was more than a mentor," says Julie Radoslovich, another South Valley student who might have slipped through the cracks. "In my senior year when my guidance counselor told me I would never get into Stanford, Alan told me to apply to any college I wanted. He wrote my college recommendations. I can't tell you how many ways he helped me be a productive citizen in this world," she says.

Radoslovich remembers the day in her senior year when she got the fateful letter from Stanford. She was thrilled to see she was accepted. But her mother was not. She was old school. Like many New Mexico mothers, she didn't want her child to leave the state for higher education. Crestfallen, Radoslovich called Marks.

Within an hour he was at her mother's door, with a chocolate cake.

"I don't know what he said, but all I remember is washing a sink full of chocolate-covered plates…and when he said goodbye to my mother, I was going to Stanford."

Marks soon became well known among families as a great teacher and mentor, with connections in the right places.

"Everyone knows Alan," said Sasha Pellerin. "He's an expert at getting minorities into Ivy League colleges and he coined the idea of going away and then coming back." Pellerin, who met Marks when she was a student at the high school he started, is now the director of *Hacia la Universidad*, an organization designed to support and guide the children of low-income families from elementary school through college (see Chapter 15).

"Alan was my inspiration," she says.

Mike Ammerman, program director of the Simon Scholars, says that Marks was ahead of his time. "What he did was radical because he saw that the students were capable and all that it took was opening the door. That shifted the paradigm."

In 2000, Alan Marks and Katarina Sandoval established South Valley Academy. Marks was initially opposed to the idea of charter schools, but he eventually recognized that they could provide both the funding and the latitude to institutionalize the practices that were beginning to get more low-income minorities into college. Sandoval and Marks recruited

Alan Marks, Continues on next page

students at community events, middle schools, even South Valley supermarkets. They did not seek the high achievers, but those in the middle. And they drew on their network of recent college graduates to become the school's teachers. Julie Radoslovich was one who came back. She is now the principal/director of the school.

Marks stepped down from his position with SVA in 2010, but he remains active in the South Valley where the charter school he cofounded is an anchor for a revitalizing local community. He is still preparing kids to take college entrance exams and spreading the gospel as a consultant with the Simon Scholars Foundation, a pipeline project working to get more low-income students into colleges and build even stronger local communities.

Poverty and Demographics: Ingredients of New Mexico's Low Graduation Rate

For years New Mexico's high school graduation rate has dragged on well below the national average of 83 percent. In 2015 New Mexico hit rock bottom, with the worst rate in the nation—69 percent. And while the overall rate has crept up slightly in the following years, the disparity between students of different incomes and races remains. In 2016, the graduation rate for Hispanics was 66 percent; for low-income students 64 percent; for African Americans 54 percent; and for Native Americans 47 percent.[42]

The bad news didn't stop there. Only a fraction of high school graduates finish postsecondary schools (college) in six years or fewer. The graduation rate for college students is even lower than for high school. For first-in-their-family, low-income college students, it is about 10 percent.[43]

Policymakers at the federal and state level have struggled with the problem for years. But with the political blame game in full swing, their efforts have largely failed. Now, at the community and neighborhood levels, a number of pipeline programs and charter schools geared to these "forgotten kids" are making headway—one student at a time.

In Albuquerque, the mayor, social service leaders, school administrators, and business leaders began "Mission Graduate" in 2010. It is a community collaborative in which each organization tackles the problem from a different angle. The Rotary Club provides tutors. The local PBS station runs public service announcements. Businesses provide internships. The civic leaders have set a goal of sixty thousand new graduates by 2020. Recently, in the summer of 2017, there's a push to help returning students.

The needle is moving, slowly.

South Valley School Gets Results for Low-Income Hispanic Students

The South Valley Academy (SVA), a charter school started by Alan Marks and Katarina Sandoval in 2000 on an old tree farm in the area, was specifically designed to prepare the area's low-income kids to enter college without remediation. Over 90 percent of the school's six hundred students are Hispanic, and the majority of those are the children of Mexican immigrants. Most of their family members never attended college, and many did not graduate from high school themselves.

"Any kid who came to us was treated like an honors kid," says Sandoval, who turned in her principal's badge for a curriculum post with the Albuquerque Public Schools and then the Native American Community Academy in Albuquerque. College is an expectation for all students at SVA, and standards are high. At the same time, students get a lot of support, with daily advisories, college seminars for juniors and seniors, and mentors from the community. Students are constantly making presentations to families and school partners, who come and go on the sprawling, farm-like campus. The connections are built in.

"One of my mantras has been 'high support, high expectations,'" says Sandoval. It's a heavy lift for the teachers, since students come there three to four years behind in math and reading. But in SVA's environment they improve. The school offers AP Spanish courses, an honors

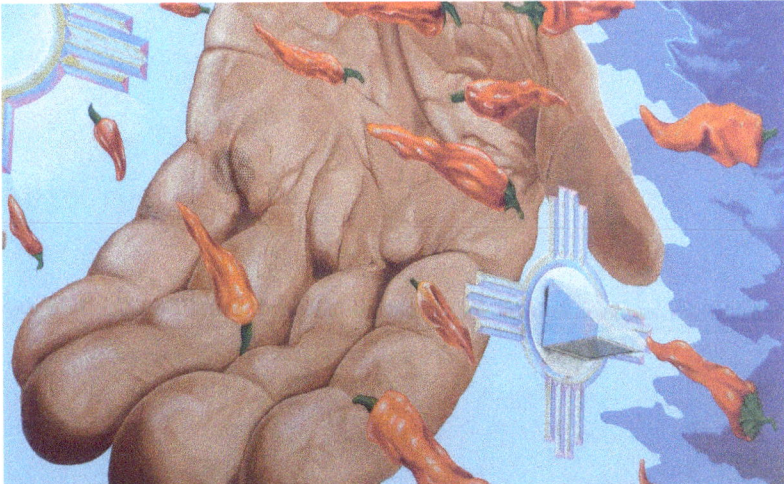

Mural at the South Valley Academy. A local farmer lent a hand.

program, and dual college-credit classes. Counterintuitively, the students rise to the challenge and do well.

Along with the emphasis on achievement, there's a safe, family feeling. Many of the teachers are former students and the school's community partners are sometimes graduates. In 2013, SVA opened a middle school. Almost all students come from the South Valley, and now, with six hundred students, there is always a waiting list.

A key component of the program is community involvement and service. In 9th grade, students are unpaid literacy tutors in local elementary schools for three hours each week (9th grade boys shine in this area, says principal/director Radoslovich). As sophomores, students are placed in non-profit agencies like the Roadrunner Food Bank or Catholic Social Services. As juniors, they write their own resume and job applications and interview with local organizations where they would like to (and do) work. For their senior projects, they research pressing social problem (such as domestic violence or drug abuse). In the second semester they put together an action plan, which is assessed in a high-stakes public presentation to community members, professionals, and peers.

This year, says Radoslovich, as tensions mounted over deportations in the South Valley, a number of seniors partnered with El Centro de Igualdad y Derechos to interview undocumented residents and create plans of protection for families. The projects presented opportunities to learn about powers-of-attorney, custody, and financial and criminal-justice issues. It was also an opportunity to use Spanish, a language spoken at SVA almost as often as English.

South Valley Academy teacher Jennifer Chavez-Miller and middle school student Esteban Casas

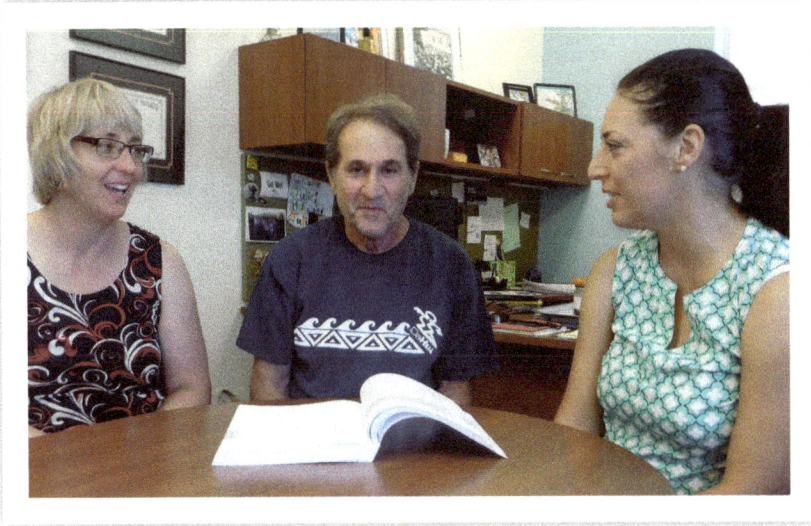

Former Rio Grande High School teacher Alan Marks (c) is flanked by two protégées: Julie Radoslovich, now principal at the South Valley Academy (l) and Katarina Sandoval (r), a founder and former principal.

With engaging projects like these, students are empowered, says Sandoval. "Young people begin to see themselves as agent of change, not victims of circumstance."

Eighty-five percent of SVA's students graduate and 90 percent of those go on to college, a remarkable statistic given the composition of the student body (90 percent eligible for free lunch; 90 percent Hispanic, the vast majority children of Mexican immigrants). A number of the school's graduates go to impressive, small colleges like Cornell College in Iowa, Occidental, Swarthmore, and Amherst. Radoslovich says the school doesn't systematically track college graduation rates, but she knows they are not good enough.

South Valley Academy has been recognized by *US News and World Report* as a top New Mexico School for four years in a row. But Radoslovich knows that is not good enough, either.

"All students deserve this," she says.

Creating a Pipeline with Safe Spaces Along the Way to Explore, Gain Skills

A number of programs to create a college pipeline, with safe spaces along the way for kids to learn how to become good college candidates, are working together in northern and central New Mexico. The programs, including AVID (Advancement through Individual Determination), Breakthrough Santa Fe, the New Mexico Simon Scholars, and the Davis Foundation work within the context of the public schools and focus on the least served student in the academic middle.

AVID, the largest of these programs, was started in 1978 by a single high school teacher in southern California who believed that if you hold students accountable to the highest standards, and provide academic and social supports, they would rise to the challenge. Started here in 2002, AVID now offers electives in fifty-six New Mexico secondary and elementary schools.[44] Teachers trained in the AVID method work with small classes to improve study skills, provide tutorials, and help students collaborate and advocate for themselves. Often the same small group moves through the grades together as a cohort, with the same teacher and sometimes a college student serving as a tutor and role model.

Del Norte High School science teacher Michael Mendoza, an AVID teacher in the large Albuquerque high school, says the AVID classrooms have a family feel, which builds trust and opens the door to learning. "It creates a sense of belonging for everyone involved, which in turn increases attendance and ultimately graduation rates."

In Albuquerque, where approximately two thousand students participate in the program, AVID sponsored ten college field trips this year to regional colleges—including New Mexico State University in Las Cruces, the University of Texas at El Paso, Texas Tech in Lubbock, and Fort Lewis in Durango, Colorado. Funding for the trips came from the APS Education Foundation's Varsity Award Program, which previously made grants of $1,000 each to thirteen high school counselors to give to low-income high school students to defray costs for pre-college tests.

The field trips can be very important in matching students to the proper college. Aside from the big universities, the New Mexico students often know little about colleges other than, maybe, their athletic teams. "It's one thing to say I want to go to college and it's another to understand exactly what that entails," says Larry Pavatt, AVID site coordinator at Valley High School.[45]

Nationwide AVID boasts big results. Of 42,418 seniors reporting data in 2015–2016, 95 percent planned to go to college. In New Mexico 94 percent planned on going to either four- or two-year colleges.

The New Mexico Simon Scholars, headquartered in Santa Fe, initially started in 2005 to provide scholarships to a handful of students from a local charter school. But the family foundation soon found money alone was not the answer. It now works with a cohort of first-generation college hopefuls, twenty of them each year, starting the summer of sophomore year with a retreat and continuing for the next two years with Saturday tutoring sessions, college tours, summer programs, ongoing mentoring, test prep, college guidance, team building, and life skills. It continues to provide scholarships (up to $16,000) and places its graduates into supportive programs in college.

To recruit the scholars, the program works with a group of about seven or eight high schools in Albuquerque and Santa Fe where it has established relationships or where there is an existing pipeline program like AVID or Breakthrough Santa Fe.

The key is the sense of community created within the cohort, says Mike Ammerman, Simon Scholars program director. "We become a home base, a connection point with people who have already done it, who come back and tell their own stories."

That, he says, allows the students to dream. "We're all about creating a culture of dreaming."

Another program, Breakthrough Santa Fe, is affiliated with Santa Fe Prep, a private school in Santa Fe. It is a six-year, afterschool and weekend program aimed at motivated but unsupported public school students. Started in 2004, it has guided 250 students from 6th grade through high school, with afterschool, summer and weekend sessions, college field trips, exam prep, and community internships. College students act as tutors, and the award-winning program has met with considerable success—92 percent of its graduates go to college. Of those, 86 percent are the first in their families to do so.

Breakthrough Santa Fe is affiliated with the Davis Scholarship, a new program that provides full-ride scholarships to seniors enrolled in that program as well as College Horizons (New Mexico students only), New Mexico Simon Scholars, the MASTERS Program, the Academy for Technology and the Classics, the South Valley Academy, NACA Inspired Schools Network, and the New Mexico School for the Arts. The full scholarships are only for a small group of participating colleges: Loyola Marymount in Los Angeles, the University of Denver, Laurence University (Appleton, WI), St. Edward's (Austin, TX), and the University of Portland. The Shelby Cullom Davis Charitable Fund, college readiness non-profits, and partner colleges fund the scholarships.

The $5 million per-year program awarded eighteen scholarships in its first year of operation (2016) and it is looking for partner schools that serve first-generation, low-income students.[46]

College Horizons Expand for Native American Students

Native American students face tough challenges when it comes to higher education, and it is reflected in the graduation statistics. In New Mexico, only 47 percent graduate high school (51 percent nationwide) and a mere 5 percent go to a four-year college. Of those, only 10 percent graduate.[47] Often, schools serving Native Americans are isolated and too understaffed to offer meaningful advice or college counseling. Many of the students have no access to college prep or Advanced Placement (AP) courses. And it is likely that no one in their families has gone to college.

Carmen Lopez, the executive director of College Horizons, is familiar with the challenge. A Navajo who graduated from Harvard and Dartmouth, she now directs the small non-profit out of Pena Blanca, NM. It started at the Native American Preparatory School on Rowe Mesa in 1998 and has expanded from forty-eight participants to serve twenty-eight hundred Native American high school students nationwide. While the scale is bigger, the format is the same.

Each year College Horizons operates an intensive five-day workshop on a college campus where Native American high school sophomores and juniors get a crash course from college counselors, essay specialists, and admissions officers from around the country. They learn about suitable colleges, how to take the ACT and SAT, navigate the financial aid process, interview successfully, and write winning essays. They meet admissions officials and they bond with one another. Originally the workshops were held at St. John's College in Santa Fe and Washington University in St. Louis. This year's workshops (2017) will be held at Princeton University and Whitman College.

The premise of the program is that Native American students do not receive quality college counseling and academic advising. Appearing on KUNM's *Native America Calling*, Lopez explained how complex the process is and how little details like applying early for student aid are crucial.

"Two-point-seven billion dollars in federal student aid goes unclaimed," she said. "The earlier you apply using the FAFSA (Free Application for Federal Student Aid) the more likely you are to get help."

College Horizons is aimed at high achievers who can afford the $450 workshop tuition, plus airfare. Over 50 percent of the students get scholarships, but the program is not free. It's a great opportunity for college recruiters to meet promising students all in one place. Ninety-five percent of the students who have attended have been admitted to college, with 85 percent graduating in four years.

For Communities to Thrive, a Critical Mass Makes a Difference

After living for years with an intractable problem, a sense of resignation often sets in. Some people even ask, "What difference does it make if most New Mexicans—particularly those who are low-income or from minority backgrounds—don't go to college?" That's the way New Mexico has operated for generations, and we know the result: economic stagnation, and a growing divide between the educated haves and the uneducated have-nots.

More and more, a postsecondary education is a necessity in the new economy that, even in 2017, seems to be passing New Mexico by. Even more important is its role in community development.

J. B. Schramm, the founder of a national college readiness program, College Summit, summed it up. "Teenagers are the single most influential group in a low-income community. If the teens are well engaged, it shifts the dynamic in that neighborhood. You are never going to see a lasting transformation in low-income communities until there is a critical mass of college-educated youth in those communities."[48]

In New Mexico the high school graduates from low-income backgrounds who headed to college thanks to Alan Marks, AVID, Breakthrough Santa Fe, the Simon Scholars, and the untold English teachers who helped their students write college essays are beginning to lift their communities and inspire their families and peers to dream big and reach high.

The hundreds of students reached by these programs could have languished in the forgotten middle, and our communities would have been that much poorer. Instead, Julie Radoslovich came back to lead a South Valley charter school; Santiago Macias is a family practice doctor in the South Valley. Many others are working in non-profits or starting businesses.

In the South Valley of Albuquerque, the critical mass is taking shape.

In a Nutshell

Problems

- Intergenerational poverty connected to low educational levels
- College attendance gap
- Lack of support for low-income and minority families navigating the elementary to college pipeline

Big Ideas

- Personal mentoring
- Better advisement system
- Use of student cohorts that travel, prepare for college together

Partners

Teachers, parents, non-profits, foundations, South Valley Academy, AVID, Simon Scholars, Breakthrough Santa Fe, College Horizons.

What You Can Do

- If you are a teacher, mentor, or church volunteer, look around for promising teenagers who need help—talk to them, mentor them through a community organization or just by yourself.

- Take students from your child's school, your neighborhood, or extended family on trips, turn them on to local museums, concerts, arts, and culture—widen their horizons.

- Volunteer to go on school trips to colleges, or organize one yourself for students identified by community organizations. Contribute money for travel expenses.

- Support and contribute to scholarship and pipeline programs.

Resources

New Mexico Simon Scholars
524 Don Gaspar Ave.
Santa Fe, NM 87505
505-982-0733
http://www.nmsimonscholars.org

College Horizons
P.O. Box 1262
Peña Blanca, NM 87041
505-401-3854
www.collegehorizons.org

NM MESA Inc.
2808 Central Ave. SE
Albuquerque, NM 87106
505-366-2500
www.nmmesa.org

AVID
Western Division Office
5889 Greenwood Plaza Blvd.,
Suite 210
Greenwood Village, CO 80111
303-436-2200 • www.avid.org
Denise Campbell, NM Director
dcampbell@avid.org

Breakthrough Santa Fe
1101 Camino de la Cruz Blanca
Santa Fe, NM 87505
505-795-7517
www.breakthoughsantafe.org

Davis NM Scholarship
A Breakthrough Santa Fe affiliate
www.breakthroughsantafe.org

South Valley Academy
3426 Blake Road SW
Albuquerque, NM 87105
505-452-3132
http://www.southvalleyacademy.org

College Summit
1763 Columbia Rd. NW 2nd floor
Washington, DC 20009
202-319-176
www.collegesummit.org

Mission Graduate
2340 Alamo Ave. SE 2nd Floor
Albuquerque, NM 87106
505-247-3671
https://missiongraduatenm.org/

PART SEVEN
Creative Enterprise Unleashes a New Kind of Economic Animal

For me, entering *The House of Eternal Return*, Meow Wolf's incomparable, interactive exhibition on the south side of Santa Fe, was like opening the door to new possibilities, not just in art, but in tourism, job creation, and economic development, all rooted in New Mexico's often quirky, out-of-the box spirit.

Meow Wolf is unlike anything I'd ever seen, and judging from the crowds it has attracted this year, its unique character is a magnet for thousands of others, young and old. Its popularity among young people, in particular, is amazing. It has attracted 3 million to its web site and is rapidly outpacing major tourist attractions in the number of posts on Instagram and Facebook. Photographs of it are everywhere, and the once ragtag collective to which it traces its origin has raised $6 million from investors this year (2017).

The phenomenal success of Meow Wolf, is based on many of the principles of appropriate community development that characterize the social enterprises we've visited in previous chapters: collaboration, use of existing assets, passion, and a sense of place. Beginning as a tribe of young creatives disenchanted by the traditional arts scene, the group collaborated to transform rooms into mini-environments, creating a sense of place with whatever materials available—mostly trash, giveaways, or items scored on the cheap. Everything they have created was done collectively, and they are the first to tell you that's their strength. Now they are passing on their passion, their optimism to others. They are mentoring children in art and technology. They are spinning off new businesses and supporting fellow artists. Most important, they are creating the kinds of meaningful jobs in the arts that young people usually leave town to get.

And who are these Meow Wolfers? They are not highly educated, refined artists or exiles from the coasts. They are our children spinning new worlds on a shoestring, sparking the imagination, creating something out of nothing. Now, with more experience and a little business training under their belts, they are quickly making the transition from a tribe to a larger enterprise that is a vital ingredient in the revitalization of Santa Fe.

It is a story that should inspire other entrepreneurs at the edges of the tourist, entertainment, and art sectors to take a big idea, get some partners, and go forth. And don't be afraid to be different—that's your strength.

CHAPTER 17

Meow Wolf:

Together We Can Build Spectacular Worlds

*"They have the courage to be different.
No one said to Meow Wolf that's not what
they are doing in New York or L.A."*

— Alice Loy, cofounder, Creative Startups

The crowds keep coming. They are children, teenagers, yuppies, boomers, and retirees. They line up in the parking lot, sample the food truck fare, gaze at the huge robot, and then enter *The House of Eternal Return*. Many will come back again and again to follow another route through the wild, interactive art experience created by the art collective Meow Wolf.

Their inner child, or maybe their real child, will insist.

The exhibit, created by hundreds of young Santa Fe artists, is set in the home of a family where something has gone terribly, delightfully wrong. Visitors follow the story, charting their own path through ice caves and fluorescent forests, passing through unexpected passages through refrigerators, entering different dimensions, flicking switches, triggering sounds, climbing trees, solving the mystery behind the house.

The exhibit is the first built in Meow Wolf's permanent home, an old 22,000-square-foot bowling alley purchased for the local arts collective by *Game of Thrones* author George R. R. Martin in 2015. It has been a huge success. Opened in March 2016, it has attracted four hundred thousand visitors in its first year, generating $7 million in revenue and employing approximately one hundred fifty Santa Feans—most of them millennials. Its website has attracted over three million visitors and it has over fifty thousand Instagram followers.

With hundreds of galleries, museums, the opera, and the Indian Market, Santa Fe has been an arts mecca for years. Indeed, the whole state is known for its creative arts. According to a 2015 study by the New Mexico's Bureau of Business and Economic Research, creative industries employ about seventy-seven thousand people and contribute about $1.3 billion in wages and salaries to the state's economy. That makes the arts a major economic driver.[49]

But for many locals, the art market is not all it's cracked up to be, and many young people are leaving the state because they cannot find work in a creative field. The Santa Fe scene is dominated by high-priced, traditional galleries featuring paintings on walls. The mystique is fading, especially for a new generation. "Canyon Road is art with a capital A, with big names and high prices," says Mary-Charlotte Domandi, the former producer and host of Radio Café, a popular show broadcast from the Santa Fe Baking Company.

Meow Wolf was started, in part, as a protest against the established art world.

"We all know that the art market is impossible for young artists," says Vince Kadlubek, cofounder and now chief administrative officer of Meow Wolf. "Meow Wolf is not just an exhibit but a new model of how new artists can create work and get paid for it."

The very name of the group, Meow Wolf, was almost random, drawn out of a hat by a group of twenty-somethings who spurned college and formal training, subsisting on part-time work and the creative energy of the group.

A Walk on the Wild Side
Step-by-Step With Meow Wolf

2008 A small tribe of twenty-somethings, loosely affiliated with Warehouse 21, an all-ages performance venue for electronic music, punk bands, and other acts, begins to take shape out of four houses gathered around a parking lot in Santa Fe. Together the group rents an old barbershop for concerts, then starts to do art shows. Beginning with murals and sculptures coming off the walls, the first shows, *Meowzorz* and *Biome,* fill the space with small environments. The shows are constructed with materials retrieved from dumpsters.

Evicted, the group paints the walls a stark white and holds one final show, *Everyone Only*. Everyone who wants to hangs artwork on the walls in protest of the traditional, exclusive art world. No one is excluded.

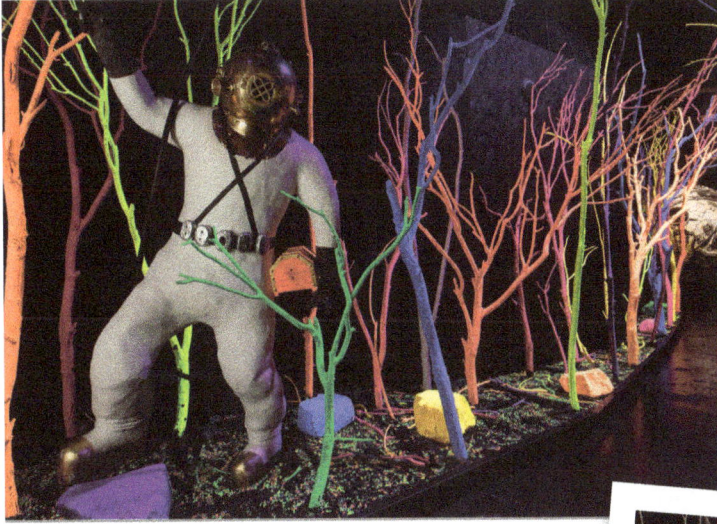

Diver in
Meow Wolf's
Glowquarium.

Photos by
Kate Russell

No Hierarchy,
No Dollars, No Heat

Meow Wolf did not start as a struggling Santa Fe art gallery. It grew organically out of a tribe of Santa Fe young people who coalesced around music in 2008. The weird, the psychedelic, and the fluorescent were all part of the attraction, and having their own space for concerts, raves, and the group's own kind of art was a dream. It was a dream that came true in an old barbershop at 2nd and Cerrillos, the first of many cold warehouses to serve as home for the art collective.

2008 The group, now calling themselves Meow Wolf, moves to a run-down warehouse at 2nd and Hopewell and stages the first show there, *Horror*. It is followed by dozens of others including *AutoWolf* and *Geodecadent I*.

2010 *The Moon is to Live On,* a multimedia play, is produced and presented at the Center for Contemporary Arts (CCA), sparking a trend toward more structure, planning, and formal roles in the collective.

"We weren't there to start a business or make money," recalls Corvas Brinkerhoff, an early Meow Wolfer. "It was about getting a bunch of people together and having a really good time making these insane pieces of artwork that none of us could ever conceive of, much less deliver on our own."[50]

The group had no budget and no formal leaders. They started with the space itself, covering every inch with materials found in dumpsters or donated by parents and friends. There was little advance planning, lots of collaboration and spontaneity.

"We started creating with nothing," says Kadlubek. "We were at the bottom of the barrel. It created momentum and gave us an appreciation for creating something out of nothing."

It was chaotic, but a unique style began to emerge, with the group creating an outrageous, overarching structure subdivided into a multitude of idiosyncratic separate worlds, little forts, trees, houses, and more—each inhabitable by the mind, and sometimes the body, of the viewer.

The amazing thing, says Mary-Charlotte Domandi, who followed the group from its beginning, is the mix of individual expression with an artistic whole. Scores of artists contribute their talents, time, and energy to the exhibits, yet they are not recognized individually. And the work of one blends into another. "They work anonymously for the overall project—for the group," she says.

A multimedia play staged by the group at the Center for Contemporary Arts in 2010 was a turning point, tempering the group's spontaneous, chaotic process with more planning and specific roles for collective members. "Meow Wolf is the play between the spontaneous and the planned—with an emphasis on the yes, the positive, the joyful, and the awesome," Kadlubek says.

2010 *Geodecadent II* opens at the Linda Durham Gallery.

Simultaneously, *Habitats*, a multilevel interactive installation of structures and environments, opens at the Hopewell space. Over twenty-five artists create an imaginary shantytown from scrap wood, mud, abandoned couches, telephone books, and assorted items, still from dumpsters or donations. The installation includes sound and video elements, and it invites viewers to inhabit it.

2011 *Due Return* opens at CCA to rave reviews

and wild success. With twenty-five thousand visitors in three months, admissions revenue is a complete surprise. Collective members debate over what to do with the money and whether artists should be paid. Meow Wolf is invited everywhere and does temporary installations in Las Cruces (*Glitteropolis*), San Antonio (*Nimbus*), and Chicago (*Nucleotide*).

Meow Wolf's breakout exhibit, *The Due Return*, a 75-by-25-by-14-foot time-traveling, interactive sailing ship, was also a turning point. The installation threw a narrative into the artistic mix, and that appealed to the public, particularly children. "We want to put the audience into an understandable space—a ship, a house—not an abstraction, but a world. And we want it to be connected," Kadlubek says.

The Due Return brought in admissions revenue and a new audience—kids, who helped construct the ship and returned again and again. The collective then began an educational outreach program, Chimera, and with one thousand school children, built an imaginary supermarket, *Omega Mart.* The children's connection was to prove important.

The successes—and the tragic death of one of its key members—brought the group, which still had no financial structure or bank account, to a crossroads. Tired of piecemeal projects, Kadlubek was searching for a big idea, a more-permanent, stable solution to keep the group together and provide revenue. In spite of his initial distaste for the professional world, Kadlubek sought help. He and cofounder Sean DiIanni learned about entrepreneurship, fundraising, debt, branding, and marketing at a business incubator for arts groups, Creative Startups. They were mentored, attended a boot camp, and got a $25,000 grant from the Santa Fe-based organization. The group decided to incorporate as a for-profit arts production company, with two non-profit educational arms, Chimera and Make Santa Fe. The business plan was based on charging admission to an immersive, multimedia experience for all ages similar to an amusement park or children's museum. But the group still did not have a building to provide the framework for its visionary ideas and the springboard to a stable future.

2012 *Omega Mart,* an imaginary supermarket, is built with one thousand Santa Fe school children as part of Meow Wolf's new educational outreach program, Chimera.

2013–2014 Spread thin, unable to simultaneously travel, work day jobs, and create a more permanent installation, the group begins to splinter. Then, a much-loved member of the group dies, and cohesion returns. Vince Kadlubek, a founding member, emerges as chief rainmaker, connecting with Santa Fe Mayor Javier Gonzales and *Game of Thrones* author George R. R. Martin.

2014 Kadlubek attends Creative Startups, an incubator for arts projects.

Neon arches in Meow Wolf's Glowquarium.

Photo by Kate Russell

A Partnership with George R. R. Martin

In 2013 Kadlubek began reaching into the community, supporting Javier Gonzales, then a candidate for mayor, and meeting with George R. R. Martin, the author of *Game of Thrones*, and the owner of a local arts cinema. Now aware of the need to raise capital for the start-up, Kadlubek pitched Meow Wolf to one of the state's most famous storytellers. After negotiations, a Kickstarter campaign, and accelerated lobbying by the newly incorporated business, Martin agreed to supply $2.7 million to buy the Silva Lanes, a deteriorating bowling alley on the south side of town, and fund renovation. Meow Wolf would lease the building from him for ten years.

2015 George R. R. Martin buys an old 22,000-square-foot bowling alley on Rufina Circle in Santa Fe and agrees to fund an extensive remodel and lease it to Meow Wolf for ten years. To seal the deal, Meow Wolf raises $2 million through local investors and a Kickstarter campaign. The city invests as well.

March 2016 Meow Wolf's *The House of Eternal Return* opens, attracting four hundred thousand visitors in its first year and generating $7 million in revenue including $800,000 in gift shop sales. Social media is the chief marketing mechanism. An on-site "Make-Space" allows children and community members to learn the three-dimensional printing and digital skills that made Meow Wolf what it is. Meow Wolf creates several charitable foundations to benefit children and artists.

After building *The House of Eternal Return* for 18 months, the installation opened in March 2016 to rave reviews and record attendance. The warehouse district around the old bowling alley had already been undergoing a renaissance, with a brewery, artists' studios, and coffee houses. Meow Wolf accelerated the trend. New music and theater venues sprang up, and the area has become trendy, an alternative to the rail-yard district and the tourist-oriented Canyon Road. The youthful spirit, symbolized by Meow Wolf, is everywhere in the neighborhood.

"The buzz around Meow Wolf is really positive," says Kate Nelson, Santa Fe's economic development director. "Meow Wolf has shifted the perception and identity of the city to youth, vibrancy, innovation, brilliance...that's a new path for the city's identity."

In recent years the population of Santa Fe has become older and older, and its culture and social life often reflects wealthier, boomer tastes and interests. It's something that political leaders and people like Kadlubek are trying to turn around.

Giving Millennials a Platform and a Chance

"We give millennials a platform, a brand," Kadlubek says. More than that, Meow Wolf has given them paying jobs — one hundred fifty of them so far. Half of those are operational, working at Meow Wolf itself, running the gift store ($800,000 in sales the first year), taking tickets, booking DJs and bands, keeping the social media buzzing. The other half are lighting engineers, ceramic or fabric artists, video technicians, and others in creative fields. Meow Wolf projects it will triple the size of its team in the next few years. It is branching out to support local spin-off enterprises — food trucks, wearable art, music videos, toys, and playgrounds. Meow Wolf has already constructed exhibits in Chicago, Las Cruces, and San Antonio and, with $1 million in new state and local funding, it has announced it is renovating a warehouse to fabricate even more exhibits for shows outside of New Mexico. One will open in Denver in 2019 and another in Austin in 2020. Construction of the exhibits, done under the aegis of Meow Wolf Creative Studios, is expected to create about seventy jobs for artists, technicians, and craftspeople.

2017 Meow Wolf renovates *The House of Eternal Return* and plans to expand to Austin and Denver. It diversifies into producing toys, playground equipment, music videos, and food trucks while still offering a performance space and immersive multimedia art experience. In May, it purchases and renovates a warehouse in which to construct exhibits, using $1 million in state and local funding. The enterprise has created one hundred fifty jobs — with more to come.

Chimera continues its work with local schools, most recently working with students at the Nina Otero Community School to create a Mad Bubble in the cafeteria. Meow Wolfers take seriously their role as mentors to the younger generation. The Make It space near the entrance to *The House of Eternal Return* is always busy, with classes and people of all ages learning three-dimensional printing and other skills.

In the wake of the December 2016 warehouse fire at Oakland's Ghost Ship, a facility very much like Meow Wolf in its earlier days, Meow Wolf set up a $100,000 fund for rent, materials, and equipment at art spaces around the world. It has dedicated other funds to local schools and charities as well.

"We're hoping to leverage our momentum, our revenue and our skill set to generate a more entrepreneurial spirit in Santa Fe," Kadlubek says.

Kadlubek explains that he feels Meow Wolf crashed through the fortress of Santa Fe identity and created an opening that wasn't there before. "It's an opportunity for others to rush in," he says.

A New Paradigm for Young Entrepreneurs?

What lessons can the phenomenal ascent of Meow Wolf teach other young adults intent on creating a career or a business rooted in artistic expression? Is it just too unique to be a model for anything else?

The importance of collaboration, synergy, and excitement about what the group could accomplish together created a buoyant momentum that carried the original core of twelve creative young people from project to project on no money and few resources except innate creativity and youthful energy. Drawn by the unique vision, the fun and the excitement, volunteers were there at every step of the way.

"It's is a good example of what our generation can do, technically and emotionally, when we work together," Meow Wolfer Megan Burns told Radio Café a few years ago.[51]

Meow Wolf's extraordinary early years as an alternative art collective are reminiscent of the 1960s protest against the established order. What's different is the group's ability to survive the down times, regroup and make the transition to a sustainable, successful company that is driving economic development in Santa Fe. Meow Wolf's partnership with George R. R. Martin was a key ingredient. The business accelerator, Creative Startups, and the transformation of Vince Kadlubek and a few other key leaders into fundraisers, planners, marketers, civic leaders, and, yes, businesspeople, made the transition possible.

Vince Kadlubek now talks about branding, managing budgets and employees, and expanding to other cities. He is the chairperson of the Santa Fe Planning Commission. Members of his team are now mentoring others, helping them market their products on the Internet or start a food truck business to serve the patrons of Meow Wolf.

The new endeavors often bear the wild, wacky style of Meow Wolf. And audiences continue to respond with a new group of customers—Santa Fe children—in the pipeline. "Twenty years from now, I would love to say that Meow Wolf created a whole new market for storytelling, entertainment and art," says Kadlubek.

Meow Wolf's success, built on the courage to be different, has come quickly in the past two years. Economic developers cite it as one of New Mexico's best start-ups. And there are ambitious plans for the future. How Meow Wolf balances the growth with its inclusive, core values of artistic expression will be tricky in the future.

"It's inevitable that their success will change them," says Mary-Charlotte Domandi. "They are no longer 20 somethings...but in the past, they have always risen to the occasion."

In A Nutshell

Problems

- Lack of meaningful, paid work for young Santa Fe artists and musicians

- Lack of outlets for non-traditional, immersive art projects

Big Ideas

- An Art Fun House—based on a narrative and the group imagination of Santa Fe millennials

- Creating something out of nothing

- The power of the collective

- An admissions-based business based on an interactive art installation for all ages

Partners

George R. R. Martin, Creative Startups, a collective of millennials, City of Santa Fe, State of New Mexico

What You Can Do

- Visit Meow Wolf in Santa Fe — open every day except Tuesday.

- Invest in Meow Wolf during one of its periodic offerings through www.wefunder.com/meowwolf.

- Encourage young artists with your purchases and attendance at their events.

Resources

Meow Wolf
1352 Rufina Circle
Santa Fe, NM 87507
505-395-6369
https://meowwolf.com/

Creative Startups
A Business Accelerator for Creative Entrepreneurs
Santa Fe, NM
Online courses, mentors, and boot camps
http://www.creativestartups.org/

CONCLUSION

Social Entrepreneurs, Change-Makers at the Grassroots Have Left a Map to a New Kind of Society

In the past few years, there have been plenty of reasons to despair about New Mexico's future. We have never really recovered from the 2008 recession, and all systems seem to be in free fall. A few years ago I was spurred to write this book after reading a collection of essays edited by Fred Harris, *New Mexico 2050*. It outlined our problems in a dozen areas and suggested policy alternatives to avoid a bleak 2050. The policy directions charted by experts have not been heeded. We are at the bottom in unemployment. Dependence is the main characteristic of our economy. Oil and gas slumps and federal spending cuts are major problems. Global warming portends drought, and our schools continue to struggle. Political leaders at the state level seem paralyzed. The election of Donald Trump and a Congress determined to roll back the significant progress the state has made in health care and other fields has been a heavy blow. Hope is in short supply, and for me, and maybe for you, too, there's been an emotional reaction that's hard to shake.

And yet, I know that in Albuquerque and around the state good things *are* happening. Against all odds, people are organizing, building on their own strengths, and not waiting for Washington or Santa Fe. Usually they are even fighting the headwinds emanating from those directions. Their determined spirit, their creative initiatives have given me hope for the future, and the idea of sharing their stories has propelled me forward from northern New Mexico through Jemez Pueblo to Hidalgo County.

In this final section I hope to share some of the ways that these leaders and organizations have solved social problems and created organizations that, taken together, can create alternatives to the current political and economic trajectory. Taken together, they point a way toward a New Mexico where everyone has the opportunity, the skills, and the knowledge to achieve economic security and build healthy communities, right here, close to home.

Two years ago when I started my visits with these innovative leaders, I had never heard the term *social entrepreneur*, which, as you know now, is someone who establishes an enterprise with the aim of solving a social problem or advancing social change. I had never thought much about what a community-medicine project might have in common with an emerging arts organization. But now I realize that there are common traits that social entrepreneurs have and there is a common pattern that successful grassroots organizations go through when they set out to solve a problem. Here it is.

A Common Pattern

Usually, it starts with a frustrated individual. Sometimes there is a precipitating incident. For Max Ramirez and Debbie O'Malley, it all started with the sawdust from a neighborhood sawmill coating their cars and even penetrating their homes. It got them asking, why should their low-income Hispanic neighborhood be the victim of environmental injustice? (Chapter 4) For Rio Grande High School teacher Alan Marks, it came with the discovery that only thirty out of the eleven hundred entering freshman at his high school ever saw the inside of a college classroom. "I looked around at the kids who were going to school there and just said, 'this is unacceptable,'" Marks recalled thinking. (Chapter 16)

For both Charlie Alfero, who started Hidalgo Medical Services, and Sanjeev Arora, who founded Project ECHO, it was a profound sense of inequity. Rural patients were at a dangerous disadvantage, and they set out to remedy the situation. Alfero sought to build a rural health-care service that put patients first, and that quest went deeper—to address the shortage of rural health-care providers and to rearrange medical training to get doctors and dentists to locate in places like Silver City or Lordsburg. (Chapters 7 and 10) It led Sanjeev Arora into a program to address inequities on a global scale (Chapter 2) and to ask profound questions about the nature of medical knowledge.

"How do we conceive of a world where half of the people are dying and the others are benefitting from this medical knowledge? Is knowledge for sharing or for private gain?" Arora answered his own question with a program whose hallmark is "de-monopolizing knowledge."

For firefighter Andres Mercado it was the expensive transports of people who didn't really need to go to the emergency room. The EMTs were required to take the 911-callers to the hospital, but it made no sense. "I was a cog in a machine," he said. "On the one hand, I was helping people but really I was complicit in a broken system." (Chapter 9)

Of course there are lots of frustrated — even outraged — people who recognize problems when they see them. But what allows some to come up with big ideas to solve social problems like persistent poverty, the achievement gap, or a shortage of jobs for disillusioned young artists?

Characteristics of Social Entrepreneurs and Change-Makers

Vision

Visions are good dreams of how things could be different — in the long run. Sometimes they occur to people in surprising ways. Sanjeev Arora's idea for using teleconferencing to move medical knowledge to patients instead of moving patients to the specialists in the urban medical centers came to him during a meditation session. (Chapter 2) Carl Colonius "hatched" the idea for the Rocky Mountain Youth Corps after brainstorming with a group of outdoor and youth advocates in Taos who saw idle young people around them being pulled in the wrong directions. Their vision was linking idle youth to the outdoors via community service. Colonius tried it out for himself by serving in a corps in California to make sure his vision wasn't just a daydream. (Chapter 13)

Cliff Crawford spent years thinking about the bosque, developing an overall management plan, then working with teachers and graduate students to incorporate kids. He knew it would take many generations to protect one of New Mexico's endangered resources. The result was the Bosque Ecosystem Monitoring Program (BEMP), which engages students, collects data, and cultivates a crop of citizen scientists and bosque stewards. (Chapter 12) The Sawmill Neighborhood had a dream of an urban village and they kept at it even when many thought the city would never cooperate. (Chapter 4)

Ambition

Ambition is sometimes a dirty word, but for change-makers it's an asset — especially when an opening presents itself. Sanjeev Arora aims to touch one billion lives with Project ECHO by 2020. First Choice Community Healthcare CEO Bob DeFelice is not satisfied with a successful primary-care clinic. He wants a health commons "with a heart" that will incorporate a food hub, an early childhood center, a health leadership high school, and a wellness center—all to address health in a holistic way. He refuses to see health care as just another "widget"—a product delivered to consumers in the form of pills and procedures. (Chapter 5)

The leaders of Hidalgo Medical Services in Silver City do not see their efforts to create a medical home and draw health-care professionals to underserved rural areas in isolation either. "Our vision is about fundamentally changing health-care delivery in the state and the nation, not just in Hidalgo and Grant counties," said Dan Otero, CEO of Hidalgo Medical Services.

Sawmill organizers also see a broader purpose.

"We are building a community, not just selling a house," said Sawmill's Debbie O'Malley.

A Plan to Continue

Ambition, drive, determination have their downside. Starting fires is easier than keeping them burning. Fire in the belly can only last so long. It's exhausting to start a new enterprise, get funding, advocate, testify, and keep going out on a limb. Debbie O'Malley decided she would move on from the Sawmill Community Land Trust in 2002, but, like Cliff Crawford, she made sure that a new leader was ready to assume the reins. Ken Balizer, Connie Chavez, and a team of the original board members picked up the task, and O'Malley found a way to help from her new position as city councilor. Cliff Crawford groomed one of his graduate students, Kim Eichhorst, to become the director of BEMP. Carl Colonius was glad to hand over the reins to Ben Thomas when Carl was ready to leave the Rocky Mountain Youth Corps. Alan Marks initially paired with one of his mentees, Katarina Sandoval, to lead the South Valley Academy, and then another one of his students, Julie Radoslovich, became the principal. The mentorship that the founders provided was key to continuing the enterprises.

The second generation of these leaders had different skills than the founders. Often they were more practical. The day-to-day operations, the nuts and bolts of regularly meeting a payroll, maintaining relationships with public and private partners, and marketing the organization takes energy, focus, and team building skills.

The Use of Overlooked Community Assets

One of the hallmarks of social entrepreneurs is that—rather than dwelling on the negative—they rearrange overlooked assets in a community to solve a problem in a new way. Kristyn Yepa, of Jemez Pueblo, calls it a *strength-based approach*. "We look at our cultural strengths and values in the pueblo and try to use those to foster the health of individuals and the community," she told me. For the Jemez

Comprehensive Health Center this has led to a fitness program that features running—a traditional activity. (Chapter 6)

For Ona Porter, the whole premise of Prosperity Works is that given the right tools and a little seed money, poor people are their own best asset. "These are whole and complete people, with goals," she said. "They know how to make their money go further." The proof is in the seven hundred businesses started and the 1,150 jobs created. (Chapter 14)

For Carl Colonius and the Rocky Mountain Youth Corps, the asset is young adults who often do not fit in to the traditional educational plan or employment market (Chapter 13). For Andres Mercado another existing asset—a network of emergency medical technicians, already funded by our tax dollars—is sitting around in firehouses waiting for fewer and fewer calls to put out structural fires. His program puts EMTs to work as community paramedics, who prevent hospital admissions and follow up on patients who may need nonmedical help. (Chapter 9)

Dr. Will Kaufman at First Choice Community Healthcare and reformers Charlie Alfero and Darrick Nelson in Silver City use another overlooked resource to rearrange the health-care delivery system: community health workers. These nonmedical professionals address the social determinants of health and help solve underlying social problems in a way (and in a language) that patients can understand. In so doing they are beginning to prevent disease and reduce costs. (Chapter 8)

Collaborative

Another critical characteristic of social entrepreneurs is that they are collaborative. They know they can't solve deep-seated problems alone, so they build teams or work within a network to develop a sense of group entrepreneurship and team spirit. The Agri-Cultura Network comprises nine community farms and community-supported agriculture entities (CSAs). Rejecting the competition found in a traditional marketplace, the members don't compete with one another, but find ways to market their products together to large institutions like schools or hospitals. (Chapter 3) In Santa Fe, Meow Wolf's key is its collective, almost tribal spirit. The group's quirky artistic installations encompass room after room, each created by individual artists. But they are not recognized individually, they share credit as a group. (Chapter 17)

"You must partner up," says First Choice's Bob DeFelice. A holistic approach is needed to make an impact on a community. "I hope our legacy will be that we've shown people how they can work together and maximize their collective resources to impact the wellness of communities.... One person can't do it alone and it's not just health care that's going to increase the wellness of a community. It's jobs, education, and all the other pieces." (Chapter 5)

Flexible and Experimental

When one approach doesn't work, try another—that's often the mantra of social entrepreneurs. Politicians, bureaucrats, and institutions get stuck—but those who want to make change can't afford to.

MoGro modified its approach of taking fresh produce to the pueblos in giant beer trucks. Too bulky. Too expensive. Rick Schneiders instead developed an online ordering system and partnered with Skarsgard Farms, which already had a fleet of smaller trucks. (Chapter 3)

Leaders of the Wild Friends program realized quickly that advocating for endangered species before the New Mexico legislature was a dicey proposition that could result in discouraged—rather than empowered—students. So they changed the approach, avoided the sacred cows, and stressed a consensus approach. The result is a record of legislative success, and students who feel they have a place in the decision-making process. (Chapter 11)

A Strong Ethical Core

It's impossible to spend any time at all with Ona Porter of Prosperity Works, Alan Marks, the founder of the South Valley Academy, or many of the other project directors included in this book without recognizing some core beliefs at work. Most prominent is a belief that everyone—no matter their income, race, sex, or where they live—should have an opportunity to work, to succeed, to be healthy, and to provide for their families. The need for equity, opportunity, and empowerment are key motivators.

And all you have to do is look at the Principle Values of the ECHO Movement (posted prominently in every office) to realize that service, sharing, mutual respect, and knowledge are the coins of the realm in that endeavor. (Chapter 2)

A Sense of Place and a Desire to Protect It

Another characteristic of organizations examined here is their dedication to their local community, or their own place in the world. Sometimes that place is a natural one. The BEMP project is based in the middle Rio Grande bosque, youth conservation projects like the Rocky Mountain Youth Corps work the national forests, and agricultural networks nurture farms and gardens. Sometimes the place is a neighborhood like the Sawmill; often it is a larger community like the South Valley or Grant County. Saving the place becomes a platform to build housing developments, schools, clinics, and other enterprises.

A Big Idea to Solve the Problem

Innovative ideas are the fuel for social enterprises. They are not always original ideas, but they are always tailored to a particular problem facing the community. Usually, they are difficult to accomplish because problems like poverty, the achievement gap, or chronic disease are not susceptible to a quick fix.

Here are some of the big ideas we've discovered in previous chapters:

- A community land trust to keep local control and provide affordable housing (Sawmill Community Land Trust)

- Using nonmedical professionals to reduce health-care costs and serve patients more personally (community health workers, community paramedics)

- Moving specialized medical knowledge to patients in rural areas via teleconferencing (Project ECHO)

- Using students as scientists to collect data for natural resource agencies (BEMP)

- Combining environmental education with civic engagement in the New Mexico Legislature (Wild Friends)

- Getting institutions like schools, hospitals, prisons, and public facilities to purchase locally grown food (Farm to Table New Mexico, Agri Cultura Network)

- Creating art collectively (Meow Wolf)

- A wellness ecosystem that incorporates jobs, education, healthy food, and exercise to prevent illness (First Choice Community Healthcare)

- Providing affordable daycare and counseling to support low-income, working women (Southwest Creations Collaborative)

- Providing assets and training to allow low-income families to get ahead and not just get by (Prosperity Works)

- Creating intergenerational wealth through accessible college guidance for low-income families (Alan Marks, South Valley Academy, College Horizons, Hacia, AVID)

- A new kind of medical residency program that encourages doctors and dentists to locate in rural areas (New Mexico Primary Care Training Consortium)

- A health commons where resources for patients are aggregated (Hidalgo Medical Services, First Choice Community Healthcare)

- The use of an Indian Health System clinic to serve rural residents as well as tribal members (Jemez Comprehensive Health Center)

- Community service that puts young adults to work outdoors, builds infrastructure in parks, forests, and preserves, and trains a new generation of resource mangers (Rocky Mountain Youth Corps, Forest Stewards Guild, Southwest Conservation Corps).

What many of these big ideas have in common is an attempt to address the root causes of a problem. Ona Porter of Prosperity Works and Arturo Sandoval of CODECE were tired of the traditional welfare approach. "I'm tired of band aids," Sandoval said. So was Porter, so she tried something new—individual development accounts.

Sandoval draws on Hispanic traditions in rural communities to start rural cooperatives. Susan Matteucci of Southwest Creations Collaborative tried out another approach to lift low-income women by addressing a key priority for her employees: their families. She created a program to combine steady income with social programs like daycare and assistance with education. They are both paying off in steady jobs and increased income.

"The trick is taking an idea, proving it works and following it until it becomes a best practice," said Charlie Alfero. "But it has to be good policy to begin with, based on equity, outcomes, and results, otherwise don't do it." Alfero and other rural health advocates took awhile to examine the reasons health-care professionals were not locating in rural places like Lordsburg, despite loan forgiveness programs and other incentives. And once they devised a program they built in periodic checks to measure the number of placements. How is the big idea working? Enterprises like Prosperity Works, the Sawmill Community Land Trust, and Wild Friends measure success on their own terms—in the number of businesses created, houses sold, or bills passed in the legislature.

Building an Organization, Overcoming Obstacles, and Moving Forward

The organizations profiled in the preceding chapters include both non-profit and for-profit organizations. Regardless of their tax designation, they develop in a common pattern, starting with a frustrated individual and a big idea.

First they have to get off the ground, which means persuading potential allies and funders that the need is there, the idea is sound, and the founder is capable of putting together a program and a team to solve the problem. Even before the first elevator speech to a potential partner, social entrepreneurs must do their homework and find out all about the problem and previous attempts to solve it. A blind faith that their idea is the only approach and confidence in one's own ability are not enough.

Many of these leaders got help and technical support from consultants who specialize in building the capacity of promising start-ups. Meow Wolf benefitted from Creative Startups, a group that helps arts and cultural organizations. Southwest Creative Collaborative got help from Social Venture Partners-New Mexico. The Sawmill Community Land Trust was guided by the Center for Community Change.

Others got initial grant funding, which was often attached to advice and performance following an approved plan. The W. K. Kellogg Foundation initially subsidized La Cosecha's food boxes; Presbyterian Healthcare Services helps to fund summer farmers' markets at First Choice Community Healthcare centers and in low-income Albuquerque neighborhoods. Sometimes early support came in the form of in-kind donations—a room at the back of the parish hall for Southwest Creations Collaborative, or classrooms at the Bosque School for BEMP project in its early years. Usually, the idea is to provide seed funding until the enterprises can generate revenue from sales of food or other goods and services.

But not every social enterprise will be able to sell products, and it is naïve to believe that small initiatives can single-handedly turn around huge marketplaces that have failed to deliver accessible health care, affordable housing, or healthy food. To get off the ground and gain the impetus they need to provide alternative models, most will need government funding in one form or another. Community development has always been a partnership between private and public organizations. But the problem for social entrepreneurs is that most of the government funding goes into a status quo that doesn't work well for everyone.

Of necessity, change-makers have to persistently advocate for the right kind of innovative state, local, and federal funding. And they have learned to do it. Debbie O'Malley became a burr under the saddle of the City of Albuquerque until it signed a memorandum of agreement, which opened the way to a community land trust. Community health advocates like Bob DeFelice and Venice Ceballos continue to push policymakers for Medicaid reimbursement for community health workers. Andres Mercado and Vince Kadlubek rely on funding from the City of Santa Fe, but they must guard it carefully and maintain the relationships that secured it; youth advocates lobby for service projects like the Rocky Mountain Youth Corps rather than unemployment relief and funds for juvenile incarceration. Ona Porter is at the NM legislative session every year trying to lower the interest rates of predatory loans that affect her organization's constituency.

These social entrepreneurs have learned the skills of persuasion, co-alition building, relationship cultivation, lobbying, testifying, public speaking, and messaging. To raise private donations and get government funding, they have had to.

Team Building

Social entrepreneurs have used a number of different strategies to both build their organizations and overcome obstacles. The chief strategies have been to create strong internal teams and operate within broad community coalitions. "Never doubt the ability of a dedicated team to change the world," says Sanjeev Arora, paraphrasing noted anthropologist Margaret Mead.

Arora and many of the health-care projects detailed here have created interdisciplinary teams to tackle complex health problems from many different directions. "The conventional approach is not working," said Brad Moran, a pharmacist working with Project ECHO in Montana. "Healthcare wants to go to a team based approach." Hidalgo Medical Services utilizes that approach as well—and patients like it. "We don't have clearly delineated scopes of practice here...we use 'warm hand-offs' of patients to other team members like psychologists or community health workers," says HMS doctor Dr. Rachel Sonne.

Corps is the most important word in the title of the Rocky Mountain Youth Corps, and everything is built around a group endeavor. BEMP, Wild Friends, and AVID are all programs that are founded on a team of students to take measurements, pass legislation, or prepare for college entrance tests. *Esprit de corps* is the key to reaching ambitious goals. It was certainly important in the years-long struggle in the Sawmill Neighborhood of Albuquerque. "We threw our feet in the fire and stuck together like glue, and the neighbors kept going," recalls Debbie O'Malley.

Social enterprises become even more likely to produce social change when they partner with even larger teams to form a network like a food hub or a wellness ecosystem like the one First Choice is establishing in the South Valley of Albuquerque. The South Valley is "blowing up" Don Bustos told me at the beginning of my own path through these organizations. But it's not just because of the Agri-Cultura Network. It's because that network, in combination with First Choice Community Healthcare, the South Valley Academy, the South Valley Economic Development Center, the Valle de Oro, and other community groups like Encuentro, the Partnership for Community Action and Koremi, are creating a critical mass. And that critical mass amounts to community development for the entire South Valley.

Partnering with a large institution like a bank (Prosperity Works), a hospital (La Consecha), or a university (BEMP) can also yield great returns for patients, students, and low-income clients served by the social enterprises. And the association lends both stability and credibility, which are essential for further growth.

Difficult as it may seem, these small initiatives keep plodding along, step-by-step. The BEMP program has expanded from a few classrooms at the Bosque School to over 35 schools. The Sawmill Community Land Trust keeps venturing into new building types—lofts, senior housing, mixed commercial and residential projects. Project ECHO is spreading to other countries. Meow Wolf is scaling up to open exhibits in Austin and Denver.

"It takes intention and a determination to overcome obstacles and put all the pieces together. You have to believe it's doable," says Debbie O'Malley. "I learned by throwing my feet in the fire, and what a learning experience it was."

O'Malley's can-do spirit is alive and well in most of these enterprises, as they break objectives down into smaller steps. And the determination that comes from the leaders helps overcome obstacles. The Agri-Cultura Network's Jedrek Lamb repeated his mantra for me: "Educate, co-ordinate, and make it happen." Brad Knipper, program coordinator of the Rocky Mountain Youth Corps, vows to "just keep showing up," even if government funding is reduced. And Rick Schneiders says that MoGro may change its tactics but it will not go away without a fight. "We'll keep trying. We'll keep changing with a cock-eyed sense of optimism," he said.

The flexibility to change the approach is key to survival for these enterprises, especially in more traditional businesses like farming. New skills or knowledge from finance or marketing courses, or specialized training from mentors like the American Friends Service Community's (AFSC) Don Bustos can help. In northern New Mexico Bustos encouraged the switch from traditional farming to specialty items like asparagus and blackberries, popular at the farmers' markets. "We learn from our ancestors, but we are not born knowing everything. It's just trial and error," said Martin Loretto, the head farmer at Jemez Pueblo.

Mentoring and Empowering New Leaders

Mentoring new leaders is also part of the survival strategy of most of these organizations, and, for organizations focused on education and youth development, it's part of their core mission. Both Prosperity Works and Southwest Creations Collaborative coach their clients and employees, helping develop financial and educational plans. Sawmill Community Land Trust provides classes on home ownership, and Hidalgo Medical Services is entirely focused on making formal medical training more relevant to rural areas. Alan Marks directly mentored his high school students, enabling them to become viable applicants to Ivy League colleges. College Horizons, Hacia, and AVID are all built on the premise that it takes personal guidance to close the achievement gap.

One mark of success for the youth programs, especially, is the sense of empowerment that participants gain from the experiences the programs provide. When Esteban Casas, a soft-spoken middle schooler from the South Valley Academy faces a senate committee to testify for his Wild Friends bill and concludes, "I knew this would be easy," it was a victory for students and future advocates throughout the state. (Chapter 11) And when Augustine Quintana, a Rocky Mountain Youth Corps member from Santo Domingo Pueblo, says, "I'm stronger and smarter than I thought," (Chapter 13) it's good news for New Mexico pueblos and tribes.

Empowering hundreds will speed the slow process of community development and enable the creation of new leaders and new enterprises to take on new social problems.

Sustainable Solutions

Many small grassroots organizations devoted to radical big ideas or to changing long-standing social ills last only a few years. Some of them actually want to work themselves out of business. Poverty alleviated, chronic health conditions addressed, the achievement gap closed, they can close up shop with the satisfaction of a job well done. Yeah, right. Real reformers know that those problems are not likely to be solved in a short time frame. Community development aimed at changing the systems that created these problems takes a long time. Meanwhile, grassroots organizations need to sustain themselves to make a difference.

Many of the groups profiled in this book are travelling a familiar path. They start with a big idea and assistance from foundations or government grants. Then they prove themselves by generating results or revenue. They spin off new jobs or businesses, and their efforts are replicated in one form or another, creating new institutions and community wealth in different local settings.

Some of the efforts profiled here are small scale, but they are sustainable nonetheless. Southwest Creations Collaborative's social mission, initially supported by foundations, is now sustained by the sales of its products. Meow Wolf gets both private and public funding, but its ticket sales are going through the roof, generating revenue with which to expand. The Sawmill Community Land Trust is self-supporting. Home sales continue as it partners with private developers to diversify offerings. BEMP sells its data to the United States Army Corps of Engineers and United States Fish and Wildlife Service; Rocky Mountain Youth Corps gets funding from national monuments, forests, and parks, which benefit from its trail construction and other services.

Small farmers who participate in the Agri-Cultura Network or who have been trained by AFSC sell their produce more widely, and they are beginning to cobble together a modest livelihood while remaining in their own communities.

Primary health-care clinics, fire departments, community medicine, and public-health projects have traditionally relied on government funding to protect public health and safety, even as they innovate to serve clients smarter and better. Often private partners like insurance companies or public universities have stepped in to help these organizations create innovative models that save money and increase the quality of care. But not always. These are difficult times. Federal and state programs like Medicaid and Medicare are not shifting the focus to prevention quickly or reimbursing community health workers and paramedics with funds now used to perpetuate more expensive, non-coordinated patient care. And although the Veterans Administration uses Project ECHO, adoption by other government agencies is spotty and funding is uncertain. Wild Friends always depends on funding from the New Mexico Legislature and Prosperity Works is not a priority for those who see economic prosperity trickling down rather than springing up from the bottom.

All of these enterprises—and more—are threatened by the current effort to defund and discredit all types of government assistance. Someday, as the pendulum swings, this will change.

But social entrepreneurs do not wait for a perfect opening.

"You can't wait for somebody else to do it. You've got to create the program—what's best for you...you've got to sustain and grow it," says Charlie Alfero. For the big changes to happen, he says you have to be a policy advocate, especially in the health care area. "It's only sustainable if it's in state law or federal policy...if it's in the financing system, in the payment contracts, or if it's revenue—not subsidized or expense-based."

Even if the individual enterprises don't last for decades, they are providing models for state and national policy changes, and their leaders are advocating for broad based policies that will make a huge difference nationally. Local food advocates like the New Mexico Farmers' Marketing Association and Farm to Table New Mexico got the state to allow food-stamp use at farmers' markets and then helped create a "Double Up Food Bucks" program, which allows recipients to buy double the amount of fresh fruits and vegetables. The first in the nation program is a national model, which is now being replicated in other states.

The use of community health workers to address the social conditions underlying chronic diseases and other health conditions has attracted attention nationwide, with Molina Health Care and other HMOs requesting training from Project ECHO and the University of New Mexico. Other states' Medicaid programs are beginning to reimburse these nonmedical services.

Charlie Alfero and other rural health-care advocates in southwestern New Mexico are chipping away at the traditional model of graduate medical education—a national system in need of reform. And now they have a model that's working.

The daycare provided at Southwest Creations Collaborative–and the permanent workforce it creates—is attracting the attention of other area employers and lawmakers who are interested in family-leave policies. The popularity of hands-on learning projects like Wild Friends and BEMP is spurring changes in the science and civics curricula one school at a time. With the help of a network of public and private partners, including the New Mexico Legislature, the projects may stimulate wider changes in state education policy.

Final Thoughts

I wrote this book to cultivate a sense of hope during a time when cynicism is growing and community development that is based on the ideals of equity, empowerment, and justice has become more difficult. In 2017, as I write these words, President Trump and the Republican Congress are threatening to undo generations of programs, cut back on Medicaid, community service, and environmental protections.
I hope the stories I've shared, and the examples of how grassroots groups are solving problems without giving up on their ideals, give you hope that change is still possible and courage to take your own small steps to make our world a better place.

Now it's your turn to be a part of the solution, to look for alternatives to the traditional trickle-down economic development model and toward endeavors like the ones in this book that lift struggling citizens, build community, and offer another way forward.

The following two sections will get you started.

Bottoms Up:
20 Tips for Budding Social Entrepreneurs and Change-Makers

I hope you've been inspired by the sampling of grassroots leaders in health care, housing, hands-on learning, art, and poverty alleviation presented in the preceding chapters. Now you know for sure that one person really can make a huge difference. But you don't have to be a Sanjeev Arora, a Cliff Crawford, or a Susan Matteucci. If you have a big (or even a little) idea to solve a problem or create a social enterprise in New Mexico, here are twenty tips based on my observations of how the New Mexico change-makers I've interviewed operate.

1. Start with where you are—your home, your family, neighborhood, school, or community.

2. Study the history of the problem you are attacking, including previous attempts to solve it.

3. Assess and build on existing strengths.

4. Volunteer or apprentice yourself to a master in the field.

5. Search out unlikely allies, partners from other sectors, different points of view, and different backgrounds.

6. Listen and learn.

7. Keep talking, networking, and knocking on doors. Practice your elevator speech.

8. Ask advice from people you admire.

9. Break it down into doable steps.

10. Learn to work as a team member, part of a network or alliance.

11. Share credit and celebrate every success.

12. Commit to the long haul even if it means making sacrifices in the short run, taking a part time job, living with your parents, or spending your own money.

13. Mentor team members, young people, or other partners.

14. Be resilient, try new approaches. If one doesn't work, try another. Roll with the punches.

15. Get hard skills. Take a finance or marketing course.

16. Advocate for your idea. Learn who the political players are and how public agencies affect your project. Lobby, testify in committee or before the city council, petition, organize.

17. Learn how to negotiate.

18. Renew your initial inspiration regularly.

19. Hold fast to your principles but not to specific methods.

20. Be generous, not competitive. Be open and transparent.

Fostering Community Development

Your Role

It takes many actors to advance economic and social change. It wasn't just visionary leaders like Charlie Alfero, Andres Mercado, or Debbie O'Malley who built those organizations that are now making a difference in affordable housing, hands-on learning, and health care. It took collaborators to build and carry on organizations like the South Valley Academy, First Choice Community Healthcare, the Rocky Mountain Youth Corps, and the Bosque Ecosystem Monitoring Project (BEMP). And it takes an even larger group to support these organizations at different stages and in different ways. That's where you come in.

Ordinary citizens who believe that where they spend their money, what food they eat, where they live, and how they spend their time are important decisions are the keys to solving problems in their own neighborhoods and communities. You don't need to have a "big idea." You can support others who do. Lift them up by buying their products, investing in their enterprises, volunteering your skills, bringing them into your network, or buying a ticket for their event. We already have a network of grassroots projects in New Mexico and we can build upon what we have—regardless of what is happening elsewhere.

11 Ways to Help

1. Think about who is addressing the root causes of the problems you are concerned about in your town, neighborhood, school, or organization. Connect with them, volunteer, or contribute. Concerned about health care but frustrated by the complicated maze of hospitals, HMOs, and pill pushers who don't seem to care on a personal level? Check out your community health-care clinic. Are your kids restless with the traditional education offerings? Check out programs like BEMP, Wild Friends, or charter schools like the South Valley Academy and the Health Leadership Academy. Volunteer, join a board, mentor a student, or provide transportation.

2. Choose to support local farmers by shopping at a farmers' market or a food co-op, by joining a CSA, or by persuading your employer or organization to "go local" instead of buying from large food distributors or grocery stores.

3. Invest in a non-profit tackling one of New Mexico's problems or convince the larger organizations you belong to do so. Wild Friends, Prosperity Works, the Rocky Mountain Youth Corps, MoGro, and others are always in need of financial or in-kind contributions, particularly as government funding dwindles.

4. Advocate for policies that invest public funds in organizations that create opportunities for affordable housing, health care that is affordable and accessible to underserved areas, or programs that empower students while they learn about the environment or wildlife. Lobby, write letters, call state legislators, and sign petitions. As an individual you can have a much bigger impact at the local level than at the national level. Responding to constituent pressure, Bernalillo County and the University of New Mexico Hospital committed mill levy funds to an array of programs for low-income people called Pathways, which partners with First Choice Community Healthcare and other local groups. In 1999, the City of Albuquerque partnered with the Sawmill Community Land Trust to allow the group to develop land owned by the city. It didn't just happen as a result of Max Ramirez and Debbie O'Malley. The arrangement was preceded by months of community meetings and pressure from local neighborhoods.

5. Partner with a social enterprise or non-profit to provide services, clothing, or food to your agency. The Army Corps of Engineers buys data from BEMP; Valle de Oro employs Rocky Mountain Youth Corps members to build fences; Albuquerque Public Schools contracts with Agri-Cultura Network to buy food for students.

6. Use the assets you have, whether they are time, skills, knowledge, or even a car. Become a mentor, a tutor, a volunteer. Drive Wild Friends to the legislature, tutor students at the South Valley Academy, judge student presentations at the Health Leadership High School, or do something closer to home at your local school or senior center.

7. Do business with those who support the organizations and causes you love. Spend your money at La Montañita Food Co-op, bank with the Rio Grande Credit Union, and thank the foundations, loan funds, United Ways, and others who contribute to the groups trying to make change. A complete list is provided in the Acknowledgments section of this book.

8. If you are a journalist, write stories about solutions as well as problems, scandals, and investigations. There are good things going on everywhere and many unsung heroes working to promote sustainable communities and lift up individuals who have never had a chance to contribute.

9. If you are a philanthropist, consider a bequest, a trust, or a gift in memory of someone who died of a chronic disease, because of an injustice, or due to inadequate food, housing, or care—all the problems that social entrepreneurs are tackling.

10. If you are a techie or have an online network of your own, help these organizations connect, build websites, databases, and online newsletters or start Kickstarter campaigns.

11. If you are an educator, incorporate hands-on learning and practical skills into the curriculum as much as possible. Investigate whether Wild Friends, BEMP, AVID, or the MESA program would fit your classroom.

Acknowledgments

nother Way Forward is not just about whether the local projects described here work to drive community and economic development. It is also about the partnership between supportive foundations, institutions, and businesses and the social entrepreneurs. And mainly, it's about citizen activists, ordinary people doing extraordinary things in community medicine, housing, arts, education, and the environment. Meeting these unsung heroes has been a key part of my own way forward. They have renewed my faith in the citizen sector and the grassroots. I want to thank all of them for their inspiration and drive to improve the lives of everything and everyone in their path.

Dr. Art Kaufman, the Godfather of community medicine in New Mexico, has led me down the path of public health. Although he is not the subject of any one chapter, many of his ideas — the health commons, the use of community health workers, and innovative ways to recruit rural health-care providers are embedded in the health-care chapters of this book. I had heard of many of these ideas when I was in the New Mexico Senate but had never observed them in action as I did at the First Choice Community Healthcare clinic in the South Valley and Hidalgo Medical Services in Silver City. Thank you Bob De Felice and Charlie Alfero, Darrick Nelson, Kristyn Yepa, Cornell Magdalena, and all those who work at primary health-care clinics. You are moving mountains and turning battleships around. I admire you so much.

The foodies and farmers from the Rio Grande valley, people like Don Bustos, Pam Roy, Anzia Bennett, Sayrah Namaste, Robin Seydel, Rick Schneiders, Leigh Caswell, Micaela Fischer, Henry Rael, Jedrek Lamb, Monte Skarsgard, Pilar and Marisella Trujillo, Ann Simon, Arturo Sandoval, Eileen Shendo, Martin Loretto, and many others taught me about networking to create a viable system that will last to provide public health and economic security right here, starting in our gardens.

Cliff Crawford the University of New Mexico biologist who began the Bosque Ecosystem Monitoring Program (BEMP) over twenty years ago passed away in 2007, but his big idea lives on in the heart of thousands who have used it to learn about the bosque and, more important, science. I got to experience Cliff's passion firsthand as we worked together in the late 1990s. His successors, Dan Shaw, Kim Eichhorst, and the scores of other BEMPers have grown the unique program, and Cliff's sons and daughters are everywhere in agencies like the United States Fish and Wildlife Service and the Army Corps of Engineers. His curiosity, joy, and scientific method have been embedded into a program that will create new scientists and stewards of New Mexico's natural resources.

Another local hero, Alan Marks, a lawyer, teacher, philanthropist, and friend, created another institution in the South Valley of Albuquerque—a charter high school. It is furthering his dream of seeing a critical mass of first generation Hispanic college graduates return home to better their communities. What's remarkable about Alan is that most of his early efforts were solitary—except of course for the families that he helped.

There are so many local heroes. I have covered only a few of them in the course of writing this book Here are just a few of these remarkable people who I salute for changing the face of our state: Sanjeev Arora, Venice Ceballos, Andres Mercado, Debbie O'Malley, Max Ramirez, Connie Chavez, Yvette Tovar, Ken Balizer, Chad Rennaker, Ona Porter, Barbara Lopez, Susan Matteucci, Flor Lopez, Michelle Melendez, Ben Thomas, Wendy Kent, Sue George, Julie Radoslovich, Sasha Perrin, Katarina Sandoval, Ruth Musgrave, Carolyn Byers, Dr. Will Kaufman, Brad Knipper, Kim Score, Carl Colonius, Richard Noland, Dr. Rachel Sonne, B. J. Ciesielski, Sylvia Sapien, Daryl Smith, Les Rubin, Harvey Licht, Eytan Krasilovsky, Rashan Jones, Kristina Leeder, Judith Phillips, Mike Ammerman, Blanca Lopez and many more. They serve as role models, and many were kind enough to help with interviews, get photo permissions, and read chapter drafts.

Special thanks to all the charities, foundations, and government programs that support these social entrepreneurs and innovators. Social change is always a partnership between the public and private sectors. The foundations and government institutions listed in the following pages have been key partners.

Finally, I am grateful for the support that the Con Alma Health Foundation, the McCune Charitable Foundation and the Thornburg Foundation gave me to write this book, to Fred Harris for his unfailing support, and to John Byram for his editorial assistance amid a time of change at UNM Press. As always, my greatest thanks go to Mark Feldman, my husband and partner in all things for almost fifty years.

Local Food

American Friends
Service Committee (AFSC)

The Thornburg Foundation

The Marshall L. and Perrine D.
McCune Charitable Foundation

The W. K. Kellogg Foundation

Presbyterian Healthcare
Services/Community Health

Blue Cross and Blue Shield
of New Mexico

Santa Fe Community
Foundation

Notah Begay III Foundation

Johns Hopkins Center for
American Indian Health

March of Dimes

Rick and Beth Schnieders

The Kaiser Family Foundation

The Simon Charitable
Foundation

The La Montañita FUND

Robert Wood Johnson
Foundation

New Mexico
Department of Agriculture

Albuquerque Public Schools

The Mid-Region Council of
Governments of New Mexico

South Valley Economic
Development Center

Center of Southwest Culture

Education

New Mexico Simon Scholars
Program

College Horizons Scholars
Program

Davis New Mexico Scholarship

The Albuquerque Public
Schools Education Foundation's
Varsity Awards Program

Bosque School

Santa Fe Preparatory School

The Marshall L. and Perrine D.
McCune Charitable Foundation

Shelby Cullom Davis
Charitable Fund

Housing

The New Mexico Community
Development Loan Fund

Center for Community Change

Institute for Community
Economics

Grounded Solutions Network

City of Albuquerque

Enterprise Community
Loan Fund

Community Development
Block Grant Program

Design Workshop

The New Mexico Legislature

Health Care

The Kresge Foundation

The de Beaumont Foundation

Presbyterian Healthcare Services

Blue Cross and Blue Shield of New Mexico

The University of New Mexico Health Sciences Center

The New Mexico Area Health Education Center (AHEC)

The University of New Mexico Health Sciences Center Health Extension Rural Offices (HEROs)

The University of New Mexico Combined BA/MD Degree Program

Bernalillo County Pathways Program

Wells Fargo

United States Economic Development Administration

New Mexico Department of Health

New Mexico Human Services Department

The New Mexico Legislature

General Electric (GE) Foundation

City of Santa Fe Fire Department

City of Santa Fe

CHRISTUS St. Vincent Regional Medical Center

Public Service Company of New Mexico

The Leona M. and Harry B. Helmsley Charitable Trust

Robert Wood Johnson Foundation

The Merck Company Foundation

Bristol-Myers Squibb Foundation

St. Vincent Hospital Foundation

Youth

The University of New Mexico Department of Biology

The University of New Mexico School of Law's Institute of Public Law

South Valley Academy

AmeriCorps

Corporation for National and Community Service

Valle de Oro National Wildlife Refuge

City of Santa Fe

George R. R. Martin

New Mexico Energy, Minerals and Natural Resources Department

The New Mexico Local Economic Development Act capital outlay (LEDA CO) funds

The New Mexico Job Training Incentive Program (JTIP)

The New Mexico Legislature

Assets and Livelihood

Charles Stewart Mott Foundation

New Mexico Community Development Loan Fund

Rio Grande Credit Union

MyBank

First American Bank New Mexico (Las Cruces)

Southwest Capital Bank

Levi Strauss & Co.

United Way

The Frost Foundation

Social Venture Partners International (SVPI)

Prosperity Now

The Atlantic Philanthropies

The W. K. Kellogg Foundation

Tides Foundation

New Mexico Community Foundation

The Marshall L. and Perrine D. McCune Charitable Foundation

Ford Foundation

Central New Mexico Community College (CNM) Foundation

Bank of America Charitable Foundation

Endnotes

1 This study was quoted in David Bornstein, "Power to Cure, Multiplied," *New York Times*, 11 June 2014. (http://opinionator.blogs.nytimes.com/2014/06/11/the-doctor-will-stream-to-you-now/)

2 Sanjeev Arora et al. "Outcomes of Treatment for Hepatitis C Infection by Primary Care Providers," *New England Journal of Medicine* (9 June 2011). (http://www.nejm.org/doi/full/10.1056/NEJMoa1009370)

3 According to a 2013 Center for Medicaid and CHIP Services (CMCS) *CMCS Informational Bulletin*, a disproportionate share of health-care spending in the United States is used to provide care to a relatively small group of patients, with 1 percent of the population accounting for 22 percent of total health care expenditures annually. The distribution of spending is even more uneven within Medicaid, with just 5 percent of Medicaid beneficiaries accounting for 54 percent of total Medicaid expenditures and 1 percent of Medicaid beneficiaries accounting for 25 percent of total Medicaid expenditures. Among this top 1 percent, 83 percent have at least three chronic conditions and more than 60 percent have five or more chronic conditions. (https://www.medicaid.gov/federal-policy-guidance/downloads/cib-07-24-2013.pdf; accessed 19 December 2016)

4 Diane Johnson et al. "Community Health Workers and Medicaid Managed Care in New Mexico," *The Journal of Community Health* (2011).

5 Statistics in this section are from the *2012 Census of Agriculture* (New Mexico section) and the *Power of Public Procurement: An Action Plan for Healthier Farms and People in New Mexico*, New Mexico State University and Farm to Table New Mexico (September 2014); 45–51.

6 Acequias are traditional irrigation ditches or canals used by farmers in New Mexico. An elaborate interconnected system fed by river water, they are maintained by farmers and are now recognized as an official governmental unit in New Mexico.

7 *La cosecha* means "the harvest" or "the crop" in Spanish. Norte is north.

8 Monte Skarsgard says that just one Whole Foods supermarket in Albuquerque sells about $52 million worth of groceries annually. Interview with the author, 17 August 2016. The New Mexico Department of Agriculture estimates

annual sales of the 150 organic producers in New Mexico at $40 million.

9 The Business Alliance for Local Living Economies has documented that for every $1 spent with local farmers and food producers, the value is multiplied in the community up to four times, staying in the community and creating greater community wealth as it supports local taxes, first responders, parks, libraries, etc. This multiplier effect can have significant impact in a state such as New Mexico, where many urban and rural communities are looking to create jobs. In contrast, only thirteen cents of every dollar spent with a chain retailer or corporate distributor stays in the community. From "NM Local Food Development Initiative Press Kit," Delicious New Mexico, May 2016. (http://www.deliciousnm.org/2016/05/12/lfdi-press-kit/)

10 "$2.1 Million to Boost Double Up Healthy Food Program," Albuquerque Journal, 9 June 2016, B-1.

11 E-mail communication to the author from Micaela Fischer, 1 September 2016

12 Business Alliance for Local Living Economies, op. cit.

13 Rick Nathanson, "Study: Cost of NM housing out-paces minimum wage," Albuquerque Journal, 6 June 2016, D 1.

14 Mark Suazo, "Mobilizing in Defense of Community," Master's thesis, University of New Mexico, 2002.

15 Janet Guokas, "No Hand-outs," Crosswinds Weekly, 28 December 1998–7 January 1999, 8–11.

16 Editorial, "Americans don't have a big place in their heart for communal ownership," Albuquerque Journal, 19 April 2001. Days before the opening, this editorial congratulated the trust on the obstacles overcome. It quoted Karen Seabury, program officer for the John D. and Catherine T. MacArthur Foundation, who said

that CLTs have to jump a psychological and cultural challenge. The editorial is quoted in Mark Suazo's master's thesis.

17 Paul Lusk and Alf Simon, eds., Building to Endure: Design Lessons from the Arid Southwest, 230. Albuquerque, NM: UNM Press. I am indebted to Ken Balizer, whose chapter on the Arbolera de Vida, "A Case Example of Community Development," informed this chapter.

18 "Community Profile," submitted by First Choice Development Director Michelle Melendez for the Build Health Challenge grant. The grant, funded by the Robert Wood Johnson, Kresge, de Beaumont, and Colorado Health foundations was awarded to First Choice and several community partners to "Address Healthcare's Blindside" in Albuquerque's Southside in 2015.

19 The Many Farms Project was an experimental program started by Cornell University doctors to treat tuberculosis, then rampant on the Navajo Nation's reservation. The project lasted from 1952–1962. Annie Wauneka enlisted the help of traditional medicine men.

20 The percentage of overweight/obese people in Jemez Pueblo in 2009 was recorded in a Jemez booklet, "FITT Trails," published by the JHHS Public Health Program. The booklet also includes trail maps, categorized by fitness level, and the number of miles. Many of the trails are suitable for strollers and bicycles.

21 There are a number of historic photos of Jemez runners at the Walatowa Visitors Center, 7413 HWY 4, Jemez Pueblo, NM, 87024, 575-834-7235.

22 Kristina Ortez De Jones and Megan Lawson, "Trail System Needed for Better Health," Albuquerque Journal, 27 November 2016, A-11.

23 Charles Sallee and LFC program evaluators, "Department of Health and Allied Agencies Adequacy of New Mexico's Healthcare Systems Workforce," 15 May 2013.

24 Pathways is funded by a portion of a county tax levied to support the University of New Mexico Health Center, which cooperates—and benefits—from the program. The logic is that the more social support patients receive, the more guidance into the proper "pathways" (e.g., education, safe housing, etc.), the fewer admissions to UNM Hospital's emergency room. Pathways is a national model originating in Cleveland, Ohio.

25 Bureau of Labor Statistics, *Occupational Employment Statistics, Community Health Workers,* May 2016. (www.bls.gov)

26 Diane Johnson et al. "Community Health Workers and Medicaid Managed Care in NM," *The Journal of Community Health*, published on line 28 September 2011.

27 Mattie Quinn, "A New Kind of Paramedic for Less Urgent 911 Calls," *Governing Magazine*, September 2016.

28 http://naemt.org/docs/default-source/MIH-CP/naemt-mih-cp-report.pdf?sfvrsn=2

29 Michael Ollove, "Reports detail how various disease rates vary by state," *Albuquerque Journal*, 13 December 2016, A 4.

30 Arthur Kaufman et al., "Health Extension in New Mexico: An Academic Health Center and the Social Determinants of Disease," *Annals of Family Medicine* 8, no. 1 (2010). (www.annfammed.org)

31 These statistics are drawn from a 1998 study conducted by the National Constitution Center and a 2006 National Assessment of Education Progress (NAEP) report on civics competencies. Both were cited in a presentation by Wild Friends, which may be accessed at: http://wildfriends.unm.edu/.

32 Two recent Crawford symposia have included student presentations on pharmaceuticals and personal care products in the Rio Grande, flower preferences of butterflies in the bosque, the shell length of turtles, tamarisk leaf beetle populations, and lizard movements.

33 Richard Louv, *Last Child in the Woods*, Algonquin Books, 2005. (http://richardlouv.com/books/last-child/)

34 Beth Baker, "Frontiers of Citizen Science" *Bio Science* 66, no. 11 (2016): 926.

35 R. L. Converse and D. Shaw, "Developing Natural Resource Career Pathways Through Citizen Science." Presentation at the Joint Annual Meeting of the Arizona and New Mexico Chapters of the American Fisheries Society and the Wildlife Society, Las Cruces, NM, February 2015.

36 Marie C. Baca, "Underbanked households on the rise in NM," *Albuquerque Journal*, 27 October 2016, B-1.

37 Center for Public Policy Priorities, *Individual Development Accounts*. Austin, TX, 2005. (http://library.cppp.org/research.php?aid=88&cid=2)

38 Ida Rademacher et al., "Weathering the Storm: Have IDAs Helped Low-Income Homebuyers Avoid Foreclosure?" Washington, DC: Corporation for Enterprise Development and the Urban Institute, April 2010. (http://prosperitynow.org/search/content?keys=Rademacher+Foreclosure)

39 Gregory Mills et al. "Final Evaluation Report, Evaluation of the American Dream Demonstration, Ford Foundation Down Payment on the American Dream," The Ford Foundation, New York, August 2004.

40 W. Elliott, "Small-dollar children's savings accounts and children's college outcomes," *Children*

Youth and Services Review 35, no. 3 (2013): 572–585.

41 Mission Graduate (https://mission graduatenm.org/bright-spots/hacia-la-universidad-toward-university/apr-29-2016)

42 2015 statistics from: Civic Enterprises and the Everyone Graduates Center at the Johns Hopkins University School of Education, "Building a Grad Nation." 2016 statistics from: NM Department of Education, cited in Kim Burgess, "New Mexico graduation rate hits record high," *Albuquerque Journal*, 16 January 2017. (http://www.abqjournal.com/928826/gov-abbiybces-record-nm-gradu-tion-rate.html)

43 Education Advisory Board, "90% of low-income, first-generation students don't graduate on time. But colleges can change that," 16 March 2016. (https://www.eab.com/daily-briefing/2016/03/16/90-percent-of-low-income-first-gen-students-dont-graduate-on-time-but-colleges-can-change-that)

44 2014–2015 figures from AVID web site (www.avid.org).

45 Quotes from *APS AVID Monthly* magazine, March 2017.

46 There are many other programs that engage students in career-related clubs or after-school academic activities. Especially when combined with mentorship, these can be vitally important in keeping kids from dropping out. Groups like New Mexico MESA engage a huge number of students in math, science, and engineering projects inspiring many to pursue college education in one of those fields.

47 College Horizons web site (www.collegehorizons.org).

48 Quoted in David Bornstein, *How to Change the World: Social Entrepreneurs and the Power of New Ideas*, 182. Oxford University Press, 2007.

49 Cited in: Kevin Robinson-Avilla, "Accelerator helping jump-start creative industries," *Albuquerque Journal*, 13 July 2015.

50 Miljen Aljinovic, "There is Magic in the World: A comprehensive biography of Meow Wolf," *Mecca Lecca*, 24 February 2016. (http://meccalecca.com/?p=25669)

51 Radio Café, Mary-Charlotte Domandi, interview with Meow Wolf, 7 January 2011.

Index

www.ingramcontent.com/pod-product-compliance
Lightning Source LLC
Chambersburg PA
CBHW042351030426

42336CB00026B/3444